CONCORDIA UNIVERSIT
GV342.F44
PERSPECTIVES AND PRINCIPLES F

T4-AEA-730

3 4211 000035730

WITHDRAWN

PERSPECTIVES AND PRINCIPLES FOR PHYSICAL EDUCATION

Perspectives and Principles for Physical Education

JANET FELSHIN

Associate Professor of Physical Education
The Ohio State University

JOHN WILEY AND SONS

New York · London · Sydney

Copyright © 1967 by John Wiley & Sons, Inc.

All Rights Reserved. This book or any part thereof must not be reproduced in any form without the written permission of the publisher.

Library of Congress Catalog Card Number: 67-21329
Printed in the United States of America

PREFACE

The goal of this book is the understanding and development of principles for physical education. Its thesis is that clarity must characterize theoretical approaches. Although physical education has dealt with principles for some time, each generation of undergraduate and graduate students is asked to define and defend the field. In *The Process of Education* Jerome Bruner suggests that the transfer of principles lies at the heart of the educational process and accounts for the broadening and deepening of knowledge. If this is to be so, principles must emerge from a process of clear and rational analysis and both process and principles must be understood.

Physical education may be considered many things: the classes taught in schools, a major in colleges and universities, a professional field, and even certain kinds of activity as they exist in society. Each of these contexts assumes a different purpose and heritage. One explanation for the lack of clarity about the nature and aim of physical education is that its perspectives have been confused or rendered uncertain. As long as principles were developed without reference to contextual analysis, they were limited in their contribution to new depths of understanding.

The major concern of this book is physical education in school programs. The related body of knowledge and the profession are also considered, but the idea of principles as purposes and as guides to action is directed toward the school. Current recognition of the demands of rationality in a world of increasing knowledge has caused all subject-matter fields to examine their goals and organization. New concepts of structure and cognition have served to spotlight the intellectual responsibilities of the schools and the curricular aspects of fields of study they include. This cannot mean that teachers will ignore the schools' other responsibilities in our society. It means that the process of teaching and learning must be clarified in relation to the pervading goals of education and to the structure and organization of knowledge in subject fields.

Each part of this book can be viewed as the development of principles on different levels within a perspective. Part One is an expression of the personal perspective of theory and process which is an underlying assumption of the book. Part Two considers the historical perspective of certain important ideas in physical education in the belief that intelligent current appraisal depends on such knowledge. Part Three develops contemporary perspective in relation to the problems of purposes of physical education which derive from its educational existence and its body of knowledge. Part Four considers principles as guidelines for action within a projected perspective.

This book reflects my own ideas in process. It is definitive in scope and enduring only in its commitment to a method of intelligence in developing theory for physical education in schools. These ideas and perspectives may be useful to others in the refinement of theoretical frames of reference. Many must undertake that task if we are to understand and explicate the ways in which the contributions of physical education enhance man's fulfillment.

The process of ideation is one of intellectual interaction and modification, and many of the concepts employed here have been developed by others. I am most conscious of my personal and professional indebtedness to Camille Brown and Rosalind Cassidy, whose recent *Theory in Physical Education* (1963) is already a landmark in the history of physical education. The men and women who have been my colleagues and students have been an important source of direction in the refinement of ideas. I am very grateful to Edrie Ferdun for her critical reading of the manuscript and her theoretical contributions to considerations of the body of knowledge. Lawrence F. Locke reviewed the manuscript at the publisher's request and offered invaluable suggestions. This would be a better work if I had followed them all. My editor at John Wiley and Sons, Joseph F. Jordan, has been continually supportive.

Janet Felshin

Columbus, Ohio
February 1967

CONTENTS

PART ONE
Perspective: Principles Within a Framework   3

1. A Point of View   5
2. Principles and Process   13

PART TWO
Historical Perspective: Principles as Essential Truths   31

3. School and Society   33
4. Teaching and Learning   68
5. Physical Education   104

PART THREE
Contemporary Perspective: Principles as Purposes   131

6. The Problem of Purposes   133
7. The Premise of Purposes   146
8. The Promise of Purposes   166

PART FOUR
Projected Perspective: Principles as Guidelines for Action   185

9. The Practice of Theory   187
10. The Practice of Profession   217

INDEX   227

PERSPECTIVES AND PRINCIPLES FOR PHYSICAL EDUCATION

PART ONE

Perspective: Principles Within a Framework

PERSPECTIVE: PRINCIPLES WITHIN A FRAMEWORK

Any study gains scope and direction when it is grounded in a well-conceived framework. A framework is the setting in which ideas or events relate to one another. To be valid a framework must reflect both conviction and knowledge and must abet the growth of principles within it. It must also be constructed by rational process.

Part 1 of this book endeavors to establish a valid framework for the study of physical education. Its objective is to provide the setting in which the principles of the subject might easily flourish. Two chapters constitute the substance of this section. The first identifies the perspective for the study, and the second develops the framework in terms of principles and process. Its ultimate aim is to strengthen the validity of our approach to physical education.

1

A POINT OF VIEW

Physical education is threatened from a number of sides. Its purpose is challenged, its cost is questioned, its value is doubted, but greater than any of these threats is the inability of its defenders to give effective expression to the essential vitality of its role in everyday life. The potential contribution of physical education in schools is enormous, yet, as things stand, the full realization of this potential grows more and more uncertain.

More than any other, physical education is a field of *action;* in it effort and achievement acquire a meaning that is rarely found elsewhere. Even the terms joy and wholeness embody a feeling experienced by the athlete perhaps as fully as by anyone else. The importance of self in activities involving movement is an exercise in growth and awareness unrivaled in most other areas of human undertaking. We know all this but rarely seem able to express it, even in teaching. If physical education is to realize its possibilities, its bases and principles will require more rational conception and understanding.

Every student and teacher of physical education is engaged in an effort to bring the potential contributions of the field to fruition. This effort must be conducted in an atmosphere of intellectual inquiry. The basis of this process might be called conceptual. A concept is the essence of an object or an idea and all things associated with it. The young child, for instance, is exposed to an orange many times before he acquires a concept of what an orange really is. He may be told that an orange is fruit with seeds. On another occasion he is told that an orange is fruit without seeds. Gradually he comes to identify the essence of an "orange," the characteristics common to *all* oranges. Once he has acquired this concept, he can easily spot an orange, even if it is a kind he has never seen before. In physical education the task is quite the same; we must identify and understand the major concepts of the field. Further, as students and teachers, we must establish desirable concepts that will find expression in the planning and carrying out of the learning activities.

Another reason why conceptual understanding and consistent interpretation is so necessary lies in the nature of the educational enterprise. Whatever its form, education is designed primarily to transmit the culture of a society, to initiate and absorb the young into that society. For primitive societies this is a simple task. Skills, knowledge, commitments, beliefs, and expectations of behavior are easily agreed on, identified, and transmitted, and the formal organization of schools is unnecessary when parents and other adults have the capacity and authority to prepare youth for its role. For complex heterogeneous societies the task is more difficult. The creation of schools becomes imperative for parents have neither the knowledge nor the time to educate their children. Indeed, the task is so great that the trend is toward lengthening the term of the school year and the number of years in which the child must remain in school. A primary task of the school is to choose those to be transmitted among the vast and increasingly complex cultural materials. All of the children of all of the people must attend school. This is the legal mandate of a complex society. What each shall learn, what each shall become, indeed, the very quality of human existence, are the responsibilities with which the schools are charged.

The teacher, as the school's agent, accepts the assignment to influence human behavior and shape human destiny. There can be no question of the ethical and moral aspects of this charge or the enormous responsibility it entails. This duty cannot be fulfilled without conceptual understanding of the nature of the task.

PERSPECTIVE

Any use of the phrase "a point of view" implies the probability of several ways of looking at something. It also reflects an awareness that a point of view is affected by many things. Such a title as "An Objective Account of the Civil War from the Southern Point of View" humorously illustrates the obvious; our ability to "see" is clearly influenced by our point of view. Likewise, the actions we choose are affected by the perspective we hold. *Perspective* might be regarded as point of view in a broader context. A point of view concerning presidential candidates, for example, is a product of perspective as a Democrat or Republican.

The facts of an individual's life may not be nearly so important in determining what he does or how he behaves as his perspective—the way in which he sees those facts. This is quite apparent in dealing with people. One adolescent girl, for instance, faced with the impending divorce of her parents may perceive the situation as a threat to herself; she may feel that her parents do not love her and that perhaps she is to blame. Her behavior may be very different from that of another girl confronted by the same situation who sees it as an unfortunate but rational decision of two adults who find they can no longer get along.

Behavior, then, must be viewed through the perspective within which it occurs, if it is to be understood. Conversely, if teaching is to reflect wise choices and actions, it must evolve from a well-developed and fully understood perspective. Valid concepts and principles of physical education can be developed only if founded on a perspective that has been subjected to reflective examination and critical insight.

Development of a useful perspective for our own operation results from an understanding of the components of perspective or its perceptual determinants. The value or importance we attach to things is likely to be central to this understanding. There is not much use in arguing about specific purposes of physical education with someone who finds no value in physical activity or in trying to help someone to bat a ball who attaches no great importance to batting skill. Unfortunately, as in many other areas of behavior, it seems natural to generalize our own values to others and to assume that they are universally accepted. Despite the numerous things said about teachers being transmitters of certain class values and about their struggles in dealing with students reared in differing class settings, the attempt to "get into the other fellow's skin" or to "see things through his eyes" has not often succeeded. When we tend to regard our own values as self-evident truths, we cannot really seriously consider opposing ones.

It is difficult to separate the components of perspective. Values are often the product of other variables of perception, such as beliefs and attitudes. In a sense the whole fabric of perspective may be said to depend on the degree of personal meaning. If the batter *believes* that by improving his skill he will achieve recognition from his friends, and this has meaning for him, he is likelier to make the effort to learn how to bat effectively. In other words, he places *value* on the recognition. When any individual understands a goal in terms that have meaning for him, it becomes important and he is ready to work toward it.

THE TEACHER

"Know thyself" has been repeated to those who have sought wisdom ever since the time of Socrates. For the teacher, to know himself is virtually a mandate. The careless, irresponsible teacher is widely condemned; yet there are too many whose choices of subject-matter content and teaching methods are not the product of a responsible system of values and beliefs.

The efforts to develop valid principles for teaching physical education must begin with an attempt to know and understand ourselves and our own behavior. Personal integrity is prerequisite to integrity of purpose and effort in teaching. The teacher must ask himself "Why do I behave as I do?" in the continuous process of understanding and evaluating himself and his own behavior. He must transcend the level of the college sophomore who frequently avows his great commitment to learning and study but spends his free time drinking beer and talking about his dedication. What we *do* is the clearest clue to our values, and there is still meaning in the much repeated statement, "What you do speaks so loudly I cannot hear what you say."

The first step in developing a consistent operational value system consists of identifying values—those that can be expressed and those that seem reflected in what we elect to do. Only by understanding the contradictions in our behavior can we attempt to change.

As an agent of knowledge and wisdom, the teacher is expected to hold valid beliefs. Anyone recognizes that believing the earth is flat is irrational and invalid; available evidence punctures such a claim. Yet, despite having gone to school and having learned how to examine and evaluate data, many of us continue to cling to beliefs that are irrational and invalid. The strong belief about the effect of milk on athletic performance and the belief that doing sit-ups will achieve a flat abdomen warrant examination in the light of all existing evidence; when found untenable they should be discarded.

Certain beliefs may be changed easily. Individuals may argue over the boiling point of water, but when clearly demonstrated the facts are accepted and the argument ends. Unfortunately, most beliefs cannot be tested so readily as degrees of temperature. In the realm of attitudes, which might be considered beliefs born of emotional influences, change is not easily accomplished. If this were untrue, we could easily eliminate all forms of prejudice and intolerance simply by documenting the historical, physiological, and social facts. However, people persist in believing even when the belief is obviously irrational.

The physical education teacher is repeatedly confronted with tests of his attitudes: toward winning and losing, toward participants, spectators, and officials, and toward work and play. To the degree that his attitudes reflect values and determine behavior, he must make every effort to understand them and modify those that prevent him from developing valid principles for teaching.

A full set of personal beliefs, values, and attitudes may be construed as a philosophy, a perspective for thought and action. They are all related. We may believe, for example, that participation in sports is beneficial to health and may value such participation as part of living fully and effectively. Perhaps we will exhibit this combined belief and value in our own lives. If not, both may have to be re-examined.

Similarly, it is almost impossible to separate a philosophy of life from a philosophy of education or to distinguish a person as an individual and a teacher. Whatever an individual is will be part of him as a teacher. In choosing to teach he accepts a moral responsibility for youth; he must therefore be a responsible person. A mature system of values and beliefs is essential to responsible human behavior and teaching.

To be sure, the days when a teacher, particularly a woman, was expected to be a paragon of virtue on the basis of a strict moral code have gone. Local laws no longer dictate the length of her skirt, but responsible behavior from every teacher is still expected. A complex society requires its institutions to espouse its highest ideals and hopes, and the teacher as the agent of a major social institution must be worthy of such a charge.

THE STUDENT

However irrational he may appear to us, the normal person does not behave irrationally. However, we cannot help anyone to act differently from the manner in which he does unless we understand what he sees and why he chooses to act as observed. It is a little like coming around a corner and seeing someone reaching out with a stick and dancing about; not until we advance and see that he is playing with a puppy do we comprehend his action. It is too easy to conclude he is abnormal until the appearance of the dog makes his behavior understandable and acceptable. Our own beliefs and values seem so obvious that we can hardly appreciate the failure of others to share them.

Until Margaret Mead showed us in her studies that adolescence in other cultures could be a relatively peaceful period we fully believed that adolescent behavior in this country was a function of adolescence rather than of adolescence *in the* United States. Thus as individuals we tend to generalize the facts of our experience and its resulting values to everyone else. However, behavior depends on perception or perspective, whether or not it is consciously identified. A process designed to *change* behavior, as is education, must therefore be predicated on a sincere attempt to *understand* behavior.

The students with whom teachers deal must be viewed as individuals with backgrounds and perceptual frameworks that may differ markedly from their own. Only as they understand and deal with these frameworks can teachers really hope to have learning. Values and beliefs give meaning to situations and subject matter, and meaning is indispensible to learning. The girl who believes that exercise will result in bulging muscles but values a "bulgeless" figure will not work hard at exercising, regardless of any outburst by the teacher. The teacher, of course, may threaten her with a low grade, and if the girl prizes a grade more than she fears bulging muscles the threat will have the desired effect—during class.

The goals of physical education are pertinent to a lifetime, not only to the school years. For this reason it is important that learning and change be attempted within those areas likeliest to result in continued desirable behavior.

Because a teacher considers a student on the basis of the student's view of the situation and the beliefs, values, and attitudes underlying that view, it is implicit that the teacher must assume the student's individuality. Each student is unique. He is whole in the syndrome of the self. The wise teacher does not try to splinter that self even for the avowed purpose of strengthening any part of it. Teachers can, of course, identify various functions and abilities of the human organism: thinking and intellectual ability; moving and bodily achievement; feeling and sensitivity; but only the total configuration of personality, the human being, is capable of all of these. The self cannot be fractionated.

SUMMARY

Public education in the United States is a vast enterprise based on social and ethical foundations and dedicated to the purpose of wise selection among a complex heterogeneous cultural heritage of those elements worthy of transmission to the young.

Within a view of education as a process of changing human behavior, it becomes necessary to examine the determinants of behavior in a perceptual context. The teacher, as agent of a social institution, accepts the moral obligation to understand his own beliefs and attitudes as part of a program to develop a mature worthy system of values and a valid philosophy for teaching. The student, as a human being with a unique personality and condition of selfhood, must be viewed through his own set of beliefs and values so that the educational process of changing behavior may be undertaken with insight and proved to have meaning.

GUIDELINES FOR LEARNING EXPERIENCES IN DEVELOPING A POINT OF VIEW

1. *List* those things you value most highly in descending order; analyze the relative position of items on the list by confronting yourself with the prospect of either/or, that is, having to choose between two.
2. *Discuss* those values that receive top priority on the list by creating situations threatening to them; for example, if honesty were identified as a high value, a situation might be suggested in which telling a lie might save a life.
3. *Write a statement* to summarize your basic beliefs about life; include such things as its meaning, purpose, and so on. Relate the choices made so far in your life to these beliefs.
4. *Describe* situations in which you believe you were unfairly treated; analyze them in terms of what you now think the other person involved believed or valued.
5. *Discuss* school experiences in physical education classes as they

seem to indicate the values the teacher held; the values the students held.
6. *Discuss* techniques that various teachers use to help students learn: daily quizzes; course outlines; recitations; grading. Try to identify the beliefs that underlie the use of these techniques.
7. *Identify* your beliefs and values about yourself. Try to decide the first thing you would tell someone about yourself; how you would describe your appearance; what things you would change if you could.
8. *Explore* the relationship of your values to your behavior. Each time you make a choice try to decide which value was at the basis; analyze this relationship for inconsistencies.

2

PRINCIPLES AND PROCESS

In teaching and learning theory and practice are as entwined as warp and woof. Neither may be considered separately. Although procedures and behavior fall under the mantle of practices, the reasons for their choice, their aims, and the beliefs and hopes inspired by the situations to which they are applied are all matters of theory. Effective and efficient teaching occurs only within a sound theoretical framework. Indeed, practices are judgeable only by the theory behind them. Two fathers, for example, may each extract payment for a window broken by a son's baseball, but one may do so in the belief that he is helping his son accept the consequences of his actions, whereas the other may be acting because of his own distress. Practice appears to be the same in both instances, but the effectiveness of the action is measurable only in terms of the governing theory; and certainly, its worth is not apparent without some evaluation of its basis.

Without doubt, learning takes place and behavior changes during the years of school attendance. The direction learning is to take, the kind of individual to emerge from the educative process, and the attitudes, values, skills, and abilities to be developed all depend on the theory of education underlying the planning and execution of the practices of learning.

Statements such as "That's all right in theory, but look at the situation" are fairly common. They indicate a belief that theory and practice are separable and that perhaps the criterion of successful practice is that it works. What these statements ignore is the obvious relation of *every* practice to *some* theory; action always relates to some value or belief. Yet people who make statements of the kind cited would be unwilling to concede that their teaching was based on expedience; "making something work" smacks fully of that. A given practice may seem successful as a teaching method, but without the relation of its success to something desirable its accomplishments are indeed hollow.

Theory implies that a problem or a project has been thought out rationally and clearly, with every one of its elements fully considered. It has been intellectualized, and from this process has emerged some rationale or plan or guiding explanation. Like a philosophy, a well-developed theory clarifies what an individual is trying to do and helps him to perfect ways of doing it. Sometimes a theory is nothing more than an educated guess, a hypothesis or plan that results from insight into the situation at hand. The theoretical is then tested by the practical. A baseball manager, for example, might develop a theory of base stealing that simply would not work in practice. He would then discard it and begin again. Each time he must plan within a valid theoretical framework, in this case, the purpose of the game, the rules, and commonly used strategy. In baseball there is such a theoretical framework; any play developed by the manager must take cognizance of it and be planned in terms of its effectiveness within that framework.

Physical education is not so simply defined as baseball. In playing baseball, no one theorizes about the purpose of the game, its appropriateness, or even about how to proceed. Nearly everybody knows its structure and therefore tends to *assume* many things in terms of this knowledge. Rarely need anyone say to someone who is not just learning the game, "There are nine players on each team and each team gets a turn at bat until three are out."

Similarly, most of us assume that we know and understand physical education. But do we? Is physical education merely sports and games, dances and aquatics, rhythms and self-testing activities? Is it education in movement or physical fitness? Is it good sportsmanship, good group membership, or participation on a team or in a tournament? Is it release from tensions, relaxation, or good body mechanics? Is physical education all of these or only some? Why does it exist, what is its aim, and what do teachers attempt to do about it?

A second baseman on a baseball team has a fairly good idea of what he is trying to do and how to go about it. The experienced player walks confidently to his position on the field, moves according to the number of runners on base, the number of outs, etc., and works well with the shortstop and first baseman, who also have a good grasp of their jobs and how to perform them.

But what about the role of the teacher? Do all teachers know what they are attempting to do and how to go about it? Is the physical education teacher there to maintain order and make the students exercise? Is it his job to listen to the problems of his students and endeavor to understand them, or should he help them to shape up and learn obedience and respect for authority? Should the teacher inspire feelings of friendship in his students, or does fear help students to learn more effectively? What does the teacher want his students to learn? Skill in hitting a ball? Proficiency in striking the target? How to be a good person? Is it all or some of these? How does the teacher know?

The second baseman unsure of his role would probably consult others who know. He would certainly seek information from his teammates and would watch, listen, and learn. To become outstanding he would have to develop a complete and valid insight into the playing of second base as well as the skill to handle this particular position. Without this challenge the game would lose its excitement once the rudiments had been mastered.

The challenge of being a teacher of physical education is also forever present. To the questions posed about the field and being a teacher in it there are many different answers, and the literature is often in conflict. Disagreement also appears in both theory and practice and, most seriously, in the theory and practice of the same teacher. Yet conflict should not discourage; rather it should help in the development of a theory. If two managers differ on base-stealing strategy, the observer increases his own understanding, not merely by taking sides but by trying to follow the logic of both arguments, by recognizing why each believes as he does, and making his own decision on the basis of insight and knowledge. It would be futile to wish that the two would agree and thus eliminate the need for such mental effort. It is equally futile for the physical education teacher to waste energy searching for someone to tell him what he is trying to do and how to do it. Only as a teacher employs understanding can he develop a clear and valid theory, and only then can he be effective and have a purpose.

The framework for a theory of physical education is composed of the forces inherent in the context in which it exists. When considering physical education in the schools, we obviously imply a context of culture and education. However, the heritage and substance of the field must itself be considered, and the focal point within the context is, of course, the youth of the society.

PRINCIPLES

For a framework to permit interpretation, it must be susceptible to critical analysis. "Framework" implies the erection of a structure. Here it is a structure of theoretical understanding based on an enduring foundation of thought and knowledge.

Principles are the building blocks for the construction of any theoretical framework. They are important in their own right and vital to future effort. Despite this dual value, they may be considered as fulfilling a primary role as essential truths or as guidelines for action.

Essential Truths

In this guise principles are statements that summarize an essence of knowledge. They may represent accumulated data or be highly rational beliefs based on careful reflection. Because of their rational nature in reflecting as much relevant knowledge as possible, principles emerge as existing truths at any point in time. Yet truth has been subject to revision on many occasions in the light of added knowledge. For this reason principles cannot be regarded as representing absolute truths but may be accepted as essential truths with the possibility of proving themselves enduring as well.

When they represent accumulated and usually scientific or experimental data, principles are readily acceptable. Newton's laws of motion explain observable phenomena and may be considered as enduring as long as they apply. When a principle ceases to explain, it will be modified. Essential truth in physics is readily represented by principles, but even in this area truth has been modified many times.

When they reflect human knowledge, principles are interpretations that often exist as strong beliefs. The principle of human equality is no more verifiable than that of the divine right of kings. Both represent philosophical and speculative belief. Ethical principles represent the most important aspects of human endeavor and are least subject to objective verification.

Guidelines for Action

Here the nature of principles is intrinsic. A summary of essential knowledge or a strong rational belief provides direction for action and behavior. Indeed, principles can be constructed primarily for this purpose; the Golden Rule is a case in point. The principles in the

Declaration of Independence are translated into guidelines for action in the Bill of Rights. Like other aspects of theory, principles are tested in practice; they must stand out clearly as guidelines if they are to test adequately.

It becomes clear that a valid interpretation of physical education in practice requires a theoretical framework that will find expression in principles that serve as guidelines for action. The student in physical education may wonder why he needs to do any more than learn these principles in his professional education, for in some curricula the learning of principles seems to be sufficient. The reasons should be evident. They are based on two principles already identified: (a) behavior (action) occurs within a perspective of values and beliefs and (b) in the application of insight valid principles and the necessary understanding and commitment are developed.

The process of developing principles can be clear and orderly. The framework is a vital element that consists of the existing context. Certain principles of physical education are implicit in the framework and cannot be ignored, but they are principles as essential truths, and practice grows out of theory only as these principles become guidelines for action. To consider the framework for practice the first step might be a brief analysis of the nature of the forces present in the context. Later in this book this context is explored as a source of foundations for developing principles within historical and contemporary perspectives—principles as guidelines for action. As the development of a framework proceeds, the character of the context for physical education requires identification.

PROCESS

Learning occurs on two levels. Simultaneous with actual learning, the learner learns how to learn. Because the professional bears a continuing responsibility of developing principles, as much attention must be paid to the process or method of development as to the principles themselves. The validity of a principle, its rational quality, and the consistency of its truth all suggest that its development stems from the intellect. Intellectual approaches to problems have been given various names—"the method of intelligence," "scientific method," philosophical or speculative thought," "logic," and "problem solving," to mention a few. All refer to a belief that thinking about a problem is likelier to achieve results than premature action. Even an experimental approach to solving a problem rests on a well thought out plan, and theory and practice go hand in hand in attacking all but abstract problems in logic.

If an individual built an airplane that would not fly, he might build another, altering some aspect, on a trial-and-error basis. Failing to achieve success, he might try again and again until eventually his model would fly. Discounting the time consumed, the most serious flaw in this process is that he would probably never recognize why he had succeeded in the end. Consequently, he could not easily utilize the solution he had worked so long and hard to attain.

Everyone admires the cook who does not seem to know how much she uses of any one ingredient, but consistent results require *consistent* measurements. Somehow she must know or indeed she is very lucky. On the other hand, a woman may be complimented on an extraordinary dish only to laugh ruefully and concede that she probably could not duplicate it. To repeat the attainment of a desired result, an individual has to know what he has done.

Neither the unsuccessful cook nor the builder of model airplanes must rush into a second hasty attempt. Both should intellectualize their problems. They should think about the situation and what they had done before. If a recipe is available, the cook should review them to determine whether an obvious error had been committed. Then she may indulge in an "educated guess" or form an hypothesis, a best speculation about what she must do or change in order to succeed. Such a hypothesis might state, "If I add baking powder, the cake will rise," or, "If I move the wings a half inch backward, the plane will fly." The next step is to do whatever appears indicated and to find out whether it was really the crucial factor. Even though not guaranteed, success is likelier to occur in this manner than by the use of random trial-and-error procedure. Furthermore, if success does not follow, at least the identification of the possible cause of error has been facilitated.

Cooking and building model airplanes are both examples of problem situations in which actual experiments are conducted. In them the approach chosen most likely resembles what is known as the scientific method, yet eventually the other approaches, the method of intelligence and problem solving, must also be tested in practice. Their purpose is to provide guidelines for the practice. Because of their pervasiveness, their processes themselves must be valid. They must ensure the greatest probability of consistent effort and result. Above all, they must be clearly understood.

Though the cook who disclaims knowledge of his method of achievement continues to win admiration, the physical education teacher cannot get away with not knowing what he is doing. The teacher or coach who proudly considers himself only a practitioner is out of place in today's world. More and more, educators are being required to explain and justify the contributions of their fields in terms of the whole educational effort. Each teacher must be able to articulate his aims and how they are to be accomplished.

Physical education will be able to define and fulfill its role in society only as each professional understands its problems and applies intellect to their solution. The first step in seeking any solution is to identify the problem to be solved. Simple as this may seem, it is usually the most difficult phase in the process, for unless the crucial problem can be identified the solution reached will have little use.

Suppose we begin by listing questions that concern the understanding of the framework within which principles evolve. These questions, of course, are influenced by the understanding already attained. From what has been learned so far the following questions could easily emerge:

1. How does an individual begin to develop principles for physical education?
2. How can he understand the framework for physical education so that he can develop valid principles?
3. How will the development of principles within a framework help him to become a good physical education teacher?
4. What is the nature of the relationship of framework to principles?
5. What are the elements of a framework for physical education and how can they be identified?
6. How can an individual understand physical education so that he can interpret the field effectively?

From identification of the problem there is no cut and dried rule for progressing to the next steps. At some point after it has been identified the problem must be stated. Assumptions must be considered and, in all likelihood, a hypothesis formed. The logic linking these steps helps to clarify them through a testing process. Let us see whether we can identify the substance of the problem as it is reflected in the questions posed.

The goal of becoming an effective teacher of physical education, which the questions imply, may be assumed. Thus it need not be included in the statement of the problem. Similarly, we may assume that we shall eventually reach an effective interpretation of physical education. What is left of the problem, then, is the nature of the elements that form its framework and how they provide a setting for the development of valid principles. The problem can be stated as follows: "What is the context for teaching physical education and how does it supply a framework in which principles may be developed?"

Once it has been stated, the problem must be closely examined to determine whether it includes every pertinent element present in its identification and whether it says exactly what is meant and is understood. The basic assumptions are implied. Others must be made clear. Unless an assumption is universally accepted, it requires support. Reasons for its employment must be given, though such support sometimes becomes superfluous as the solution of the problem becomes evident.

The question, "What is the context?" implies the assumption of a context and also that it is identifiable. Asking oneself, "How can I learn to play tennis?" assumes that by doing certain things one *will* learn or that certain actions must be pursued in learning to play the game.

Similarly, asking in relation to context, "How does this provide a framework?" assumes that somehow a context does supply a framework for the development of principles. This assumption obviously stems from the discussion of principles in which a framework was defined as a theoretical structure based on the contextual forces involved. Finally, in mentioning a framework for developing principles, we assume that principles *are* developed within a framework. This basic assumption is supported and extended as study of the problem proceeds, but it should be largely acceptable on the basis of the theoretical considerations already presented.

Let us review the progress we have made:

Identification

1. Concern with the goal of becoming a good teacher of physical education.
2. Concern with the goal of becoming articulate in understanding and interpreting physical education.
3. Concern with the nature and kinds of elements that influence physical education.
4. Concern for understanding the theoretical framework for physical education and for developing valid principles.

Statement of the Problem

What is the context for teaching physical education and how does this provide a framework for developing principles?

Basic Assumptions

1. A context for physical education can be identified.
2. The theoretical framework for physical education emerges from a critical analysis of the context.
3. Principles for physical education should be developed within a valid framework.

Hypothesis

If the context for physical education were analyzed, a framework for developing principles could be established.

The hypothesis should follow clearly from a statement of the problem and the basic assumptions. It suggests that if certain actions are taken the problem will be solved. If the solution still seems hazy after the basic assumptions have been made, the hypothesis can be presented in greater detail; indeed, it may suggest specific procedures. If at the point of formulating the hypothesis it cannot contain the affirmation that if certain things are done a solution will follow, the problem may need restatement on a simpler level.

Frequently a problem stated is based on too many other unresolved problems and is therefore incapable of solution as a single problem. This should become apparent if the basic assumptions pose problems themselves or lead to timid or unsupportable statements. If, for example, the question, "What is the relation of intellectual to motor ability?" is posed, it is assumed that such a relationship exists. If the assumption is unfounded or doubted, the problem may better be stated as, "Is there a relationship between intellectual and motor abilities?"

The statement of the problem, the basic assumptions, and most important, the hypothesis should furnish clues for action. Then a plan of action or approach, which can be as specific as necessary, may be prepared; for our purposes it could take the following form:

Plan

1. Identification of the context of physical education.
2. Brief analysis of the context in terms of its implications for the framework.
3. Establishment of a framework for the development of principles.

This method, however, may prove useless, for each step contains assumptions of its own. Step 2, for instance, assumes the ability to make such an analysis and may be premature. If it is, the hypothesis may be modified to include the qualification, "provided I know how to analyze the context." Now the plan would include an additional step that would lead to an understanding of the analysis and would be incorporated in Step 2.

Two aspects for completion of the process remain: carrying out the plan and evaluating the results. Crucial as they are, the probability of success depends entirely on how clearly the problem and its basic assumptions have been stated and understood. This cannot be emphasized too strongly. Unless the problem is key or basic, the solution will have little value. A faulty or inaccurate basic assumption which cannot be supported will lead to an inaccurate solution. At each step in carrying out the plan the logic of the process must be reviewed: the problem is the real concern, the basic assumptions directly underlie or are contained in the statement of the problem, the hypothesis includes direct guidelines for action, and the plan follows a logical sequence. Even as the solution appears, other steps may have to be modified. For this reason the process must be viewed as a whole at all times and the statement of the problem and its assumptions reviewed regularly.

The first step indicated in the plan is identification of the context for physical education. The forces concerned are believed to be culture, education, physical education, and youth, and a fuller identification of each is necessary to an analysis of the nature of its relation to the solution of the problem.

Two broad definitions of education have been presented: transmitting the cultural heritage and changing behavior. The system of public education in the United States is a social institution clearly designed to acculturate the youth of the society. Physical education falls within this broad purpose. Part 2 furnishes the foundations for developing principles as guidelines for the specific role of physical education, but within the scope of the present problem certain aspects that concern the framework must be recognized.

Acculturation and changed behavior clearly suggest the existence of goals. Because acculturation means being able to participate fully in the culture, we must be able to identify the characteristics that permit us to operate effectively as adults within the culture of the United States. Language, for example, is a part of the American culture. The ability to speak and understand English is a necessary aspect of becoming acculturated. We could certainly survive without it but could never participate completely nor really operate with much effectiveness. Because of the obvious importance of this verbal aspect, reading and writing have always been indispensible parts of the educational process.

Asked to characterize the United States, we should certainly include the democratic nature of American society. For Americans democracy is more than a political concept, more than a way of being governed. It is a way of life, and its tenets and their implications are a pervasive social *ethos*. An American who is unfamiliar with democracy and its principles and methods is at odds with his culture. Every phase of American life has some degree of democratic commitment in evidence. Though democratic principles are violated in many aspects of life in the United States, the importance of the democratic ideal as the social rationale of American culture does not diminish.

Another cultural reality in the United States is the rapidly increasing rate of change in the lives of its people. To be acculturated today means to expect the world to change and to be able to adapt to its changes. Teachers cannot prepare youth for adulthood unless they also prepare them for an ever-changing society. Indeed, the task is immeasurably complicated by the difficulty of preparing for anything very far into the future, for the nature of the future can change quickly and drastically.

Another major characteristic of the United States, which emerges from the complexity and heterogeneity of its society, is the social interrelatedness and mutual dependence of its people. Everything we are or do, everything we wear or eat, everything we see or consider reflects the extent to which our own activities depend on those of others. The future of American society, moreover, is inextricably tied to those of other societies, if not to outer space.

If we accept these obvious cultural elements as basic assumptions, the three foremost characteristics of American culture may be considered (a) the democratic nature of the society, (b) the ever-increasing rate of social and technological change, and (c) the mutual dependence of social relationships. These characteristics, along with language and other cultural factors, are the major cultural forces that bear on the selection of a framework for physical education.

The educational forces consist mainly of the legal mandate that all of the children of all of the people must be included in the vast enterprise of free compulsory education and of public education's obvious commitment to the ideal of helping each individual to develop to his optimal potential by ability rather than position or prestige. These goals of American education set it apart from many other systems of education in the world.

Physical education is part of the total educational curriculum (in many states by legal provision). Although it was not contained in early school curricula, it has come to attain widespread inclusion at all levels of education. Like educational programs in the broader sense, physical education programs differ widely. Today, greater emphasis than ever before is placed on physical activity, prompted by the greater need for health and well-being in times of national crisis and the lesser need for physical effort occasioned by the technological progress of recent years. One further cultural factor bearing on physical education is the shorter work week with its corresponding increases in leisure time for many segments of society.

The targets of any consideration of the forces pressing on physical education or education itself are necessarily the persons to be educated. The present era has been called The Age of Anxiety; certainly it must seem that growing up is not so simple a matter as it once was, though it has never really seemed so. Today's youth posess a serious and complex challenge to both school and society. The realization increases that young people are not secure in facing the world and the future. Many of the evils associated with conformity as a social trend, which are particularly prevalent among the young, seem to indicate a groping for something to count on, for something that has meaning. Never before, even when rugged individualism dominated the American scene, has the willingness to assume responsibility for oneself and others seemed so lacking as a social factor. The whole value structure of American society seems to hang more precariously in the balance as each new generation grows up.

In many respects youth's problems are heightened by greater competence and awareness. No preceding generation has had the avenues and opportunities for exposure to every fact of cultural heritage and accomplishment that now exist. Because cultural participation is based on age in American society, because it is designed on the basis of its appropriateness at the various age levels, small wonder we hear the cry, "They grow up too fast!" The cultural privileges of adulthood have been made to seem highly desirable to youth whose awareness of them has also made these privileges obtainable.

The American people have an almost unbounded faith in youth and tomorrow. Education is seen by them as the means to the end of progress, and progress is a goal highly prized. Thus the ideals and hopes of society in here most firmly in the schoolboy and schoolgirl as symbols of the brighter days to come. There is also a respect for individual personality and dignity which is one of the basic principles on which American society rests. All of these considerations certainly contribute to the establishment of a framework for physical education.

With the analysis of the contextual forces completed, the task begins of examining the implications of and establishing a theoretical framework within which to develop principles for physical education. This is the final step that leads to a solution of the problem. Now, at last, the nature of the framework comes into view. From the analysis and our own knowledge, it should be evident that a framework must not only encompass all of the elements involved but also that its function is to impose a general structure and lend purpose to the matter at hand. The framework should furnish scope and direction to the development of principles as guidelines for action. Thus the framework consists of certain principles as essential truths. Although physical education finds little parallel in established facts like the boiling point of water, the principles that emerge should be rationally conceived, fully understood, and deeply believed.

As indicated in Chapter 1, the establishment of a theoretical framework should be undertaken in terms of underlying values and beliefs. The emerging principles must be valid, based on reflection that is as rational and complete as possible. Finally, and most important, these principles should be consistent and represent deep convictions.

Having traced the steps constituting the process of solving a problem, we turn a possible solution to the specific problem posed in relation to physical education. The following statement of principles as essential truths is offered as one solution to the problem of furnishing a framework within which to develop principles as guidelines for action:

1. The value of personality is the highest of all possible values.
2. The beliefs and implications of democracy stand as the foundation of culture in the United States and serve as the basis for all social intercourse.
3. The fulfillment of the human potential is an enduring national goal which exists in harmony with humanitarian ideals of responsible social and individual action.
4. The contemporary scene is characterized by an ever-increasing rate of change.
5. Effective cultural participation involves the application of intelligence to group and individual problems.
6. The ideals and hopes of American society reside most fully in youth and education.

EVALUATION

The solution of a problem may be evaluated in a number of ways, depending on the nature of the problem itself. In the problem presented, and many like it, the process of solving it must be considered as part of the solution. Merely considering the various contexts relevant to physical education contributes breadth to the theoretical framework, even though all the intellectual effort may not be reflected in the solution itself. The real test of the framework that emerges is whether it is valid; that is, whether its principles as essential truths are believed and understood. If so, all principles as guidelines for action will be consistent with them. The key element in the evaluation of the solution is the amount of meaning and credulity an individual assigns to the principles as essential truths.

Principles as essential truths furnish a framework for theory. The principles developed within this theoretical framework to serve as guidelines for action clearly indicate the practice to be pursued. All aspects of this endeavor must reflect keen intelligence and intellectual integrity at every turn.

GUIDELINES FOR LEARNING EXPERIENCES IN UNDERSTANDING PRINCIPLES AND PROCESS

Principles

1. *Examine* practices in physical education to see if you can identify the theory that is reflected by them. If the theory stated seems to be different from that reflected, try to determine the reasons for the difference.
2. *Discuss* sports and games: analyze *context, framework, theory,* and *practice* in terms of purpose, rules, and strategy.
3. *List* principles as essential truths in which you believe and try to identify the underlying beliefs and values. *Discuss* differences in values and beliefs reflected in the principles and analyze disagreement in terms of its source and nature.
4. *Develop* principles as guidelines for action from the list; try to be consistent with the principle as an essential truth.

Process

1. *Analyze* problem questions in terms of their basic assumptions.
2. *State the problem and list the basic assumptions* inherent in the following situation (caution: state a *problem;* not a solution):

    A group of senior professional students in physical education were discussing one professor's technique of not allowing missed work to be made up. Players on the basketball team were especially upset, for the class met on Fridays and they frequently had to travel for games.
3. *Examine* the assumptions underlying the physical education requirement at all levels in your local schools; analyze the differences.
4. *Suggest* the basic assumptions for the principles as essential truths stated at the conclusion of this chapter; analyze their support.

PART TWO

Historical Perspective: Principles as Essential Truths

HISTORICAL PERSPECTIVE: PRINCIPLES AS ESSENTIAL TRUTHS

Historical interpretation has as many theories as there are reasons for being concerning with history itself. The title of this section clearly implies the use of historical perspective in the development of principles for current use. Human beings are often trapped in the heritage of traditional beliefs. Unless these beliefs are understood within a historical context, contemporary appraisal becomes difficult. Although the lessons of history are rarely applicable in a direct sense, a great deal may be learned from analyzing, in the light of the results, the forces that affected any particular event.

The teachings of the past are useful only as today's student endeavors to understand their character and their influence on the subject at hand. There is not much to be gained from judging the past from today's perspective, but there is much to be learned from judging today from the perspective of the past.

This section delves into the development of principles within the historical perspective of the relation between school and society. It deals with the nature of teaching and learning and with physical education as a field of study and a profession. The principles derived in its three chapters are more in the vein of *essential truths* than of guidelines for action. They are prerequisite to study of the contemporary perspective undertaken in Part 3. Perhaps individuals can understand the place in which they stand only by observing the path by which they arrived. Certainly, such understanding points to the right choice for future adventure.

3

SCHOOL AND SOCIETY

The actual historical relation of school to society has less importance than the manner in which individuals perceive it. Clear sight requires identification of the forces that govern the relationship. Forces that may take the form of cause, belief, value, philosophy, or rationale. Like any method used to achieve human understanding, the process of identifying them is facilitated by a thorough analysis of the problem, its assumptions, the hypotheses advanced, and the impinging factors.

In studying history facts are not always easily distinguishable from the way one sees them. Each historian writes from his own perspective, and few readers are sophisticated enough to shell the substance from its presentation. Wide investigation based on a critical approach steeped in the elements of scientific method at every turn is essential.

The historical analysis in this chapter of the relation of school to society in the United States supplies the bases for the development of principles bearing on the place of physical education in today's schools. Because no reader is presumed to have engaged in an exhaustive scholarly study of school and society, all should approach this material with a view toward understanding the broad development of American education in relation to the changing perspectives that fostered it.

FOUNDATIONS

In recent decades the concept of culture has been widened to include the total way of life of a human society. "Man alone has a significant culture; it is man's social heritage which chiefly sets him apart from all other creatures."[1] Man's social heritage also saddles him with the responsibility for transmitting culture. In simple societies this transmission is an unselfconscious process of introducing the young to the society's pattern of customs and beliefs. More complex societies, for example, the United States, require more organized means to supplement the efforts of the family. James Quillen said:

"Schools are the instruments through which cultures perpetuate themselves. They are established and maintained when the members of a cultural group believe that a special institution is necessary to insure the development of the knowledge, ideals, and competence needed to preserve and continue their way of life."[2]

Raup drew a distinction between the "education of the public" and "public education." He characterized the former as the whole nondeliberate process that causes a people to develop habits, customs, and beliefs. Public education, on the other hand, implies a deliberate organized effort within this process aimed at guiding it, with the school as the crux.[3]

The terms culture and social heritage have wide connotations which must be known in order to understand the school as a social institution. Once they have been grasped, we must recognize the school as an institution of some actual living society, not of an abstraction of society. The school is an institution of some human group that possesses both a past and a future.

Assuming that the school is a social institution automatically establishes its relation to society, but the nature of that relationship needs to be made explicit. Moreover, for the fullest development of the school educators must become aware of their role in fulfilling the school's responsibility to society.

As long as the social order was assumed to be of divine inspiration, as it was in the early years of the seventeenth century, an aristocratic view of society prevailed. Governments were instruments for carrying out God's laws on earth. The people were simply ordained "to carry out the decrees of God which had been embodied in the laws of

---

[1] William F. Ogburn and Meyer F. Nimkoff. *Sociology*, Boston: Houghton Mifflin, 1940, p. 15.

[2] James Quillen, Priorities in the Educational Program. *Teachers College Record*, 57, No. 6, 405 (March 1956).

[3] R. Bruce Raup, "Public Education" and the "Education of the Public." *Readings in the Foundations of Education*, Vol. I. New York: Bureau of Publications, Teachers College, Columbia University, 1941, p. 3.

the state by God's elect."[4] American education reflected this view of society during the seventeenth century, but then, as Butts and Cremin have observed, a transition began:

"Gradually, however, the belief grew that men had certain natural rights, whether accruing from God's gift or simply from natural sources, that could not be abrogated by society. In either case more and more people began to believe that men themselves, indeed the majority of men or all men, should have some share in formulating the civil policies by which they were to be governed. This outlook took the form of a belief in natural rights, in a more democratic form of government, and in a humanitarian social philosophy. Again, the emergence of these views represented a growing belief in the secular assumptions underlying organized society and resulted in demands for a greater role for ordinary men in the conduct of their own affairs."[5]

The colonies in America were not subject to a consistent form of government or social philosophy; neither was the education within them. In the South the English system of education predominated and was applied in terms of universal individual responsibility, universal opportunity for schooling, and universal training for vocation.[6] The middle colonies sought education through the churches. Pennsylvania, for instance, authorized each religious body to build up its own school system, as did Delaware.[7] Massachusetts, however in 1642 laid the enforcement of education on the selectmen or prudential men of the town. As Monroe said:

"The law primarily concerned 'the calling and employment of children' and specified parents and masters as especially concerned. So far it was the English stature of artificers in a New England setting. But one phrase was interpolated which made this a revolutionary enactment—'especially of their ability to read and understand the principles of religion and the capital laws of the country.' This is the only provision which is foreign to the laws of apprenticeship as they were enforced in England and in the remaining colonies. But it is the germ of our public school system."[8]

---

[4] R. Freeman Butts and Lawrence A. Cremin. *A History of American Culture.* New York: Holt, 1953, p. 59.
[5] *Ibid.*
[6] Paul Monroe, *Founding of the American Public School System*, Vol. I. New York: Macmillan, 1940, p. 68.
[7] *Ibid.* pp. 103–104.
[8] *Ibid.* p. 105.

The Colonial Era

In colonial America both a distinctive nation and what was to be its distinctive educational system were evolving. The education of the time reflected the guiding beliefs of the society. The view that "all men should have some share in formulating civil policies" reached fruition in the American Republic. During the colonial period America had not yet taken on its unique character, but from the very first, it should be noted, the principle of equality was germinating. Tocqueville said:

"The emigrants who colonized the shores of America in the beginning of the seventeenth century somehow separated the democratic principle from all the principles that it had to contend with in the old communities of Europe, and transplanted it alone to the New World. It has there been able to spread in perfect freedom and peaceably to determine the character of the laws by influencing the manners of the country." [9]

Certainly, the establishment of democracy was not quite so simple a matter as Tocqueville seems to suggest, but the directions of the future were clear.

The Declaration of Independence presented the rational philosophy; man had inherent rights as an individual. The natural laws of human rights and the inherent dignity and worth of men, simply because they were men, served to support a whole new concept of government and education. The statement, "We hold these truths to be self-evident, that all men are created equal, and that they are endowed by their Creator with certain Unalienable Rights, that among these rights are Life, Liberty, and the Pursuit of Happiness," has been the prevailing rationale of American society.[10]

Yet America did not acquire a distinctive democratic character with the signing of the Declaration of Independence or even on ratification of the Constitution. The significance of these documents lies in the philosophy they expressed. It is worth noting that the Constitution contains the phrase "we, the people," for here again is reflected a belief in the role of ordinary men in the conduct of their own affairs.

Similarly, an educational system did not emerge quickly or clearly

---
[9] Alexis de Tocqueville, *Democracy in America*, Vol. I (revised by Francis Bowen). New York: Knopf, 1946, p. 13.
[10] Arthur Henry Moehlman, Fifty Years of Educational Thought, *Phi Delta Kappan*, 37, No. 4, 134 (January 1956).

in the new nation. Just as Monroe found the germ of the public school system in the Massachusetts law of 1642, other events and philosophies also marked the beginning of public education. These beginnings, however, were not consistent expressions of principles and theories. The young nation was diverse, and its education developed with a complexity and diffuseness not unlike the diversity it envinced in the seventeenth century. Curti cited Thomas Jefferson as "the first American to emphasize public education as an instrument for the realization of democracy and the furthering of social reform.[11]

Jefferson advanced the idea that a single system of schools would bridge the gap between rich and poor, and he considered education as a sure means of promoting human happiness, freedom, and democracy. Benjamin Franklin also proposed a policy he called "Americanization through education." Both men, however, were circumscribed by their times and their own backgrounds. Franklin could not envision a free and universal education for all children. He contented himself with the charitable institutions typical of a class society to minister to the poor. Jefferson did advocate elementary schooling for all, but his intense individualism impelled him to oppose compulsory school attendance.[12]

"It is significant too that while Jefferson kept alive for fifty years the ideal of universal elementary education, free to all alike and bearing no stigma of pauperism, and while in theory he regarded schools for the people as more important than a university, yet in actuality he devoted his major efforts, particularly after his retirement to Monticello, to the founding of an essentially exclusive institution of higher learning." [13]

The most important idea bearing on the relationship of education to society lay in Jefferson's recognition of public education as a vehicle for the realization of democracy and the advancement of social reform. Even as abstract as the concept was at that time, public education was intimately related to society. This much is reflected in the factors that contributed to the defeat of Jefferson's plan. The plan lay before the public from 1778 to 1826. Although Jefferson put his faith in general enlightment, the influence of wealth on political action most likely prevented his educational plan from receiving a fair trial. The ruling

---

[11] Merle Curti. *The Social Ideas of American Educators.* New York: Scribner's, 1935, p. 45.
[12] *Ibid.* pp. 38–45.
[13] *Ibid.* p. 43.

class, which still existed, saw no need for public elementary schools for its children, and a democratic conception of education was felled by its hands. In addition, sectional antagonisms had been inherited from colonial days, and integrated planning and centralization were abhorrent to many in a nation in which nationalism had yet to acquire strength.

In 1795 the American Philosophical Society held a prize essay contest designed to "promote an American system of education." The essays discussed a free and universal school system that espoused a humane and enlightened American nationalism. The writers urged the achievement of human welfare and social progress through education and conceived of democracy's being attained by the development of every individual. Many of the obstacles that Jefferson's plan encountered also proved effective against this proposal. Perhaps of paramount significance was the opposition to its democratic aspects, which envisioned "the continuous remaking of society through science and education," by long-established and still widely entrenched class and religious concepts of education.[14]

America now began to don a democratic mantle, and many of the principles of liberty and equality which had provided a basis for life in the New World were achieving realization. Suffrage was gradually extended in the general direction of universality. Political processes became democratized, and a growth of vigorous nationalism accompanied the growth of industrialization.[15]

"As the movement to extend the suffrage and liberalize politics progressed during the 1820's and 1830's, these demands received ever wider enunciation. Moreover, the problem itself became more and more complex. An intelligent electorate was now far from the only need. With the growth of the idea that any citizen could hold any public office, or serve on juries, or in the militia, the dangers of ignorance could only be multiplied. Furthermore, as political power gradually began to slip from their hands, many upper-class people came to realize that popular education was actually to their own advantage. If the people were going to rule, they ought at least to rule well. More than ever, the education of all was clearly the interest of all."[16]

There is little doubt that universal education was conceived as an instrument to serve society. Many arguments supported this notion.

---
[14] *Ibid.* pp. 45–49.
[15] Butts and Cremin, *op. cit.*, p. 141.
[16] *Ibid.*, p. 191.

Widespread schooling was expected to increase national prosperity by raising the productivity of the people. It was also expected to stem crime and prevent poverty. Further, education was claimed to be the right of every individual, and the public was charged with the duty to furnish it.[17] The opposition to universal education, and public education in particular, was not basically at odds with this concept. Rather it was concerned with the ideals and realities that education was to serve and for whom it would serve.

Education in America needed definition. All the arguments for and about it dealt with the character of American society. Both proponents and opponents of universal public education realized that American education had to be based on American ideals and that it had to contribute to the formation of American society. The idea of universal public education was the source of much debate in early nineteenth-century America. One factor aggravating the problem was the dominant laissez-faire philosophy, which regarded education as a private rather than a public matter. The prevailing ethic, however, was one of individual human perfectability. Man was thought to be capable of enlightment. A laissez-faire philosophy coupled with a strong belief in individualism seemed to lead to the view that each man was free to do what he could, according to his ability.

Mursell said of laissez faire:

"Nevertheless, it was essentially a doctrine of optimism and faith in human nature. And it was the key motive of the great educational movement of the nineteenth century; for the impelling desire which that movement expressed and embodied was to bring out the best and most typically human in individual men and women: to make them good enough and wise enough for freedom." [18]

Whether this was true or the public schools were victors over laissez faire is hard to determine. At any rate, the way was prepared for the acceptance of public responsibility in matters involving individual well-being, especially for the less fortunate.

The Common Schools

Numerous developments led to the crusade for common schools. Religious and philanthropic societies maintained Sunday schools and

---
[17] *Ibid.*, pp. 193–194.
[18] James A. Mursell. *Education for American Democracy.* New York: Norton 1943, p. 58.

day schools in which children of the poor could acquire some education. In the Lancastrian or monitorial plan large numbers of children received instruction at one time by working in small groups with monitors who had already learned the lesson from the teacher in charge. Groups and organizations like the Pennsylvania Society endeavored to extend educational opportunity. Workingmen's associations were concerned with the problem. The popular lyceum movement begun in 1826 was dedicated to the "advancement of education, particularly in common schools, and the general diffusion of knowledge." French and Prussian methods of organization and administration of schools were becoming known and subject to wide discussion.

All of these factors influenced the fight for common schools. Demands were pressed by leaders in many states of the Union: James G. Carter and Horace Mann in Massachusetts and Henry Barnard in Connecticut were keenly influential; Calvin Wiley of North Carolina and Charles Fenton Mercer in Virginia, Calvin Stowe in Ohio, and John Swett in California all worked incessantly for reforms with the help of friendly public figures and middle-class groups.[19]

Horace Mann is generally considered to have taken a leading part in the formation of universal common schools. As Secretary of the State Board of Education in Massachusetts from 1837 to 1848, he was able to exert strong influence. In his *Second Annual Report,* for the year 1838, Mann wrote:

"Knowing as we do that the foundation of national greatness can be laid only in the industry, the integrity, and the spiritual elevation of the people, are we equally sure that our schools are forming the character of the rising generation upon the everlasting principles of duty and humanity? It becomes, then, a momentous question, whether the children in our schools are educated in reference to themselves and their private interests only, or with a regard to the great social duties and perogatives that await them in after-life." [20]

Others were saying essentially the same thing. In the same year, 1838, the people of New Jersey heard an address called, "The State and Education":

"Omitting all considerations, then, of what has been or of what may be legislative enactments on the subject, we address you as the

---

[19] *Ibid.,* pp. 61–63. See also Butts and Cremin, *op. cit.,* pp. 242–243.
[20] Horace Mann. *Second Annual Report Covering the Year 1838.* Boston: Dutton Wentworth, State Printers, 1839, p. 4.

Sovereign People, and we say that *it is your duty and your highest interest to provide and to maintain, within the reach of every child, the means of such an education as will qualify him to discharge the duties of a citizen of the Republic.*" [21]

The struggle for support of public education was long and bitter. Educators had to rally the support of a public composed of varying interests. As a result, most controversial questions other than the of universal schooling were avoided. They stressed the social importance of education and, more cautiously, the idea that the free common school would break down the barriers of caste and promote democracy "by equalizing opportunity for every rank of life." Faith in the idea of progress led to the adoption of public education as "the chief instrument for realizing a middle-class utopia in which morality and religion would be respected; in which every citizen would be law-abiding, orderly, industrous . . . in which property and life would be secure." [22]

Beginning in 1821, during these same years the public high school emerged. It was supported by public funds and existed as an adjunct of the common schools. Tuition fees were paid in the early high schools, but like the rate fees in the elementary schools they may be regarded as a vestige of private support that was soon removed. Butts and Cremin said of the American high school:

"Finally, the high school, as an institution beyond the common schools, removed the threat of a dual system of education implicit in the private academy. No longer did those who could afford it send their children to one school and those who could not, depend on the public school. Now, in theory at least, everyone was free to avail himself of the public elementary school first, and then, if qualified, of the public high school. If the student were further qualified, the way was open from that point to the public university." [23]

So was public education established in nineteenth-century America, a period of stress and controversy. Those engaged in the fight were so concerned with the establishment of schools and the recruitment of public support that little headway was made in formulating an educa-

---

[21] "The State and Education," an address to the people of New Jersey in 1838. Henry Barnard (ed.) *The American Journal of Education*, Vol. XV, Hartford, Connecticut: published by Henry Barnard, 1865, p. 8.
[22] Curti, *op. cit.*, p. 197.
[23] Butts and Cremin, *op. cit.*, p. 263.

tional policy for the new system. Clearly, education during the Civil War did not foster the nationalism it claimed.

Some social progress had been made in the field of education. A single system of schools which dealt a blow at the class system had been developed and, for the most part secular considerations replaced the religious. Educational opportunities for women evolved. Mann and Barnard pioneered in this endeavor, and Emma Willard, Catherine Beecher, and Mary Lyon established seminaries.

But much had not been done. There was still crime and pauperism and other evils that education had asserted it would relieve. By the time of the Civil War, however, a great victory had been won—the establishment of a public school system as a social institution which stands as a tremendous and singular achievement. This gave the promise of the beginnings of democracy in America a frame of reference for its realization. Fulfillment of the promise remained to be seen.

New Forces

American faith in education was made clear by the accomplishments of the nineteenth century. A crude educational structure appeared with the acceptance of public education and developed quickly, in part because of the growth and expansion of the nation. As the century reached its twilight, however, it became evident that diffuse improvised efforts were not enough. Some of the bases of tax-supported education recently won demanded attention. Wrote Cubberley of this development:

Beginning back about 1880 to 1885, however, our schools began to experience a new but steady change in purpose and direction along the lines of the new social and democratic forces, though it is only since about 1900 that any marked and rapid changes have set in." [24]

The strong influence of these new social forces cannot be ignored. Cremin has said:

"An expanding industrialism, a changing immigration, and a vigorous democracy exerted fundamental new demands on American schools between 1893 and 1918. Equally important in the evolving pedagogy of the era, however, were changes in the conception of the

---

[24] Ellwood P. Cubberley. *Public Education in the United States*. Boston: Houghton Mifflin, 1934, p. 505.

school itself—of its relationships to society and to the individuals who attended it." [25]

As these social forces exerted influence on the schools, they commanded greater attention. Reisner suggested that four aspects of social revolution had had great effect: political development in terms of the nation-state, extension of the right to participate in political government, the establishment of universal suffrage, and finally, "the changing modes of economic production with the related social and ideological changes." [26]

In describing the school as it existed in 1890, Rugg suggested that it failed to dip into social matters:

"The school of our fathers' children had no consciously designed theory of the social institutions of the day. As a consequence the curriculum of the schools did not bring young Americans to grips with the actual social scene in which they lived—the problems of their industrializing society, their economic system, changing government, family life, press, the schools themselves, nor any other institution of the day. Not even a chapter could be found in the American histories of the determining role of the Westward-moving frontier nor of the gigantic waves of recurring immigration which were playing such a vast role in the formation of the new national society." [27]

A paradoxical situation pervaded American education. Great social changes were affecting education, but what was education's response to these forces? In the main, as Rugg intimated, it ignored the whole problem. Actually, this is not a fair indictment. Education did respond, but in a practical manner, without a guiding theory. On the high school level educational opportunity widened as society demanded more and more people to fill the positions created by the expanding commercial life born of the industrial revolution. Americans in great numbers were becoming literate, and the masses of new immigrants were joining them in learning the three R's.

At the opening of the twentieth century the clamor increased for a closer relationship between the education offered and the society

---

[25] Lawrence A. Cremin. The Revolution in American Secondary Education, 1893–1918, *Teachers College Record,* **56,** No. 6, 301 (March 1955).
[26] Edward H. Reisner. A Century of Universal Education. *Readings in the Foundations of Education,* Vol. I, p. 823.
[27] Harold Rugg. *Foundations for American Education.* Yonkers, New York: World Book 1947, pp. 526–527.

America was becoming. The report of the Commissioner of Education for 1899–1900 contained this statement:

"A prevalent view is that, because in times past the 'three R's' constituted all elementary instruction, therefore any education which occupied itself with these would be sufficient. To suppose this is, however, to close our eyes to the changes which have been wrought in the world. . . ." [28]

In addition to the changes in American society at the close of the nineteenth century, experts had advanced new discoveries and theories. Rugg and Withers suggested that by 1890 America had developed the capacity to produce a theory of education based on a science of society and culture, a science of behavior, and the art of expression. Darwin published his theories of evolution in 1859; the pre-Gestaltists and the Behaviorists had pioneered in psychology; there were new theories of political science, economics, and anthropology; and the art of expression in architecture, dance, and music underwent exploration.[29]

Two issues were identified. First, some voices urged an educational program that was more aware of society. Second, these voices pressed for the consideration of new knowledge on the basis of its implications for education.

No doubt John Dewey exerted the greatest influence on education at the turn of the century. Dewey took cognizance of both desires in his conception of education. We shall turn to his philosophical outlook presently, but here it is important to examine his book, *School and Society*, first published in 1899. This book was one of the first efforts to challenge the tradition that the schools supported by society were to be concerned only with the responsibility of handing down a fixed body of knowledge. Dewey was interested in all available knowledge and questioned the faculty-psychology viewpoint that prevailed at the time. He recognized the needs of the individual but was concerned for all. In discussing school and social progress, Dewey wrote:

"Yet the range of the outlook needs to be enlarged. What the best and wisest person wants for his own child, that must the community want for all of its children. Any other ideal for our schools is narrow

---

[28] H. H. Morgan. The Justification of the Public High School, Chapter XI. Report of the Commissioner of Education for the Year 1899–1900, Vol. I, Washington, D.C.: U.S. Government Printing Office, 1901, p. 636.
[29] Harold Rugg and William Withers. *Social Foundations of Education.* Englewood Cliffs, New Jersey: Prentice-Hall, 1955, pp. 492–493.

and unlovely; acted upon, it destroys our democracy. All that society has accomplished for itself is put, through the agency of the school, at the disposal of its future members. All its better thoughts of itself it hopes to realize through the new possibilities thus opened to its future self." [30]

Many other educational problems were developing. During this period the ideas of Pestalozzi, Herbart, and Froebel were imported to America. With them came a need for closer examination of educational ideas. The diversity of students turning up in the high schools generated an increase in speculation about curricula and deepened the study of them. Such groups as The National Society for the Promotion of Industrial Education exerted pressure on the schools, and the National Educational Association appointed committees to investigate some of their problems. The turn of the century was steeped in controversy. It was not whether education for all should exist, it was the form education should take.

The School Explosion

The record of growth stands as the strongest testimony to the faith of the American people in the school as a social institution. This growth is manifested in the 19,000 existing public high schools, their nearly 2 million yearly graduates, and the 41.8 million pupils enrolled in public elementary and secondary schools.[31] Though the population of the United States has little more than doubled in the twentieth century, the increase in the number of high school graduates has approximated fifteenfold. The expansion in educational spending has been staggering. The 1960 White House Conference on Children and Youth showed that in the preceding decade expenditures for elementary and secondary schooling increased $6.48 billion, or 152 per cent.

Both the growth and magnitude of public education in the United States define it as one of the most vital social institutions imaginable. One aspect of the functions of such institutions is their policing role:

"They are . . . a means to the reconsideration of the rules and for the changing of the rules. They operate in that frontier of rule-making

---

[30] John Dewey. *The Child and the Curriculum and the School and Society.* Chicago: University of Chicago Press, 1943, p. 7.
[31] Research Division of the National Education Association. *NEA Research Bulletin*, 42, No. 1, 3–4 (February 1964).

and rule-observing where conflicts occur, or at least differences of opinion, and the enforcement and interpretation of the rules helps to keep at least some of the people conscious of them, and so pushing to change them." [32]

The functions of any social institution all relate to those of others, and education is no exception. Education's functions are considered in relation to many other institutions. Indeed, education has been a function of various agencies at different stages in its development. However, the school is an institution "exclusively and deliberately devoted to the formal process of education."

"Schools are institutionalized ways through which a particular society seeks to influence the development of its people. The influence upon people which a given society prescribes, prefers or permits are conditioned both by the established goals of life which characterize that society and by the institutionalized ways through which people in it are allowed or encouraged to reach these goals." [33]

As Ogburn and Nimkoff put it, "One of the best ways to discover the goals in a society is to examine its educational setup. The group is always interested in transmitting its ideals to the young, for only in this way can the group standards be preserved." [34]

It is also expedient to accept the view of Ogburn and Nimkoff with respect to the interrelatedness of institutions:

"The interconnection of institutions is best seen from the point of view of function rather than structure, for the correlation of the different parts of culture is a functional one. The relationship of schools to industry in modern society is a matter of the functions performed by industries and the functions of the schools exercise in equipping the young for earning a living in industry." [35]

Though the interrelationship and interdependence of institutions seem inescapable in a complex modern society, schools have not always taken full cognizance of them. Since colonial times, however, one such relationship has been respected, that between education and

---

[32] Robert Redfield, How Human Society Operates. In Harry L. Shapiro (Ed.), *Man, Culture, and Society.* New York: Oxford University Press, 1956, p. 361.
[33] B. Orthanel Smith, William O. Stanley, Kenneth D. Benne, and Archibald W. Anderson (Eds.). *Reading in the Social Aspects of Education.* Danville, Illinois: Interstate Printers and Publishers, 1951, p. 12.
[34] *Op cit.,* p. 360.
[35] *Ibid.,* p. 744.

government. This view is not unlike one expressed by Jefferson in the eighteenth century or by Horace Mann a century later.

"Human reason creates, modifies and perfects the instrument of government. Mere men may destroy it without sacrilege and constitute another in its place. Briefly, it rests on the will of men who agree to act collectively to form a common law for their security. The stream of legislative power is continuous, is not exhausted by exercise. Education, to serve such a society, must be continuously preeminently concerned with perfecting men's rational capacities on which the conduct of government depends. This can be done only under conditions of freedom." [36]

In 1955 the Educational Policies Commission stated the following:

"The history of education in the United States makes it clear that the American people have evolved educational ideas and practices that are unique. Keyed to the development of responsible citizens and based on equality of opportunity in a democracy, the public schools are indiginous to the American way of life.

"America's public schools embody the time-honored values of freedom, equality, and self-government. Indeed, the nation's program in education, as organized in public institutions for all American youth, is itself one of the essential values and distinguishing characteristics of the American tradition." [37]

Although the colonies had enacted legislation for the establishment of schools, the Constitution failed to mention education, and its control was thus reserved for the states. This was contrary to European practice in which highly centralized control was exercised.

Jesse H. Newlon has reviewed the development of support for the schools:

"Support was, in the beginning, entirely by local taxation. In time, as the system expanded, school administrators drawn from the ranks of the teachers became a necessity. In time state departments of education were established and given control over many matters. State-supported colleges, universities and professional schools were established. Grants of land were made by the Federal government for

---

[36] Thomas Woody. Education and National Culture. In *School and Society,* 52, No. 1342, 183 (Sept. 14, 1940).
[37] Educational Policies Commission. *Public Education and the Future of America.* Washington, D.C.: National Education Association and American Association of School Administrators, 1955, p. 79.

the support of schools in the newer states, and especially in recent years state taxes have been levied for the support of the common schools." [38]

It might be noted that Federal participation in the support of various phases of education has increased but that control has remained in the hands of the states. Boards of education were organized under state laws and are chosen by the people to control the public schools. Within an institutional setting education thus enjoys a high degree of independence.

The School as a Social Institution

The necessity for defining the relationship of the school to society in the United States has rapidly increased because of the urgency of the problem. The twentieth century has produced a society of greater complexity, and the rate of change seems to increase continuously. New knowledge about learning, individuals, and society and many other developments cannot be ignored. In describing education as a fixed process of transmitting culture, Margaret Mead said, "Thus we avoid facing the most vivid truth of the new age: no one will live all his life in the world into which he was born, and no one will die in the world in which he worked in his maturity." [39] The Committee for the White House Conference on Education in 1956 made this statement:

"Although it is new, this ideal of schools which do everything possible for all children is a natural development in the United States. The moving spirit of this Nation has been from the beginning a sense of fairness. Nowadays equality of educational opportunity for children. Ignorance is a greater obstacle than ever to success of most kinds. . . . In still another way, this new ideal for the schools is a natural development of this century; it recognizes the paramount importance of the individual in a free society. Our schools are asked to teach skills currently needed by the Nation, but never at the expense of the individual. This policy of encouraging each child to develop his individual talents will be of the greatest use to the Nation, for in

---

[38] Jesse H. Newlon. Dominance of Local Control of Schools. *Readings in the Foundations of Education*, Vol. II, p. 596.
[39] Margaret Mead. A Redefinition of Education. In C. Scott Fletcher (Ed.), *Education for Public Responsibility*. New York: Norton, 1961, p. 56.

the long run, if no talent is wasted in our land, no skill will be lacking.

"This great new goal for our schools is unanimously approved by the committee." [40]

Although the ideal of schools "which do everything possible for all children" may be a natural development, it creates still another dimension to the problems confronting them. As Quillen said:

"The question of educational priorities becomes increasingly important as contemporary culture becomes more complex and more tasks are thrust upon the school. The identification of priorities is difficult, however, and, in an age of ideological conflict, almost inevitably controversial. Decisions concerning priorities in the school program need to be based on the characteristics of contemporary culture, some conception of ideals and values, and the best available knowledge regarding the nature of individual growth and development and the learning process." [41]

The ideal of schools doing everything they can for all children is relatively new and so is the recognition that the school cannot do everything. In the opinion of Butts and Cremin, "In spite of growing attacks on traditional conceptions of human nature and learning, religious-moral development and mental discipline remained paramount aims well into the twentieth century." [42]

Another factor that has contributed to this complex relationship between school and society has been the practical nature of education. Said Havinghurst:

"The reasons for such general approval of educational expansion have been mainly selfish, because of its usefulness in improving the economic and social status of the individual, and partly because it was thought to improve his civic and cultural behavior." [43]

The Committee for the White House Conference on Education endorsed the concept of improving social status in the statement:

---

[40] The Committee for the White House Conference on Education. *A Report to the President.* Washington, D.C.: U.S. Government Printing Office, April 1956, pp. 9–10.
[41] Quillen, *op cit.*, p. 404.
[42] *Op cit.*, p. 433.
[43] Robert J. Havinghurst. Social Foundations of General Education. In *General Education,* Fifty-first Yearbook, Part I, National Society for the Study of Education, 1952, p. 73.

"The schools have become a major tool for creating a Nation without rigid class barriers. *It is primarily the schools which allow no man's failure to prevent the success of his son.*" [44]

This dual concept of public education as a means of improving social and economic status and contributing to individual success has been well-documented in the twentieth century. Education has symbolized one of the channels to a better life for Americans no less than for immigrants. Said the Educational Policies Committee:

"In these ways and others have the public schools justified the faith of the American people. Like other institutions, they are not perfect; like any institution, they have shortcomings. But their contributions have been significant and lasting. The United States would not be so democratic, so prosperous, so satisfying to the individual, and so strong in mind and spirit as it is today were it not for the nation's record in developing and supporting public schools." [45]

Before turning to the functional relationship between school and society let us reflect briefly on the democratic basis of American society. Many current arguments in support of the school's obligation to the development of democracy strongly recall those of the eighteenth and nineteenth centuries. Basically, however, the intent differs. In the early days of the United States democracy meant little more than teaching people to read and write. This concept has slowly broadened. The Educational Policies Commission commented:

"Owing to the nature of popular usage, there is danger that the term *democratic society* be taken too narrowly, in a mere political sense. Society is more than politics. It embraces all culture. And democracy implies the widest possible diffusion of culture and all the means essential to the good life." [46]

The Commission stated further:

"Democracy is more than institutions and ways of life. It is a great social faith which, in response to the yearnings and struggles of many races and peoples, has been developing through the centuries." [47]

---

[44] *Op. cit.*, p. 9.
[45] *Op. cit.*, p. 76.
[46] Educational Policies Commission. *Policies for Education in American Democracy.* Washington, D.C.: National Educational Association and the American Association of School Administrators, 1946, p. 93.
[47] *Ibid.*, p. 103.

American society is thus both complex and changing. Its predominant values contain a concept of democracy that stands as a social faith. It is the relation of school to this society that mainly concerns us. Margaret Mead characterized that relationship:

"If we turn from images to look formally at the history of American education, of its theory and its practice, the conflict between the school oriented toward the past and the school oriented toward the future, with the seldom obtainable dream of a school which would hold the world steady, will be found to be a prevailing theme." [48]

Nathan M. Pusey has said:

"The age-old conflict within education about its ultimate purpose will, I fear, still be unresolved in 1980. Almost from the beginning there have been those who have believed that everything needful is said when it is stated that education's function is to serve society. . . . Opposed to them are the humanists who, while not explicitly denying any of these aims, resolutely insist that education needs no such justification, that it is an experience valid for its own sake, and that its proper function is simply to help individuals to grow as individuals." [49]

To understand the nature of the conflict to which both Mead and Pusey refer requires us to examine the possibilities inherent in the relationship between school and society. Cuber and Harper isolate this issue in terms of three conceptions:

"1. That education should be concerned solely with the *indoctrination of the young into the culture of the group which* controls the educational system—that is, that the schools should teach each new generation to be precisely like its predecessor in as many ways as possible. This we may call the 'function of indoctrination.'

"2. That the function of education is not merely to perpetuate the existing culture without bias, but to *evaluate* it—that is, to analyze it, to raise questions concerning the relative worth of things, and to *consider various proposals* for *the perpetuation or modification of the society* in which the student lives. . . .

"3. That it is the function of education to *direct social change* along lines which appear to be desirable in the interest of public

---

[48] Margaret Mead. *The School in American Culture.* Cambridge, Massachusetts: Harvard University Press, 1951, p. 13.
[49] Nathan Marsh Pusey. The Exploding World of Education. In David Sarnoff et al., *The Fabulous Future. America in 1980.* New York: Dutton, 1956, p. 75.

welfare—that is, the schools should take the attitudes and skills of children so as to facilitate an emerging but different society. This too is a type of indoctrination, but it is a dynamic rather than a static orientation. It warrants the term indoctrination, however, because the emphasis is placed upon teaching people what they ought to think, rather than simply training them to be critical, analytical, and open-minded about social issues." [50]

Because these authors have apparently made a value judgment, let us digress a bit to note that *all* education implies prediction and control, with the concept of indoctrination quite implicit. Evaluation presupposes indoctrination as surely as change. Thus it becomes necessary to recognize formal education as indoctrination of some sort, whether it be to one doctrine or to open-mindedness. The mere existence of an evaluative process indicates a bias. None of these possibilities suggests that education is not in some way related to society. This is Glenn Austin's view, as we can see from what he has said:

"Education and society are ceaselessly interacting with each other, each affecting the other. Social change is taking place and education can react to it in at least three ways: (1) ignore it and thus tacitly approve it; (2) re-enforce social change indiscriminately; or (3) strive to help people to operate with an awareness of the alternatives available and what can be done about them." [51]

Austin also drew on a concept of democratic society in establishing this view:

"A democratic society is not one which must conform to any prescribed, predetermined pattern. It is a society which emphasizes participation of all its members in developing the values to be cherished (in that society) and in selecting the most desirable of the alternative directions for social change. And perhaps most important of all, the criteria for what is improvement and what is desirable are determined by the members of the society." [52]

What, then, are the *commitments* of public education in the United States? As we have seen, certain commitments have been implicit

---

[50] John F. Cuber and Robert A. Harper. *Problems of American Society: Values in Conflict.* New York: Holt, 1948, pp. 224–225.
[51] Glenn Austin, Freedom, Conformity, and Uniformity. *Teachers College Record,* 58, No. 4, 210 (January 1957).
[52] *Ibid.,* p. 207.

throughout the history of this relationship of school and society. The Educational Policies Commission in its 1946 report refers to them in this statement on public education:

"It is committed to the maintenance and improvement of American society as now constituted and unfolding . . . the sharp antithesis sometimes drawn between those who would have the schools create a new social order and those who would confine them to a mere defense of the status quo does not correspond to the known facts in the case." [53]

Whether or not the conclusion in this statement is warranted, the schools are certainly committed to American society.

Two points have primary importance. First, public education is committed to doing everything possible for all children, and, second, the necessity for priorities in education is implied. It becomes obvious that the status quo cannot be maintained. Even without the element of change, modern society is too complicated for transmission as a whole. Because the schools must of necessity be selective and public education is inextricably related to society, it behooves us to pay heed to the relation of the school to social change.

Describing the first half of the twentieth century, Butts said:

"The most thoughtful approach among professional leaders was to try to understand clearly the basic intellectual forces at work in our society and to make informed choices that could be defended judiciously yet fearlessly. Three general types of orientation were discernible in their influence upon education. Some educators and philosophers relied on the authority of tradition for their principle assumptions concerning educational content and method. Others looked to modern science for their authority in describing the world, human behavior, and the educative process. Still others appealed to the cultural conceptions of man and society as providing the basic ingredients of a defensible philosophy of human nature, knowledge, and education." [54]

These philosophical views are pursued presently. However, they provide some basis for the substance to follow. It is significant, though sometimes overlooked, that much of the difference of opinion

---
[53] *Op. cit.*, p. 67.
[54] R. Freeman Butts. *A Cultural History of Western Education.* New York: McGraw-Hill, 1955, p. 554.

in this area stems from differences in philosophy. Havinghurst and Neugarten raise an important point which bears on the problem.

"In a changing society there is always some difference between what the society is and what it wants to be, between its practice and its ideals. Thus the educational system, being part of the culture, has two supplementary functions: to be a mirror that reflects society as it is, and, at the same time, to be an agent of social change and a force directed toward implementing the ideals of society." [55]

This supports Margaret Mead's view of a conflict between schools oriented to the past and schools oriented to the future, "with the seldom obtainable dream of a school which would hold the world steady." The statement also sums up a whole realm of images, among them, the "American dream" and the cultural lag. Even the American classless society must be classified with ideals, as research in the social sciences has demonstrated. Many claim that universal education is not a reality in the United States, or at least that it is not free so long as so many young people drop out of school because they cannot afford the luxury of not working.

The Educational Policies Commission contributed this statement to the matter of ideals:

"Ideals and values derive their entire practical importance from the behavior which results from them. The expression of high ideals accompanied by the doing of wrong is thoroughly vicious. Education, therefore, seeks to encourage the mastery of such knowledge, the acquisition of such attitudes, and the development of such habits as make a socially desirable way of living likely to be followed by the learner. . . . The definition of this scale of values is a continuing and crucial problem of both social and educational policy." [56]

Edwards and Rickey also identified this sense of values as being of the utmost importance:

"It must not be supposed, however, that education is always caught in the iron grip of the present, that it has no obligation to the future. Quite the contrary is true. In any civilization that has a sense of direction, that has moral commitments, the school has an important role to play in the processes of social transition. Certainly, in an age such as ours, when the economic, political, and ethical foundations of soci-

---

[55] Robert J. Havinghurst and Bernice L. Neugarten. *Society and Education.* Boston: Allyn and Bacon, 1957, p. 201.
[56] *Policies for Education in American Democracy,* p. 187.

ety are undergoing profound changes, teachers have a responsibility for the shape of things to come which they cannot in good conscience evade. They need to know where they are going and why, and they need a set of values that will give them a sense of direction at all stages of the journey." [57]

Some of these values have already been documented.

"Instead of mere teaching institutions, engaged in imparting book information and imposing discipline, our schools have been asked to grasp the significance of their social relationships, to transform themselves more fully into institutions for the improvement of democracy, and to prepare the young who attend them for greater social efficiency by teaching more that is directly useful and by training them better for citizenship in a democracy such as ours." [58]

Cubberley's comment re-emphasizes the need for the schools to define their purpose as social institutions. Gordon Blackwell has made two noteworthy points. The first restates the interrelatedness of all institutions of society and that schools must recognize this fact; the second concerns the schools' responsibility for social change:

"Several basic assumptions underlie my approach to this discussion: (1) Education does not function in a social vacuum but in and for a given society. (2) Education should be directed toward the needs of the group, the community, and the society fully as much as toward the individual. (3) Individuals must continually work out adjustments to the culture and social organization in which they live. This is a matter of accommodating individualized drives and goals to the expectations, values, regulations, and sanctions which society has developed to control human behavior. (4) Education as a means of influencing human behavior must be considered in relation to other forms of socialization and social control in a society." [59]

He further stated:

"If individuals, in the course of their personality development, frequently find themselves on shifting sand, this is of considerable concern to education. If the teacher is to understand and work ef-

---

[57] Newton Edwards and Herman G. Richey. *The School in the American Social Order.* Boston: Houghton Mifflin, 1947, p. 840.
[58] Cubberley, *op. cit.*, p. 502.
[59] Gordon W. Blackwell. New Social Patterns. *Teachers College Record,* **57**, No. 6, 392 (March 1956).

fectively with his raw material—the students—he must give attention to these problems of social adjustment on the one hand and to the development of individuality and personal integrity on the other. There is also the responsibility of education for helping to mold new social patterns within which individuals of the future may work out their adjustment and integrity with higher chances of success." [60]

Blackwell's contribution is highly pertinent. First, he said that education "should be directed to the needs of the group, the community, and the society fully as much as toward the individual." This is a twentieth-century concept. As we have seen, the belief at the beginning of the public school system in America was that developing the individual in certain ways would ensure the progress of society in the same manner. This is not necessarily true. Imbuing the individual with a belief in democracy does not ensure the development of a democratic society. Second, education must be considered "in relation to other forms of socialization and social control in a society." This is another point about which educators have not seemed to show sufficient awareness.

The interrelatedness of institutions is moot; it is inescapable; and if these relationships are to be exploited for the greatest good, they must be recognized. Blackwell also makes a point that was only implied in the Havinghurst and Meugarten statement: that education has a responsibility to the future and to the implementation of social ideals, but that it also has a responsibility to the acculturation of students. It follows, therefore, that education would indeed have "to be a mirror that reflects society as it is" for students to take their places within that society. Whether it can at the same time "help to mold new social patterns" is debatable. Caswell said:

"When in a period of momentous social change, people can make only the roughest approximation of the significance of the events transpiring around them. Yet we must seek within the limits of our vision to understand them in their long-range implications, or it becomes impossible to influence to any extent the future course of events." [61]

This much would seem true: an effort must be made to understand the events of the present or it becomes virtually impossible to affect their future course.

---

[60] *Ibid.*, p. 399.
[61] Hollis L. Caswell. Achievement and Challenge. *NEA Journal,* 46, No. 3, 143 (March 1957).

The Role of Philosophical Belief

No one can overemphasize the importance of philosophical belief in the development of education. Theodore Brameld wrote:

"Philosophers have sought steadily to give distinctive expression to the beliefs, attitudes, and functions of the young nation from the earliest pre-Revolutionary days to our own. Education, too, has been regarded as one of our chief instruments of cultural solidarity and progress. The history of American *philosophy,* interpreted in the perspective of American *education,* is at the center of the adventure which is American *culture.*" [62]

With this in mind, it becomes necessary to examine philosophical orientations in connection with the relationship between schools and society in the United States.

Brubacher has remarked that the "study of educational philosophy has flourished in the twentieth century as never before in the whole history of education." He attributes this interest to the rise of progressive education. The controversy between progressive and traditional educational practices, of course, only oversimplifies the issues at stake. Brubacher said:

"The experimental schools which made up progressive education were but the vanguard of the larger twentieth-century endeavor to assume more and more intentional control of the social process. Traditional methods of cultural transmission and renewal, once left to automatic processes, now became the object of conscious consideration. Progressive schools, for instance, deliberately fashioned their practices on scientific findings. As these often were in conflict with cherished traditional convictions there was an urgent demand for a fresh philosophical approach to resolve the conflict." [63]

Many factors contributed to the differences between progressive and traditional education. For the most part, traditional education had ignored the development of a scientific psychology and its conceptions of human nature. The Darwinian view of development had not impinged on traditional beliefs about education, nor had the cul-

---

[62] Theodore Brameld. *Philosophies of Education in Cultural Perspective.* New York: Dryden, 1955, p. 67.
[63] *Modern Philosophies and Education,* Fifty-Fourth Yearbook, Part I. Chicago: National Society for the Study of Education, 1955, p. 5.

tural relativity espoused by anthropological and sociological studies been adopted.

Furthermore, the twentieth-century setting for these differences was one of political and economic upheaval. Democracy pervaded a variety of courses: laissez-faire individualism, benevolently paternal newdealism, and pragmatic liberalism. Strife between capitalism and socialism infected the economic system. These factors all accentuated the difficulties of a period of accelerated social transition. Although men had long been interested in the direction education should take, Brubacher ascribed the present tensions to the conscious use today of education "as a tremendous instrument of public policy." [64]

John Dewey's challenge to traditional education has probably been the largest single influence of the century on the philosophy of education. Because he accepted the Darwinian theories, Dewey regarded human intelligence as a relatively late development and considered it to be instrumental. In *Democracy and Education* he said:

"Thus we have completed the circuit and returned to the conceptions of the first portion of this book: such as the biological continuity of human impulses and instincts with natural energies; the dependence of the growth of the mind upon participation in conjoint activities having a common purpose; the influence of the physical environment through the uses made of it in a social medium; the necessity of utilization of individual variations in desire and thinking for a progressively developing society; the essential unity of method and subject matter; the intrinsic continuity of ends and means; the recognition of mind as thinking which perceives and tests the meanings of behavior. These conceptions are consistent with the philosophy which sees intelligence to be the purposive reorganization, through action, of the material of experience; and they are inconsistent with each of the dualistic philosophies mentioned." [65]

In accordance with his instrumental view of knowledge, there could be no absolute truth in Dewey's philosophy. Therefore process became important, and the contribution of his thinking was to be found in "growth." Concerning the social dimension of Dewey's philosophy, Curtis and Boultwood have said:

"In the struggle for stability, Dewey has no doubt that there must be aroused an awareness of individual responsibility in an enlarged

---

[64] *Ibid.*, p. 507.
[65] John Dewey. *Democracy and Education*. New York: Macmillan, 1916, p. 377.

and complex world. The school can contribute by training the young in specific and experimental thinking and by helping them to experience the need for democratic co-operation. He sees human progress as dependent upon the opening up of lines of communication between peoples—nations, classes, and all smaller groups. Early in the century he expressed his hope that American schools, in bringing together children of many nationalities, languages, traditions, and creeds, would demonstrate the development of social unity through the culture common to all groups. How far this has yet been achieved must be decided by the Americans themselves, for the course of American education was destined to be influenced by other conflicting philosophies." [66]

Before dealing with these "other conflicting philosophies," let us note the inescapable conclusions of pragmatic philosophy in regard to the relation between education and society and social change. Childs summarized this position:

"The new education has not only conceived of the work of the school in social terms, it has also suggested that the focus of the curriculum should be on those areas in the life of a society where reconstructive activity is in process because tensions have arisen between new inventions, new knowledge, new ways of life with their as yet unrealized possibilities, on the one hand, and inherited traditions, customs, institutions, and group habits and attitudes on the other. It is clear that an educational program which is thus centered in the changing and growing points of a society will not be content with mere transmission of meanings; it will also be concerned to indicate the nature of these conflicts, the institutional and ideational factors involved in them, and the direction in which reconstruction should move if these conflicts are to be overcome in a way that will preserve essential democratic values." [67]

In the Great Depression of the 1930's progressive education, which had assumed many forms in distortion of Dewey's views, was scored by many for its failure to include a social element. Led by George S. Counts, this group stressed the collectivistic character of American society and championed the notion that the school should take the initiative in planning and achieving a new social order. It was attacked from many sides. Robert Maynard Hutchins, president of the

---
[66] S. J. Curtis and M. E. A. Boultwood. *A Short History of Educational Ideas.* London: University Tutorial, 1953, p. 476.
[67] John L. Childs. *American Pragmatism and Education.* New York: Holt, 1956, p. 348.

University of Chicago, was one of its major critics. "The neo-Thomism of Hutchins and his associates, including Adler, Barr, and Buchanan, was not indifferent to the depression and the quest for security. But it looked not to some golden age in the future in which security would reign but to a golden age of the past." [68]

In the opinion of these neo-Thomists the mass should receive training for vocations and citizenship with an emphasis on essentials in the elementary schools and on subjects of general significance in high schools and junior colleges. By such a reformation of education they hoped to subordinate excess materialism, loose and out-of-hand individualism, and false democracy to what they considered the "intellectual verities." [69]

Perhaps it is true, as Brubacher said:

"From the objections to the theory that the school should give direction to social progress, it would be unfair inference, in most instances, that these same critics did not think the school had any role to play in social progress. . . . Or perhaps more accurately yet, one should set aside as futile any discussion of which is cause and which effect, education or social change. The two are mutually interactive, circular, never-ending. Each cross-fertilizes the other." [70]

Havighurst offered this same divergence of opinion in another way:

"The extent of divergence among the educators . . . is best seen by studying the actual content and methods which they advocate for general education. In general, the group who think of education as closely and reciprocally related to society favor a curriculum centered on the present society, its problems, achievements, values, and operations; while those who think of general education as ideally the same everywhere favor a curriculum centered on the past, its values, problems, achievements, and operations. Yet all agree that a good general education should result in improvement of the present society." [71]

The key phrases from our standpoint are "yet all agree" and "should result." None would argue that society does not affect the schools;

---

[68] Merle Curti. *The Growth of American Thought.* p. 733.
[69] *Ibid.,* p. 744.
[70] John S. Brubacher. *Modern Philosophies of Education.* New York: McGraw-Hill, 1939, p. 225.
[71] Robert J. Havighurst. *General Education.* p. 79.

and when the concept is added that the schools, by content and method, should contribute to an improved society, we are back at Brubacher's "mutually interactive" position in regard to education and social change.

This interactive position has been expounded by many writers. Butts said:

"The interactive process means that individuals realize their potentialities in and through a genuinely democratic social participation. The well-developed individual cannot be considered apart from a consideration of a desirable social order, in which individual needs are fulfilled by a democratic society. All good education rests upon a good society." [72]

Kandel added:

"The school, then, cannot build a new social order. . . . This is not a matter of courage or cowardice; it is a question of fact which all history of education has proved and which the study of any educational system, even the most radical and revolutionary confirms . . . the school reflects social demands but does not initiate social change. A new education can be developed when the public has determined what the nature of the new America will be; . . . nor does it mean that education and the school have no concern with social progress; it does, however, mean that they are confronted with the task of discovering how social progress can best be promoted within the fabric of society as it now is." [73]

Kandel's views might be considered to agree with the dual purposes of education pointed out by Havighurst and Neugarten: that the school must reflect society as it is and be an agent of social change. This would presumably support an interactive position. In reflecting society the schools must be sensitive to it as it exists, and in contributing to social change they must be sensitive to what society will become. As Kandel asserted, there can be no social progress that is not based on the "fabric of society as it now is." This view is well put in two basic assumptions underlying a recent work devoted to education in the face of a changing society:

"1. At all times, society and not the school is responsible for its deepest problems.

---

[72] R. Freeman Butts. *A Cultural History of Education.* New York: McGraw-Hill, 1947, p. 643.
[73] I. L. Kandel. The School Cannot Build a New Social Order. In *Readings in Foundations of Education,* Vol. I, pp. 904–905.

62   Historical Perspective: Principles as Essential Truths

2. If schools are to serve society well at any time, and crucially in times of change, the schools should be given a clear mandate to inculcate values appropriate for continuing the growth of society." [74]

Clearly, the divergent views on the purposes of education depend on the various philosophical conceptions of the individual and society. Pragmatism has been the dominant philosophy in twentieth-century education, but no matter how divergent the views have been there seems to be agreement that (a), notwithstanding degree, the school cannot be wholly divorced from society and (b), notwithstanding differences over method and content, the school should contribute to the improvement of society.

This would tend to support an interactive approach to the relations between school and society. In the extreme we can envision the school alone building a new social order or schools doing nothing but attempting to transmit a social heritage intact. These extreme positions are virtually impossible of attainment. Even the neo-Thomists support interaction, though in a less positive form than the pragmatists. In his exposition of Thomist philosophy Jacques Maritain said:

"As concerns the social change in the contemporary world, teachers have neither to make the school into a stronghold of the established order nor to make it into a weapon to change society." [75]

Summing up an historical view of philosophy and science in the western world, Reisner said:

"It is highly improbable that all of us will be satisfied with the same intellectual formulas, but there is more reason to believe that men of good will may lay hold in our changing social order upon the same system of human values. If such be the case, the prospect of uniting the forces of good conscience and good will in support of a system of education which will lead to better social arrangements . . . is good indeed." [76]

PRINCIPLES

Before turning to the development of principles in the foregoing framework, let us consider a brief account of a lost cause as an exam-

---

[74] August Kerber and Wilfred R. Smith (Eds.). *Educational Issues in a Changing Society*. Detroit: Wayne State University Press, 1962, p. 11.
[75] National Society for the Study of Education, *op. cit.*, p. 69.
[76] *Philosophies of Education,* Forty-first Yearbook, Part I. Chicago: National Society for the Study of Education, 1942, p. 37.

ple of the pitfalls to avoid. This case is drawn from the book *NEA: The First Hundred Years;* it follows several educational movements which over the years have lost their passion, such as temperance and simplified spelling. This account deals with thrift.

School savings accounts were initiated in 1885. Eight years later some 33,800 pupils had $345,634.52 on deposit in their own names. By 1913 about 1500 participating schools in 30 states and about 150 cities had adopted school savings plans. As late as 1956 schoolchildren had $156,600,000 in bank savings accounts, yet by 1925 the movement had essentially ended in spite of the fact that the NEA had published an 80-page book reporting the results of a National Conference on Thrift Education held in 1924.

The school savings plans were predicated on the importance of the habit of "thrift." At the 1916 sessions of the National Council of Education papers on thrift called the habit an educational necessity and dwelt on its relation to home, country, industry, health, and character. The participants extolled thrift as a virtue, "a discipline and an exercise of the will, a developer of moral stamina, and a protection against the temptation to waste and squander."

Following the outbreak of war in 1917 President Wilson declared thrift a national goal and school officials developed many novel plans for its practice in school administration. Bank balances were taken to exemplify the virtues of thrift, and some school districts made provisions for overseeing pupils' accounts during summer work periods. Thrift outlines were prepared for various grades, and universities and teacher-training institutions were condemned if they failed to offer courses in the teaching of thrift.

Ultimately the death of the movement seemed predestined by organic failure. Thrift education became a lost cause because it did not cure all the ills of society; wasteful spending as well as criminality persisted. A post-mortem examination of its basic assumptions turns up a perhaps more significant reason for its proving a lost cause. Does thrift really equate with bank deposits? Bankers thought so, but why did teachers? Indeed, why thrift at all? Was this truly a basic and crucial issue of its time, or was it merely a readily identifiable issue that proposed action without really altering the existing educational framework?

This chapter has sought to clarify the relations between school and society, and its purpose is to identify as essential truths the principles that have emerged from the historical nature of those relations in conception and practice. The social and educational achievements of the United States can hardly be separated, even for purposes of discussion. It is almost impossible to isolate cause and effect in the development of enlightened citizens, self-government, and unity of national purpose which have come to characterize the nation in so short a time. No one today would seriously protest universal education or public support of public education; we could scarcely visualize the United States without them. Historically, they were real, debatable social issues only a few decades ago. Nor is it possible to speculate on the direction American growth might have taken if these issues had been resolved in some other manner.

The people of the United States, whether few or many, elected officials or inspired leaders with insight and vision or a single pedestrian belief, created the vast educational enterprise which serves as the major social institution for their own betterment. However, if the developmental history presented in this chapter is to have any significance for the present, we must understand the underlying rationale and guiding theory that appeared in various stages of the process. The Massachusetts Law of 1642, for example, has often been called the "Old Deluder" law, for its very statement of purpose presupposed a belief that in the ability to read God's word lay the answer to that "Old Deluder, Satan." As one of the earliest manifestations of educational commitment in law, this indeed warrants Monroe's assertion that it contained the "germ of our public school system."

A distinction must be made, however, between legally requiring education and requiring it in order to enable people to deal effectively with "Satan." A more considered view of the Massachusetts Law of 1642 exposes its limited purpose of literacy as an outgrowth of its motivating beliefs. The point is that developmental history must be viewed within its framework. Its similarities and dissimilarities to the current situation must be understood so that it can have some value for the present and serve as a vital assumption. We cannot ask the foolish question, "Why didn't the selectmen in Massachusetts in 1642 'see' that education should have secular assumptions?" We can only ask ourselves why *we* see it and what was different in their world of values and beliefs.

The relation between schools and society is a basic assumption. Schools were created by society, and society as it is would not exist in the United States were it not for the nation's educational history. Many of the following principles are other basic assumptions, but this, in part, is the purpose of a historical perspective. Whether essential truths or implicit guidelines for action, the principles that emerge from a review of developmental history of a relationship like that between school and society become assumptions for the establishment of other principles based on functions within that relationship. Without these functions it would be very difficult, if not impossible, to develop principles within contemporary perspective which evince full understanding.

1. *The first principle is that public education in the United States is an increasingly important social institution.* This principle emerges from the place of education in society; it is documented by time, money, and the degree of involvement of millions of children and adults in its operation as well as by the laws, customs, and social factors surrounding it. As an organized institution, probably none other in the United States is more far-reaching in its impact. Its ever greater growth is easily certified.

2. *The second principle identifies education as a social institution charged with introducing the young into the complex society of the United States.* A society creates institutions to supply the influence or development private or individual sources cannot provide. The enduring purpose of education is acculturation, and the American people have organized a vast system of public education to carry out this process. Other assumptions also underlie the creation of a social institution designed to educate: the complexity of the task, the necessity for trained leadership, the importance of common or basic elements in the undertaking, hence the existence of an identifiable role.

3. *The third principle is that schools should contribute to the progress of society by the preservation and expression of enduring commitment to the ideal social values on which they are founded.* Public schools are indigenous to the American way of life. The unique concepts that produced an educational system embracing all of the children of all of the people are based on deeply rooted and time-tested values. Both the concepts and values, and their expression in the educational enterprise, stand as outstanding aspects of American tradition and society. The assumptions of American education cannot be extricated from the assumptions of American society. History reveals the faith of the American people in the values of responsible citizenship, human personality and development, democracy, freedom, equality, and progress, and their schools must reflect this commitment.

4. *The fourth principle concerns the responsibility of education to reflect the society so that young people can take their places in it.* This principle is based on the diverse conceptions surrounding the role of the schools in American society. The "thrift" experience could be duplicated over and over again in almost every aspect of American education. Although there is general agreement at the principles-as-

essential-truths level on the nature of education and its place in American society, disagreement is widespread on the role or functions of the schools. Most of this controversy revolves about teaching and learning, which is the subject matter of Chapter 4, but much of it lies within philosophical considerations of educational aims, especially in relation to social processes and social change. The importance of education has usually been stressed in terms of some idea of social good. The learning of thrift, for example, was presented on the basis of its value as an individual habit that would cure all social ills. In a similar manner education as "preparation for life" was predicated on an interpretation of acculturation as a learning of skills and habits that would be needed later. Even mental discipline as an educational aim meant the cultivation of habits of control and development for subsequent use. The orientation of the progressive educationists made this relation of education to social processes explicit and sought to emphasize the present rather than the future.

SUMMARY

In a complex and rapidly changing society in which there is a commitment to the values of human personality, democracy, and education these principles emerge from an analysis of the relationship between school and society seen from the perspective of history:

1. Public education in the United States is a major social institution of increasing importance.
2. Education as a social institution has as its primary task the acculturation of the young into the complex society of the United States.
3. Education in the United States is committed to the value concepts that gave rise to its development and is dedicated to the progress of American society founded on the preservation and expression of ideal social values.
4. Education in the United States had a dual role of reflecting society as it is and contributing to its growth and progress.
5. Public education is firmly rooted in a tradition of public faith and support.

GUIDELINES FOR LEARNING EXPERIENCES IN DEVELOPING PRINCIPLES WITHIN THE HISTORICAL PERSPECTIVE OF SCHOOL AND SOCIETY

Foundations

1. *Select* a period in American history and see if you can relate its social events and beliefs to educational events in terms of similarity of underlying assumptions.
2. *Find out* all you can about specific people of importance in education; try to identify the underlying beliefs and values in their efforts to change or reform educational practice.
3. *Explore* various philosophical positions in relation to the role schools should play in society; identify differences of belief, especially at different times in history.
4. *Discuss* social problems in the history of the United States and relate them to the ways in which education contributed to their solution; identify persisting problems and suggest ways in which education might effect change.

Principles

1. *List* the basic assumptions underlying the principles presented in the summary of this chapter; support them.
2. *Examine* the listed principles in terms of their consistency with the framework and the action they seem to imply.
3. *Discuss* the question, "Should the schools teach people how to cheat effectively on their income tax?" State the basic assumptions underlying every statement of opinion.
4. *Analyze* current arguments about what the school should teach in terms of the principles underlying the relations between school and society.
5. *Discuss* the brief account of the history of "thrift" in the curriculum; identify the assumptions underlying the events and develop principles as guidelines that would have changed the events.

4

TEACHING AND LEARNING

It is not unusual to speak of someone as having *learned* something by himself, though there may indeed be assumptions of some teaching agent. On the other hand, to have *taught* clearly implies that some person or persons have learned. Teaching and learning go together as an inseparable pair of interactive functions. In the two, as they are conceived and practiced, lie the essence and expression of the educative process.

The teaching-learning experience is one in which someone is helped to learn something. The concept seems simple enough. A mother teaches a child an infinite number of skills and transmits a vast amount of knowledge; face washing, shoe tying, and buttoning clothes are taught and learned simultaneously with the meanings of words, names of people, and beliefs about right and wrong. Yet even at this level the concept is complicated. Though the child may learn to tie his shoes exactly or very nearly as his mother intended him to, he may learn other things quite differently. He may learn that it is better to be a boy than a girl, that lying is feasible if no one finds out, or that money is the most important thing in the world. Somehow these things can be learned without anyone attempting to teach them.

Teaching and learning as part of a process of education carried on by the schools as social institutions must be carefully considered as aspects of responsible expression. The questions of how and what to teach are age-old, and their answers have been sought in how people learn and what they become. The beliefs about how learning occurs, and how it influences human behavior, and the values that suggest what should be learned serve as the basic assumptions of education anywhere and at any time. These enable us to perceive the aim and nature of education and the role of the teacher.

Understanding teaching and learning in historical perspective serves two essential objectives: (a) it permits us to relate accepted beliefs and values to the changing principles of education; and (b) it helps us to develop the principles of present-day teaching on the basis of intelligent analysis and critical review. Many current practices in education stem from obsolete psychological and social needs but will never be discarded unless seen clearly in relation to the reality on which they are based. Only as we perceive contemporary reality in valid knowledge can we initiate sound educational practices.

How people learn and what they become is not absolute at any moment of history in any society. As man contemplates his destiny so does he fashion the education of his young. The purpose of education is to shape or mold, a concept that implies change-in-process and concern with the future. But one man may view the future with confidence and another with fear, one with vision and another with conservatism, and these outlooks will influence his understanding of the nature of education. The responsibility for educational policy and direction in the United States is not clearly assigned, even in the role of schools as social institutions. Hence we must accept as a basic assumption the dual function of the schools of reflecting society and contributing to social progress.

Let us consider the teaching-learning process within the historical perspective of purpose, learning, and the nature of the learner, the methods of teaching and educational practice, and the role of educators as individuals and members of a profession. Forces of social belief and change are ever-present, for the basic assumption of a relationship between school and society is continually reaffirmed by events. By pointing out the historical relationships between underlying beliefs and values and educational practice and providing foundations for the development of principles as essential truths we simplify our task. We must remember, however, that beliefs do not categorically belong to particular periods and some often persist long after they have ceased to be valid in the light of present knowledge.

FOUNDATIONS

In the minds of most of us mention of the classroom at the turn of the century conjures up an image of rows of immovable desks, probably all the same size, a portrait of a president, blackboards, chalk, erasers, and pointer, an American flag, and perhaps a globe. We picture pupils in this schoolroom sitting attentively, hands clasped, and standing to recite when called on. If asked to describe the curricula and methods of the era, we should probably identify the three R's as the cornerstones of the programs and practice and repetition as the essence of the methods. We could not be sure whether the children who went to school at that time practiced swoops and swirls to learn good penmanship, played "red light" during recess, or even had recess.

Although the beliefs and values behind this formalized education underwent continuous scrutiny, they must be identified so that the practices themselves may be understood and evaluated. Horace Mann's dedication to common schools reflected an ultimately moral approach to education. As a forceful influence in the formation and early growth of public schools, he had unlimited faith in their power and in their ability to solve all the problems of the American republic. Mann conceived of education broadened beyond the prevailing scope of aristocratic aspects of culture. On the other hand, the naturalistic pedagogy of Rousseau and Pestalozzi was popular among educators; their predicament consisted in freeing children while developing self-discipline so that the interests of the free society would be served.

Lawrence A. Cremin, in analyzing progressivism in education, suggested that the answer to this problem lay in ". . . phrenology, as popular an intellectual fad as any that swept nineteenth-century America."[1] According to the phrenologists, the mind comprises 37 faculties which govern all of our attitudes and actions. Cremin pointed out that although phrenology is primarily remembered as a method of reading character from contours of the skull it actually provides a naturalistic and behavioristic psychology which maintains that ". . . desirable faculties can be cultivated through exercise and undesirable faculties inhibited through disuse."[2]

For most educators some form of faculty psychology furnished the rationale for teaching and learning and gave rise to a "disciplinary theory of education." John Swett, for example, referred to the purposes of education as "intellectual training."[3] Of course, training presupposes the use of discipline, and because these faculties were thought to contain innate power their exercise was clearly a function

---

[1] Lawrence A. Cremin. *The Transformation of the School.* New York: Knopf, 1961, p. 12.
[2] *Loc. cit.*
[3] John Swett. *Methods of Teaching.* New York: Harper, 1883, p. 24.

of training. It was believed that the faculties, which awaited developing influences, could be increased by such exercise.[4]

The extreme implications of a disciplinary theory of education emerge from this statement made by an educator in 1872:

"School discipline, and, indeed, discipline everywhere, in order to be thorough and efficient, must be based on authority. This implies a right to *enforce*, and the *power* to do so, even by the use of severe means, if necessary. The discipline of the schoolroom must be sustained, in some cases, by the infliction of punishment. This may be of various kinds. To some, a mere look, or word of reproof, may be more severe and more efficacious than the severest personal chastisement to others. But, while we freely admit the undesirableness of corporal punishment, and feel that it need not often be resorted to, we still contend that the right to inflict it does, and should of necessity rest with the teacher. . . ."[5]

Now an amusing symbol of the power of the teacher, the "hickory stick" was a real threat to at least a generation of children.

School practices proceeded according to educational theory, and however authoritarian they may seem today they were conceived in their own time as being good for the child. The educational theory predicated on faculty psychology did embrace aims in terms of individual development and sought to correlate the "growth of man's faculties, intellectual, physical and moral."[6] The purpose of education was primarily intellectual, but organized religion had had a strong influence on educational aims when public schools were first established. Schools continued to be viewed as instruments for the realization of a society in which morality and religion prevailed and citizens were expected to be orderly, law-abiding, and industrious.[7] As schools became secular, this view dovetailed with the disciplinary theory and became the god of character training.

The traditional curriculum consisted of cultural subjects, such as the classics, and mathematics was added for reasons of discipline.

---

[4] N. A. Calkins. The Teacher's Work in the Development of Mental and Moral Power. *The Addresses and Journal of Proceedings of the National Educational Association, Session of the Year, 1881.* Washington, D.C.: 1881, pp. 69–74.

[5] Charles Northend. *The Teacher and the Parent; a Treatise Upon Common-School Education.* New York: A. S. Barnes, 1872, p. 112.

[6] John Ogden. *The Science of Education; or the Philosophy of Human Culture.* New York: Van Antwerp, Bragg, 1879, p. 11.

[7] Merle Curti. *The Social Ideas of American Educators.* New York: Scribner's, 1935, p. 197.

The transition from the earlier rationale of culture and literacy to one of discipline was easily accomplished. True culture, it was held; would spring from well-developed faculties; discipline was only *mental* culture. Now the theory of education was complete. Furthermore, by a circuitous path of reason the disciplinary theory of education could be seen as being democratic by eliminating the caste and class connotations of culture; by being geared to the individual, for it dealt with the development of individual faculties; by contributing to society through the development of self-disciplined individuals who would be law-abiding and orderly; and finally, by fulfilling the moral purpose of education by attending to those faculties that affect character.

Imagine being a teacher committed to faculty psychology. The implications are enormous, but not unpleasant, for they seem to lead to a clear conception of the role of the teacher. Humanistic emphasis on the classics was less clear. Teachers could very well have wondered how to teach Latin in order to develop culture. For this reason, no doubt, the disciplinary theory was found easily acceptable, especially since the subject matter itself did not change. The usual subjects and forms of instruction persisted, but in place of cultivating humanistic interests and appreciation the teacher's goal was to develop the faculties by use. Discipline served both as a theoretical end and a practical method of education.

Teachers have always welcomed an educational objective that implies method. Thus the principle of formal discipline quickly took its place as an essential truth and a guideline for action. The teacher with a behaviorist outlook who believed that faculties resided in each individual and that use would develop them, whereas disuse would destroy them, easily found teaching a process of drill entailing rewards and punishments as needed. Closely related to faculty psychology was the theory of the mind as a muscle that could be developed with exercise, and this became the primary function of education within the prevailing intellectual framework.

William Torrey Harris may be identified as the man who "ultimately rationalized the institution of the public school." [8] As superintendent of the St. Louis public schools from 1868 to 1880 and as United States Commissioner of Education from 1889 to 1906, Harris exerted a profound influence on both the theoretical and practical aspects of education in this country. He reconciled his own religious beliefs with the idealism of Hegel into a practical administrative out-

---

[8] Cremin, *op. cit.*, p. 18.

look for education in an era of unprecedented immigration and educational problems. In St. Louis Harris organized graded schools and paid attention to the details of school organization in their application to courses of study, buildings, and teachers. His efforts resulted in a practical application of a theory of pedagogy in which "emphasis is on effort rather than freedom, on work rather than play, on effort rather than interest . . . on regularity, silence, and industry. . . ."[9]

Enter Physical Education

At this period in the history of American education physical training achieved a foothold as a school subject. The prevailing educational view furnished the basis for its inclusion. John Ogden wrote in 1879:

"Since there is no incompatibility between physical exercises and mental activity, but that, when properly directed, the one promotes the other; and since there is no antagonism between any of the faculties and forces that develop them; and since it does not become necessary to sacrifice one single physical power or one real enjoyment in order to educate the mind; therefore, we conclude that there *is* a special necessity for connecting physical training with, and making it a part of an educational system."[10]

In 1883 Swett noted, "One of the most hopeful features of modern education is the growing recognition of the importance of physical education in school."[11]

During this time the conception of physical training was based on a belief in faculty psychology. Because education was a process of developing or training the mental faculties, it made sense to include the physical faculties as well. Frequent allusions were made to faculties of both mind and body, and the existence of separate traits within this a dualism was generally accepted. A disciplinary theory of education was more hospitable to inclusion of physical training than was the humanistic approach.

The development of physical education in a historical perspective is examined in Chapter 5, but it concerns us here because of its significance in some of the relationships between teaching and learning. Faculty psychology or phrenology, and the consequent disciplinary theory, supplied the theoretical framework for education at the

---
[9] *Ibid.*, p. 20.
[10] Ogden, *op. cit.*, p. 121.
[11] Swett, *op. cit.*, p. 23.

end of the nineteenth century. No single theory wholly explains educational outlook or practice in any age, but this one may be regarded as a reflection of a prevailing point of view and its practices. As indicated, it was the first to offer a basis for the provision of physical training in schools.

The types of activity qualifying as physical education or play have existed to some extent in every culture in recorded history. The Grecian ideal of the harmonious development of man, especially as it was reflected in gymnastics and other sports of ancient Athens, has persisted down through the centuries. A society's inclusion of physical education in its schools may be considered as an index to the worth it places on such activities and usually results from the prevailing view of man and his destiny.

Because this study is limited in scope to education in the United States, it is important to identify the beliefs that permit the inclusion of physical education in American school programs. Humanism, of course, is not basically opposed to physical education. In its reverence of things ancient and classic humanist philosophy embraces the value of physical development as idealized by the Greeks. The course of humanism in American education, however, was influenced by other values. To begin with, the puritan or ascetic view held in Colonial America exalted work and condemned play. Further, the dualism of mind and body not only assigned mind a higher value but also invested intellectual processes with such importance that they were considered the only things worthy of cultivation. Because of the religious zeal that motivated the formation of schools, this comes as no surprise.

Nineteenth-Century Contributions

Many events occurred during the nineteenth century to alter the situation. However, they were not reflected to any great extent in public education until the closing years of the century.

In the 1820s Charles Beck, Charles Follen, and Francis Lieber introduced the gymnastics of Friedrich Ludwig Jahn to the United States. In addition to the outdoor German *Gymnasia*, which included gymnastics and games, interest grew in the physical development of students in military academies. In the following decade calisthenics were introduced to the female seminaries for the purpose of developing grace and health, largely through the efforts of Catherine E. Beecher. Increased German immigration in the 1840s precipitated the formation of the German *Turnverein,* and many of these gymnastic clubs have persisted until now. Football and baseball teams also appeared during this decade, and their formation in New York and New England marked the start of organized amateur sport.

During the 1850s the first college gymnasia were constructed. Amherst, Harvard, and Yale took the lead. Edward Hitchcock was appointed the first Professor of Hygiene and Physical Education at Amherst. By the 1860s the gymnastics of Pehr Hendrick Ling of Sweden had been imported to the United States. George Barker Winship became famous as an advocate of heavy gymnastics, and hosts of "strength seekers" patronized his gymnasium in Boston. The first impetus to teacher training was given by the Normal Institute for Physical Education in Boston founded by Dio Lewis in 1861.

The 1870s saw the beginning of the regulation of amateur sport. Associations such as the Association of American Colleges and the Intercollegiate Association for football were formed to obtain agreement on rules. Except for sporadic efforts, none of these developments or movements found expression in the public schools of the country. Although it had been used earlier, the term physical training did not really replace physical culture until the 1880s and may be considered as representing a theory of education based on a training of the faculties.

We can easily imagine the kind of curriculum stimulated by this underlying aim of physical training and the methods employed to administer it. Like academic pursuits, physical training stressed drill and repetition, and calisthenics most readily reflected this emphasis. Another purpose of physical training was corrective; it was considered necessary to counter the negative effects of the schoolroom in which children sat cramped and bent over mental tasks for long periods of time. The implied criticism of educational practice was not limited to physical training; discipline as a single educational objective was under fire.

Demise of the Disciplinary Theory

In assuming that an ultimate moral purpose was to be expressed in social behavior and that it enjoyed a clear relationship with its underlying scientific and psychological rationale, the disciplinary theory of education sowed the seeds of its own destruction. Morality had been judged by the theory's contributions to society through the development of individual character. This led Cubberley to write in 1909:

"The school now shows signs of becoming conscious of itself in a new and truer direction; its gaze is now outward instead of inward, and the relation of the school to the world outside has now become a question of the first importance in educational procedure. . . . The school must grasp the significance of its social connections and relations, and must come to realize its real worth and its hope of adequate reward lies in its social efficiency." [12]

Education's development of character was simply not sufficient to meet needs rising out of increasing immigration and the changing character of society. The schoolroom itself was directly concerned with problems of cleanliness and dress in addition to attitudes and manners, and none could be ignored. Expanding industrialism demanded preparation for work as part of adequate schooling, and the history of the manual training movements in the schools is long, involved, and fascinating. To speak of social efficiency was a challenge to the existing point of view of faculties and discipline. William Torrey Harris responded vigorously to the demands of manual training exponents by contending that they reflected a failure to distinguish higher and lower faculties and by insisting that "Education that educates the child in the art of self-education is that which the aggregate experience of mankind has chosen for the school." For Harris the business of the school lay in the cultivation of man's ability "to generalize, comprehend, relate, and idealize." [13]

There was certainly a movement for education of a practical nature. On the national level organizations like the Country Life Commission and the National Society for the Promotion of Industrial Education were extremely effective. Their leadership consisted of businessmen, labor leaders, and municiplal reformers. The Smith-Lever Act of 1914, which established a system of extension work in agriculture and home economics, recognized the place of these groups. So did the Smith-Hughes Act which became law early in 1917 and ensured vocational studies at all levels of schooling.

Manual training classes included carpentry, metal and machine work, sewing, cooking, drawing, and physical education. Originally conceived as adjuncts of the regular school curriculum, these subjects

---

[12] Ellwood P. Cubberley. *Changing Conceptions of Education.* Boston: Houghton Mifflin, 1909, p. 54.
[13] *Proceedings of the Department of Superintendence of the National Education Association 1889.* Washington, D.C.: United States Bureau of Education, 1889, pp. 126–127.

soon appeared in elementary, secondary, and college classrooms as part of the regular program. The commitment to culture and discipline could not forestall the demands of an industrial economy for manpower, and much of the movement for vocational education emphasized practical training for a trade.

Because of the influence of the colleges, secondary school curricula by the end of the century had become confused. Not only were demands made on the schools for practical training, but college entrance examinations also began to base entrance requirements on subjects included in the college curriculum. Secondary schools were obliged to expand their curricula in the direction of college courses and taught them on the same basis. Because of dissatisfaction with secondary school curricula, the National Education Association named a committee to arrange a series of national conferences devoted to a consideration of subjects taught in secondary school.[14]

Under the leadership of Charles W. Eliot, president of Harvard University, the Committee of Ten reported:

"The secondary schools of the United States, taken as a whole, do not exist for the purpose of preparing boys and girls for colleges. Only an insignificant percentage of the graduates of these schools go to colleges or scientific schools. Their main function is to prepare for the duties of life." [15]

The view of education as "preparation for the duties of life" must be supposed to have then implied the same things as it would today. William Torrey Harris, while studying the problem of a unified course of study from primary school to the university for the NEA, voiced in 1875 one of the strongest objections to secondary school curricula. The problem, as Harris saw it, was caused by the efforts of the secondary school to prepare students both for college and for the "duties of life." Because the colleges required examinations only in Latin, Greek, and mathematics, he commented:

"Hence the public high school is obliged to provide for a classical course and a general course, if it would continue its common school course, and, at the same time, prepare its pupils for college. The

---

[14] Report of the Committee of Ten on Secondary School Studies. *Report of the Commissioner of Education for the Year 1892–1893*, Vol. 2. Washington, D.C.: U.S. Government Printing Office, 1895, pp. 1415–1494.
[15] *Report of the Committee on Secondary School Studies Appointed at the Meeting of the National Educational Association, July 9, 1892.* Washington, D.C.: U.S. Government Printing Office, 1893, p. 51.

influence of higher education upon the lower is to force the latter to drop its collateral and information-giving studies." [16]

Responding to the secondary school's failure to function solely as a college preparatory agency, the Committee of Ten formulated four types of course—the classical, the Latin-scientific, the modern language, and the English. The emphasis on science was significant, and the Committee included in its report the suggestion that students could devote Saturday mornings to laboratory work. It is also significant that the Report of the Committee of Ten made no specific provision for physical training, any vocational subject, or the fine arts. There is little doubt, however, about its having perceived the relation between literacy and the "duties of life." E. M. Hartwell, an early leader in physical education, charged that the Committee was still under the influence of "the dogmas of effete humanism" and indicted the report for its omission of physical training.[17]

The Committee's report was the first of a series of recommendations that have shaped American education. Parenthetically, the problem of the effect of college requirements on secondary schools was approached more realistically in 1899 with the first report of the Committee on College Entrance Requirements.

The Herbartian Contribution

Just as faculty psychology has sometimes been attributed to the philosopher John Locke, another psychology which had great influence on teaching is linked to Johann Friedrich Herbart. Herbart's psychology which represented an early scientific approach to the study of education rested on a process of "apperception" by which new knowledge was related to old. His ideas gained currency in the United States after the organization of a National Herbart Society in 1895. The importance of the Herbartian movement is its emphasis on teaching. Herbart's followers devised five formal steps in teaching, all of which were based on the principle of apperception: preparation, presentation, comparison, generalization, and application.[18]

---

[16] *Journal of Proceedings and Addresses 1876*. Washington, D.C.: National Education Association, 1876, p. 62.
[17] E. M. Hartwell. Remarks and Discussion on the Literature Concerning Physical Education, *Report of the Ninth Annual Meeting of The American Association for the Advancement of Physical Education*. New Haven, Connecticut: Press of Clarence H. Ryder, 1894, pp. 81–89.
[18] Charles DeGarmo. *The Essentials of Method*, Part III, rev. ed. Boston: Heath, 1903.

As an educational method, these five steps achieved great popularity. They satisfied the requirements of explaining how learning takes place by apperception and how teaching should proceed by the five formal steps. Few teachers questioned the assertions of the Herbartians that at last a formula for effective instruction had been discovered. Indeed, many teachers of today are waiting for word of just such a discovery by psychologists or educational leaders. In practice, actually, the five steps were difficult to apply to existing textbooks which had been developed more or less on the basis of deductive logic. They were also found to be cumbersome when applied to teaching.

Although the Herbartian method was easily displaced by later scientific and psychological examination, its effects, like those of many educational theories and movements, are still traceable. Dozens of publications based on Herbartian method were issued before the end of the nineteenth century and some remain in use. Moreover, as we examine an individual's educational theories, especially on the basis of method, we frequently find evidence of the five formal steps. Here again, as in the theory of formal discipline, all problems of teaching seemed to be solved. Small wonder that teachers and teacher-preparation institutions, having grasped the concept, were reluctant to relinquish it.

Newer Scientific Theories

The growing impact of science, reflected in Herbartian psychology and the Report of the Committee of Ten, ultimately challenged American education with new theories of man and society. In recognizing the function of the schools in preparing children for the "duties of life," the Committee of Ten had surely been influenced by Herbert Spencer, the English philosopher. To Spencer recognition was an urgent affirmation. He believed that preparation for "complete living" stood as "the function which education has to discharge; and the only rational mode of judging any educational course is to judge in what degree it discharges such function." [19] Spencer's work on education, widely read in the United States, clearly indicated that education for complete living lay in activities for self-preservation, in securing life's necessities, in rearing and disciplining offspring, in main-

---

[19] Herbert Spencer. Education: *Intellectual, Moral, and Physical.* New York: Appleton, 1860, p. 31.

taining proper social and political relations, and in gratifying tastes and feelings.

Spencer's writings had great influence. One reason for this was the evolutionary theory in which many of his works were based. By the beginning of the twentieth century theories of Darwinian evolution were being applied to social life in the United States. "Social Darwinism" or the "culture-epochs theory" maintained that the life of the individual reprised the whole history of the life of man on earth. Spencer, for instance, concluded that because the development of the mind followed an evolutionary process education was simply a process of helping man to adapt to independent forces. In his important work in education in 1911 Frederick Bolton claimed that a study of phylogeny did not show that the individual recapitulated the entire history of the race but did reveal "analogies and retracement of the main features." [20] Lewis F. Anderson commented:

"The doctrine of evolution has made itself felt not only in a modification of the common school curriculum but in a broadening and deepening of the conception of school education. It has come to be looked upon as a phase of the evolutionary process, a process of more complete adaptation to and utilization of the environment. This environment in the case of man is, for the most part, social." [21]

Certainly, the influence of social Darwinism provided a clear departure from the concepts of teaching and learning based on a disciplinary theory.

Effects of Darwinism were immediately apparent in American psychology. G. Stanley Hall became the leading agent of the culture-epochs theory in the United States. Hall concentrated on child development and his theories strongly affected education. Because a large part of the psychology supporting the culture-epochs theory stemmed from the nature and development of the child, teaching focused on the student. This psychology also presupposed the necessity for living through each of the stages of man from savagery to civilization as part of normal growth and development. Hall said in 1894:

"A complete system of education will begin with regimen and digestion, with the habits that give strength, and end with the educa-

---

[20] Frederick Elmer Bolton. *Principles of Education.* New York: Scribner's, 1911, p. 91.
[21] Lewis F. Anderson. *History of Common School Education.* New York: Holt, 1909, p. 295.

tion of those very slight, complicated movements, which I will not quite say constitute thought, but which it is a pre-requisite to teach first, which must be taught upon the basis of the solid, all-round education of that half of the body which is made up of muscle tissue." [22]

Hall's address before the American Association for the Advancement of Physical Education indicates the importance of the culture-epochs theory to that field. Clearly the need to lead the pupil through a reprise of the history of the race involves more than intellectual activities alone. Addressing a meeting of the NEA in 1903, Thomas D. Wood said:

"School gymnastics should, if the term may be used this way, be more phylogenetic in character and progression than they are at present; i.e., they should correspond more closely to the motor activities which enabled our ancestors, amphibious and otherwise, from the more remote times to the more recent, to live successfully. The study of organic evolution, and of the life history and motor habits of animals and men at different stages of development, will give the clue to the types and sequence of movements and exercises which are best adapted to the different stages of the development of the child." [23]

Luther H. Gulick was a strong proponent of the culture-epochs theory applied to physical training. In welcoming him to his new position as Director of Physical Training for the public schools of New York City in 1903, Jessie H. Bancroft said:

"It was from you that we first heard applied to physical training the recapitulatory theory in education—the idea that in his exercise, as in other ways, the child passes . . . through the primitive stages of the race. . . ." [24]

No doubt this was an exciting theory for the young field of physical education. For the first time a dignified scientific theory seemed to

---

[22] G. Stanley Hall. Some Relations Between Physical and Mental Training, *Report of the Ninth Annual Meeting of the American Association for the Advancement of Physical Education*. New Haven, Connecticut: Press of Clarence G. Ryder, 1894, pp. 30–37.

[23] *Proceedings and Addresses of the Forty-Second Annual Meeting*. Washington, D.C.: National Educational Association, 1903, pp. 628–629.

[24] Jessie H. Bancroft. Physical Training in the Public Schools of the City of New York. *American Physical Education Review*, 8, 16–36 (March 1903).

indicate clearly that physical training was proper educational subject matter. R. Tait McKenzie suggested that the evolution of the child's physical nature was the "epitome of the evolution of the whole race." [25]

It may also be that the success of the playground movement in the United States was the result in part of a belief that "play impulse" was a manifestation of an evolutionary stage through which all children pass.[26]

The culture-epochs theory influenced curriculum and method in all aspects of education. More significantly, it made closer study of the development of the child appropriate. Emphasis on feelings and attitudes increased, and child-study in which the needs of children were a major consideration attained importance. The most obvious influences worked on curriculum more than on method. As an interpretation of the culture-epochs theory, Gulick said:

"We were unwilling to develop athletics among girls on the same basis as that on which we were developing them for boys, because we regard the biological history of the sexes as sufficiently divergent to make it improbable that athletics, which in their origin involve movements and instinct feelings of the combative and hunting type should be adapted to the feminine physiological, psychological, social or aesthetic needs." [27]

It is difficult, if not impossible, to estimate the effect of such a view on the development of physical education. Certainly, other views of sex differences at the time seemed to lead to the conclusion that athletics were inappropriate for women. In the relation of beliefs to action any view that saw all educational activities as phylogenetic could not properly provide athletics for women. Unfortunately, the history of education sometimes lends credence to viewpoints in which it is easier to accept new ideas than to relinquish old ones.

Ultimately, experimental psychology most effectively influenced educational practice and methods of teaching and, incidentally, weakened the force of the culture-epochs theory as a basis for human

---

[25] G. Tait McKenzie. The Regulation of Physical Instruction in Schools and Colleges from the Standpoint of Hygiene. *American Physical Education Review*, 14, 224–227 (April 1909).
[26] Henry S. Curtis. The Relation of the Playgrounds to a System of Physical Training. *American Physical Education Review*, 13, 245–249 (May 1908).
[27] Luther H. Gulick. The Place and Limitations of Folk Dancing, as an Agency in Physical Training. *American Physical Education Review*, 13, 377–382 (October 1908).

development. Thorndike initiated laboratory experimentation with animal learning in the United States. The value of animal learning as a subject of study for a psychologist, of course, presupposes an evolutionary theory. Using it as a corollary of scientific theory, Thorndike brought new credibility and dignity to psychology. Although employing evolutionary theory as a basis, Thorndike criticized the pedagogy to which social Darwinism had given rise. He suggested that things should not be repeated merely because they had occurred but that education should try to improve all the time.[28]

Thorndike's theories are familiar to all students of psychology. Learning involves specific responses to specific stimuli, physiological bonds form in the neural system, and reward tends to "stamp in" the tie between S and R. Thorndike's studies on the transfer of training effectively challenged the assumptions of a disciplinary theory of education. In all, his contributions to such areas as intelligence, mental testing, classroom grouping, genius, and quantified methods are inestimable.

The psychology of William James, who had made some of the earliest attempts to vest psychology with the disciplines of science, highly impressed Thorndike. James's view of the learner was much more dynamic than Spencer's or Hall's, and he concluded that habits emerged from repetition of acts and eventually became determinants of social and personal behavior. Obviously, habit formation became a prime aspect of education in this view.

Thorndike agreed with both the psychology and philosophy of James. The passive learner in an evolutionary web had no place in the thinking of either of these men, and experiences and responses by learners were of the highest significance. Cremin made another interesting observation:

"Equally important, perhaps, Thorndike's new law implied a new theory of mind. Building on the idea of a reflex arc, which connected the brain and neural tissue with the total behavior of the organism, he ended the search for mind by eliminating it as a separate entity. Mind appeared in the total response of the organism to its environment." [29]

The psychological theories of James and Thorndike characterize many aspects of educational thought and practice in the twentieth century. Behaviorist psychology, of course, is easily documented, and

---
[28] Lawrence A. Cremin, *op. cit.*, p. 113.
[29] *Op. cit.*, pp. 111–112.

animal experimentation for the gathering of learning data is commonly accepted. To be sure, behaviorist theories of learning are not the only ones to have been advanced, but their wide appeal lies in the scientific aspects of the "proof" they offer. Because behaviorist psychologists confine their concern to observable and verifiable behavioral phenomena and the forces influencing them, their findings must become acceptable. The problem arises only from the meaning of the findings and how they relate to some theoretical framework. To the extent that experimental psychologists provide learning *models* rather than learning *theories* the problem is minimized.

James and Thorndike clearly established a link between psychology and education which the passage of time has made more explicit. Because the teaching-learning process is so definitive, applications of psychology's findings to learning were promptly studied for their implications for teaching. Furthermore, both James and Thorndike were eager to put their theories at the disposal of education and devoted themselves to the task of underlining these implications. In doing so, they invested the process with philosophical aspects in addition to the psychological ones.

The transition from knowledge of animal learning to methods of teaching children was most easily accomplished by James's stress on habit formation. Thorndike's theory of S-R bonds, reinforced by rewards, would certainly be evident in repetition, both during and after learning. James expressed attention to volunteerism by emphasizing will, especially since will takes the form of attention. In a complete summary of learning undertaken in 1911 Colvin observed that although a disciplinary theory based on a faculty psychology was untenable general training was nevertheless possible. Said Colvin: "Will, in the last analysis, is a matter of attention. The education of a right will consists in training those aspects of attention that have regard for situations that are stamped with social approval." [30]

Since the time of James habit formation has been used to represent all of man's activities. In 1925 Edwards noted that, "The term habit in too many minds suggests only the narrow mechanical action of the individual. . . . But habit rightly understood means . . . the automatic activities in the motor realm to the professional attitudes and moral habitudes." [31] In 1960 Lawson, in a comprehensive work

---

[30] Stephen Sheldon Colvin. *The Learning Process.* New York: Macmillan, 1911, p. 293.
[31] A. S. Edwards. *The Fundamental Principles of Learning and Study,* rev. ed. Baltimore: Warwick & York, 1925, p. 24.

on learning, similarly indicated that, "Habit, as used here, means much more than it does in the popular vernacular." [32]

The appeal of habit formation as the business of education is understandable. Because habits are both fixed and permanent, the teacher's role is not only clarified but exalted. Thorndike's theory of "original tendencies" led to a wider view of the potentiality of education than either the disciplinary or culture-epochs theories, but it did not essentially change the concept of teaching and learning. The scientific basis of these theories also explains their appeal for teachers. Habits were readily observable in behavior and could be considered to be learned when responses that had not been evident before were present and repeated. Thus we may be said to have acquired the habit of brushing our teeth when we get up each morning and go through the brushing ritual. If we forget on occasion, the habit has not yet been truly formed.

The rationality of the reward and reinforcement theory is equally obvious. To get a child to brush his teeth each morning we reward him on his performance, having first provided a stimulus so that he will make the appropriate response. In this way the bond between S and R is reinforced, and eventually, as the habit is formed, the reward becomes superfluous. Is it any wonder that teachers grasped this conception of education with alacrity? Indeed, many teachers today view educational aims and practices in this way and strive to inculcate habits of belief and behavior in their pupils. If this guiding theory does not always work in practice, they respond by trying harder!

In physical training, so obviously concerned in all of its aspects with observable behavior, the theory of habit formation was readily accepted. We continually hear references to the aim of developing habits of exercise, though many Americans seem not to have acquired them. In physical training as well as in academic subjects the practices of formal drill changed slightly in response to this theory and were not directed toward some vaguely defined discipline but to the scientifically established purpose of forming good habits. Motor learning, mental and moral education, and all aspects of human behavior were the functions in which to develop habits. Whether a faculty or an S-R bond, repetition of a desirable act clearly would lead to good results, whereas discouraging an undesirable performance would prevent its recurrence.

The component of attention or will necessary to the formation of

---

[32] Reed Lawson. *Learning and Behavior*. New York: Macmillan, 1960, p. 25.

habits was too limited in concept to explain the failure of the habit theory to achieve educational results. Will was necessary, but how was it to be trained? A further limitation lay in the assumption that education and the teacher knew what habits were to be formed. This assumption was basic to every popular theory of education until the present century, but in affirming the role of the school only in its reflection and transmission of knowledge it did not fulfill the destiny inherent in the design of education in America.

Education and Psychology

The student of education is well advised to understand the scope of psychological theory. Processes and faculties that have been subjected to psychological study and experimentation have traditionally been most crucial to learning. Theories of learning devised by psychologists have found wide application in education. Psychological no less than philosophical views of man furnish the basis for any educational theory. In excellent historical perspective Gardner Murphy has identified behaviorism, Gestalt and field theories, psychoanalytic theory, and social psychology as differentiated and important systems of psychological thought.[33] Because these theories cannot be compartmentalized into tight historical periods, we must familiarize ourselves with the elements of each in order to understand their impact and expression in American education.

The mechanistic approach to human beings exemplified in behaviorist theories was sharply criticized by various field psychologies. "Organismic" theories assert that behavior can properly be considered only when the total organism is viewed within its whole field. Gestalt psychology and the theories of Kurt Lewin endeavor to recognize all the forces bearing on a given situation. Both insist that the individual learns by insight rather than reflexes.

The psychoanalytic theories of human behavior stemming from the work of Freud are also well known. In concentrating on motivation, drives, and instincts as vital elements in behavior, Freud drew attention to the three realms of ego, id, and superego. The psychoanalytic emphasis on unconscious motivation, of course, is the antithesis of the behaviorists' ever-increasing attention to operationally observable acts as the path to an explanation of behavior.

Social psychology developed in part in response to the findings

---

[33] Gardner Murphy. *Historical Introduction to Modern Psychology*, rev. ed. New York: Harcourt, Brace, 1949.

of cultural anthropologists and broadened psychological theory from its traditional basis in the individual. This theory grows out of a better understanding of individuals in its concern with their social and cultural milieu. Besides, social psychologists place great weight on social and group life and among them group dynamics becomes an important and useful approach.

The Progressive Movement

The progressive education movement in the United States symbolizes the changing nature of society and its education as well as the character of educational conflict. The definition to which it gave rise and the controversies it provoked centered in concepts of teaching and learning. Many groups in the early years of this century demanded educational reform, and their demands most often called for schools to expand their functions in the direction of solving real social problems.

John Dewey deplored traditional education's isolation from society and gave cogent expression to a view of the school as reflecting and contributing to it. With his wife, Dewey ran an experimental school, known as the "Laboratory School," in which the emphasis was on cooperative activities, especially as they reflected the concerns of society. The school was devoted to discovering better and more natural ways of teaching and learning. Groups were kept small, community resources were utilized, and a constant effort was made to keep the subject matter interesting and relevant.

Similar experiments took place in public schools. Francis W. Parker, as superintendent of schools in Quincy, Massachusetts, and later as principal of the Cook County Normal School in Chicago, was firm in his attempts to place attention on the child and to give meaning to the curriculum. William Wirt, superintendent of schools in Gary, Indiana, sought to expand the curriculum and make the school the heart of community life. The "Gary plan" organized each school as a community and utilized a platoon system for maximal employment of facilities.

The demands of progressive education for skilled teaching could not be ignored. Every experimental school or new pedagogical plan offered a sharp departure from traditional methods of instruction. The theories of James and Thorndike and, most important, of Dewey shifted the spotlight of education from the curriculum to the child. The social and democratic concepts which were essential aspects of Dewey's philosophy compounded the problem of defining teaching methods. In psychology Dewey had been influenced by James and Hall, but the newer principles of Gestaltism and psychoanalysis were also consonant with his philosophical views, and he perceived thinking and reasoning as processes in relation to problems and goals. Although Dewey's philosophical and pedagogical theories were clearly enunciated in his many writings, too many teachers have never bothered to read them.

The mood of the United States after World War I made it easy to grasp some of Dewey's ideas in distortion. During the twenties romanticized versions of social reform and psychoanalytic theory produced a child-centered education that was a travesty of Dewey's views. The vigorous interpretation of the needs of individuals in a social and democratic society, which Dewey wished to translate into educational practice, was never fully realized. Dewey's principle of growth stressed growth as an educational reality but related it to the necessity of teaching and its guide. In these years growth became an end in itself. Its aim was hazy and the freedom of the child was the watchword. Unfortunately, the common notion of the meaning of progressive education usually includes the child's saying, "Do I have to do what I want to today?" or a teacher smiling in a sea of bedlam.

There is no substitute for reading the works of the fathers of progressive education—Dewey, W. H. Kilpatrick, Harold O. Rugg, Boyde H. Bode—or the descriptions of Helen Parkhurst's "contract plan" developed in Dalton, Massachusetts, or Carleton Washburne's educational system in Winnetka, Illinois, for a true understanding of the progressive movement in education. The Association for the Advancement of Progressive Education, later the Progressive Education Association (PEA), was formed in 1919. The original members of this association were primarily lay citizens rather than professional educators. Their initial statement of principles indicated their dedication to the child as a future member of a democratic society.

As presented by Dewey in *How We Think* (1910) and *Democracy and Education* (1916), the progressive education movement confronted social change in a democracy with a problem-solving method of teaching. Kilpatrick is generally credited with having originated the "project" method, outlined in his *Foundations of Method* (1925). Although Kilpatrick spent his long and influential career at Teachers College, Columbia University, in interpreting the philosophies of Dewey, Cremin commented:

"But Dewey's enterprise in the Laboratory School was to develop a new curriculum to take the place of the old—a new body of subject matter, better ordered and better designed, that would begin with the experience of the learners and culminate with the organized subjects that represented the cumulative experience of the race. Kilpatrick, on the other hand, in his emphasis on future uncertainty and in his unrelenting attack on subject matter 'fixed-in-advance' ultimately discredits the organized subjects and hence inevitably shifts the balance of Dewey's pedagogical paradigm toward the child. The resultant child-centered emphasis calls to mind the very position Dewey himself rejected, first in *The Child and the Curriculum* (1902) and later in *Experience and Education* (1938)." [34]

Dewey himself had moved on to other concerns reflected in *Human Nature and Conduct* (1922), *Experience and Nature* (1925), and *The Public and Its Problems* (1927).[35] Thus the progressive education movement, though founded on Dewey's theories, was being expressed in the pedagogical theories of interpreters and sympathizers, and the efforts of the Progressive Education Association must be viewed apart from Dewey's influence.

During the twenties and thirties the Progressive Education Association was eminently successful. Its publication, *Progressive Education*, was widely read. It continues to have interest today for its reflection of educational activities of the period. The truely progressive schools were primarily private, but schools like Lincoln and the two Horace Mann schools, one for boys and one for girls, all operated by Teachers College, will long be remembered for their educational reforms and practices. The Progressive Education Association also fostered many commissions which were concerned with such problems as educational resources, educational freedom, home-school relationships, and curricula. Perhaps best known was the Commission on the Relation of School and College, which, under the chairmanship of Wilford M. Aiken, gave rise to the celebrated Eight-Year Study.

As Aiken reported, the study developed during a Progressive Education Association conference in 1930 from a consideration of how secondary schools might better serve youth. The difficulty of curriculum experimentation in the face of college entrance requirements led to the Commission's appointment some months later.[36] In addition to the usual list of criticisms of traditional education, the Commission indicted the American secondary school for failure to fulfill

---

[34] *Op. cit.*, pp. 219–220.
[35] *Ibid.*, p. 215.
[36] Wilford M. Aiken. *The Story of the Eight-Year Study*. New York: Harper, 1942, pp. 1–2.

its purpose—for failing to develop an appreciation for the American heritage, to prepare for community responsibilities, to challenge able students, to know and guide students wisely, and to create conditions for effective learning.[37]

The Eight-Year Study was begun in 1933, with 30 schools, large and small, public and private, and more than 300 colleges and universities participating. Admission to college during the experimental period was on the basis of recommendations and school histories. Only Harvard Haverford, Yale, and Princeton also required candidates to take the College Entrance Board Examinations.[38]

The story of the study is an unparalleled drama of teaching and learning. Sometimes, indeed, many times, teachers became the learners as they strove to rise to the challenge of their new-found freedom from the yoke of college entrance requirements as the rationale of the curriculum. As a human experiment in teaching, the value of the study is apparent to any reader, and many educational problems might be solved if all teachers could match the involvement that characterized it. Students were also aware of the experiment and were serious and excited in their consideration of its educational purpose.

The scope of the experiment with respect to teaching method is too wide to be described briefly. In genenal, both curriculum and method followed progressive lines. Traditional categories of subject matter were discarded in favor of units of work engendered by the interests of the students. Many schools made extensive use of community resources as laboratory experiences in a whole range of areas from economics to recreation. There were, of course, problems and mistakes. Some teachers could not adapt and schools were not equal in their departure from traditional curricula. On the whole, however, a spirit of creative adventure pervaded the study.

Did the students involved succeed in college? The Commission determined that college success would be the criterion by which the experiment would be judged. Of the 1475 matched pairs of college students, one was a graduate of one of the 30 schools in the study and the other was a graduate of another secondary school but otherwise much like the first in regard to age, sex, race, test scores, background, and interests. The graduates of the 30 schools were found to be superior in every aspect of comparison: grade average, academic honors, intellectual curiosity, thinking ability, resourceful-

---

[37] *Ibid.*, pp. 4–5.
[38] *Ibid.*, pp. 12–15.

ness, participation in student groups, and better vocational orientation.[39]

The Eight-Year Study, as well as the activities of the Progressive Education Association which followed it, attracted huge sums of money from such groups as the Carnegie Foundation and the General Education Board, and the PEA became a large professional organization with a multitude of research projects. With its new professional membership in the thirties, it became subject to controversy and its direction for progressive education lost its clarity. As early as 1932 George S. Counts had challenged progressive education to be progressive. His ideas, cogently expressed in his book, *Dare the School Build a New Social Order?*, include a reconstructionist role for American education. Counts remained active in the Association, but the ideas he represented were no longer found wholly acceptable. The PEA itself was unable to agree on a statement of philosophy or principles. Marred by criticism and impotence, the Association changed its name in 1944 to the American Education Fellowship and adopted a statement of policy.[40] In 1953 it reassumed its original name and formally disbanded two years later. *Progressive Education* suspended publication in 1957. The ineffectuality of the Progressive Education Association after the thirties is a telling commentary on the swan song of the progressive education movement as such.

Basic Assumptions of Teaching and Learning

Following World War I the character of American education itself became progressive and what had been considered radical theory acquired respectability and turned into the basic assumptions of teaching and learning. In 1913 the NEA had appointed a Commission on the Reorganization of Secondary Education. Eventually this commission consisted of 16 subcommittees with a total membership of more than 100 drawn from 30 states. In 1916 the Commission published *Social Studies in Secondary Education* which recommended a course in the problems of democracy for twelfth-grade study. "This was the first time that a responsible agency had advocated the classroom study of contemporary issues as distinguished from formalized subjects." [41]

---

[39] Dean Chamberlain, Enid Straw Chamberlain, Neal E. Drought, and William E. Scott. *Did They Succeed in College?* New York: Harper, 1942, pp. 207–208.
[40] Objectives and Program for the American Education Fellowship. *Progressive Education* 22, 9–10 (1944–1945).
[41] Edgar B. Wesley. *NEA: The First Hundred Years*. New York: Harper, 1957, pp. 298–299.

The most significant publication of the Commission contained the now famous seven cardinal principles of education: health, command of fundamental processes, worthy home membership, vocation, citizenship, worthy use of leisure, and ethical character. Furthermore, the Commission clearly indicated a role for the secondary school in a democratic society.[42] Spencer's theories of education as preparation for complete living were finally accorded full recognition in the United States in the statement of these principles.

Several factors occasioned the unprecedented shift toward the progressive bases apparent in the cardinal principles. Schools were growing at a rapid pace. More children were in school for longer periods of time, and education for all was becoming more of a reality than a goal. World War I, of course, made people more conscious of democracy and more convinced than ever that the future of the nation depended on the schools. This made sense in view of the greater social complexity and change occasioned by the war. In addition, the United States Office of Education acquired additional powers through its administration of the Smith-Hughes Act and it began to support new curricular and teaching ideas as well as the adoption of vocational programs. Professional associations of teachers burgeoned; membership in the NEA soared from 10,104 in 1918 to 52,850 in 1920 and to more than 200,000 in 1929.[43] In 1916 the American Federation of Teachers, which linked teachers with organized labor through the American Federation of Labor, was formed. It had as its slogan, "Democracy in Education; Education for Democracy."[44]

Teaching itself was becoming professionalized. Newly created state departments of instruction were setting up certification requirements to ensure minimum standards of preparation. Because these programs included more professional courses, newer concepts of teaching and learning found their way into the schools. The impact of science was felt in many places. Large-scale testing programs administered to servicemen during the war were soon applied to school children. Growing awareness of individual differences led to changing structures in educational administrative units, to expanded curricular offerings, to greater flexibility in the grouping of students, and to the development of programs of guidance and counseling. Science also contrib-

---

[42] *Cardinal Principles of Secondary Education.* Washington, D.C.: United States Bureau of Education, Bulletin No. 35, 1918.
[43] Edgar B. Wesley, *op. cit.*, p. 397.
[44] The Commission on Educational Reconstruction. *Organizing the Teaching Profession.* New York: The Free Press, 1955, p. 9.

uted new teaching materials, models, and experimental animals, as well as films and slides; and all of these things and more eventually became adjuncts of every classroom. It might even be surmised that the growth and comparison studies of fathers and sons made during the war contributed in some measure to the changing furniture of the schoolroom.

Certainly the character of American education was shaped over a span of several decades. The principle of local control was reaffirmed. Almost every state had compulsory attendance laws but provided for local school administrative units to maintain and operate the public schools. Local boards of education furnished public, tax-supported elementary and secondary education, and each of the states provided at least one public college or university which was maintained primarily with tax money.[45]

Achieving National Standards

Although the principle of local support and control of education has remained supreme, there has been a persistent effort to standardize educational practices throughout the nation. The most evident aspect of this drive has been the role of Federal government in education under state control. Many school policies have been determined by Federal courts; the decision handed down by the Supreme Court on the integration of public schools exemplifies this trend, and other examples which have affected many of the state educational systems are readily available.

Education has received Federal aid in support of specific programs and in the form of help to students. Vocational programs, school lunches, the G.I. Bill, and the National Defense Education Act of 1958 are typical. Funds have also been supplied by the Federal government for the financing of many research projects and for the attack of many programs of international scope.

Other efforts to thread educational pursuits with a common purpose have been conducted by national nongovernmental organizations, which have continually sought to refine educational theory and the approaches to educational problems. Americans have always regarded the teaching-learning process as the heart of the educational enterprise and have considered the teacher its responsible agent. Similarly, they have recognized education's obligation to society ever since the

---

[45] United States Department of Health, Education, and Welfare. *Education in the United States of America*, Special Series No. 3. Washington, D.C.: U.S. Government Printing Office, 1955, pp. 7–9.

inception of the common school. World War I showed, however, that seemingly enduring assumptions about education no longer applied in a world so overwhelmingly changed.

In the thirties and forties the Educational Policies Commission of the National Educational Association attempted to develop a cohesive theory for education in the United States. The recognition of the changes in the character of American society, heralded by the progressive education movement in the earliest years of the century, has been a strong influence in this development. War and depression had furnished urgent proof of change, and the design cast in the nineteenth century for the role of education in America finally showed its obsolescence in the contemporary world. The functions of the school had expanded in response to the demands of the changing order. It could not remain committed to intellectual pursuits alone. New organizations in family life, the shift to an urban society, technological development, lack of employment for youth, morality, scientific advance, and the expanding concepts of a democratic government all made educational changes urgent.

In 1937 the Educational Policies Commission enlisted the aid of the eminent historian Charles A. Beard in the preparation of a statement of the functions of education. The statement charged education with the explicit task of maintaining and improving American society, reminded it of its declaration of ethical purpose to be fulfilled in the "living contacts of teachers and the taught, pupil and pupil," and urged it to rededicate itself to "the whole philosophy and practice of democracy." [46]

In 1940 the Commission faced the financial problems of public education in a paper, which, like earlier publications, urged the involvement and support of the public in education:

"Fundamental changes have taken place in American life since the foundations of our educational systems were laid. We are in a period in which skill, technical and professional knowledge, social insight, and consistent and intelligent group action are essential. In developing all of these, schools and colleges made a vital contribution. Public vision and insight will determine the value of this contribution in the future." [47]

---

[46] Educational Policies Commission. *The Unique Function of Education in American Democracy.* Washington, D.C.: National Education Association, 1937, pp. 82–89.

[47] Educational Policies Commission. *Education and Economic Well-Being in American Democracy.* Washington, D.C.: National Education Association, 1940, p. 203.

It was during the forties that the Commission laid down a blueprint for education in postwar America. In 1944 it published *Education for All American Youth* and in 1946, *Policies for Education in American Democracy*. In addition, *Educational Services for Young Children* appeared in 1945, and *Education for All American Children*, in 1948. The Commission's thesis was the following:

"Schools should be dedicated to the proposition that every youth in these United States—regardless of sex, economic status, geographic location, or race—should experience a broad and balanced education which will (1) equip him to enter an occupation suited to his abilities and offering reasonable opportunity for personal growth and social usefulness; (2) prepare him to assume the full responsibilities of American citizenship; (3) give him a fair chance to exercise his right to the pursuit of happiness; (4) stimulate intellectual curiosity, engender satisfaction in intellectual achievement, and (5) help him to develop an appreciation of the ethical values which should undergird all life in a democratic society." [48]

The plan envisioned by the Commission contained a more comprehensive school system than that in existence, and there is no doubt that the growth of preschool educational opportunities, in the form of nursery schools, and postsecondary schooling, in the form of community colleges or junior colleges, sprang from this plan.

In projecting educational plans for the 1950s, the Commission obtained the cooperation of many groups such as the American Association for Health, Physical Education, and Recreation and the National Association of Secondary School Principals. Its plans called for greater public concern and support for public education and suggested that interaction by educators, boards of education, and state legislatures might result in a "federalized system of secondary education . . . ultimately to replace the traditional American system of state and local control of education." [49] Fortunately, action did result, and the consolidation of school districts, increases in Federal and local expenditures for education, and the cooperation among local, state, and Federal agencies in the postwar period helped the educational enterprise in its rededication to democracy.

Although the Educational Policies Commission laid down an essentially progressive educational program for postwar America, it did so within a setting of historical and social ethics that clearly indicated

---

[48] Education Policies Commission. *Education for All American Youth.* Washington, D.C.: National Education Association, 1944, p. 21.
[49] *Ibid.,* p. 1.

a democratic framework for educational policy and practice. Within this framework objectives of self-realization were used to describe the dynamic nature of the individual and the important relationships between self and society.[50] In addition to the objectives of self-realization, the Commission postulated others of human relationships, economic efficiency, and civic responsibility.[51] These objectives were an outgrowth of the "Imperative Needs of Youth" identified in *Education for All American Youth*.

Within the responsibilities of democratic government and the character of democratic education, the Commission outlined the obligations of the teacher:

"First, maintain a steadfast loyalty to the democratic faith. Second, achieve and sustain high professional competence. Third, participate actively and intelligently in shaping educational policy. Fourth, establish and maintain a condition of mutual trust, understanding, and sympathy with the people." [52]

The schools of two mythical communities, Farmville and American City, presented in *Education for All American Youth*, emphasize an expanding role for the teacher. Their programs show a high degree of concern with guidance and personal assistance and indicate a changed conception of the teacher's function. They also reflect a heightened community interest in the work of the schools.

The work of the Educational Policies Commission in the forties succeeded in formulating an educational theory based on the philosophy and policies of democracy and overcame the weakness of progressive education in its sole emphasis on individual development. As Cremin has noted, this issue had been pointed out by Boyd H. Bode in his *Progressive Education at the Crossroads* (1938), but his prophetic challenge went unheeded.[53]

Out of a democratically based theory of education the teaching-learning process emerged in a new perspective. The ethical bases of democracy more than any psychological theory provided a view of the learner in which he was to be accorded worth and dignity, assisted to reach his optimal potential, and helped to respect himself as well as the rights and feelings of others. The high regard for humanitarian ideals which characterize the democratic faith led to

---

[50] Education Policies Commission, *Policies for Education in American Democracy*. Washington, D.C.: National Education Association, 1946, p. 193.
[51] *Ibid.*, p. 189.
[52] *Ibid.* p. 150.
[53] *Op. cit.*, pp. 326–327.

conceptions of teaching in which the sanctity of human personality lay at the base of learning opportunities and the rights, privileges, and obligations of a democratic policy enshrouded the teaching-learning process. The importance of individual differences, the attainment of democratic human relations, the development of attitudes toward tolerance, fair play, and the like, and the use of reason and intelligence were all accepted as underlying factors in teaching and learning.

Professional educators embraced this theory. Much of the emphasis in institutions of teacher education was placed on group dynamics—on helping the teacher to understand the nature of groups and how they function in influencing joint and individual behavior. Guidance and counseling achieved importance among the functions of the school, and many teachers were heard to say, "I don't teach a subject. I teach children."

New Criticisms

No sooner had the work of the Educational Policies Commission in converting progressive education into acceptable, good, normal education been completed than education faced an unprecedented wave of general criticism. Philosophical attacks assailed the pragmatic bases of progressive education. In 1931 Herman H. Horne criticized various aspects of progressive education severely from the standpoint of an idealistic philosophy. Horne suggested that "some of our young students at least are not being adequately impressed by the intellectual element in the ideal life, and also . . . an appreciation of the true place of religion in life is almost totally lacking." [54]

Similarly, Frederick S. Breed presented the realist position in opposition to that of pragmatism.

"The most general difference between the realist and his pragmatic opponent in education is a difference of emphasis. One stresses the conservation of values; the other their improvement. One looks more to science and research for light; the other takes more readily to the free air of philosophy and speculation. The first emphasizes habituation and the permanent elements of experience; the second, intellection and a philosophy of change. One glorifies the social tradition and subjects of study; the other, the individual and his spontaneous activity. One therefore believes in a larger measure of authority; the other in a fuller measure of freedom. Effort in like manner is arrayed

---

[54] Herman H. Horne. *This New Education*. New York: Abingdon, 1931, p. 176.

against interest, repression against expression, requirement against election." [55]

The criticism of education in general did not begin to reach massive proportions until after World War II. The schools were under a great deal of pressure. Building had been postponed during the war, and the imminent arrival of the "war babies" in school and the loss of many teachers presented a grim outlook. Threats of communism, inflation, and the unrest of society put the schools in an awkward position. As usual, they were blamed for every social weakness exposed by the war. For the most part, the conclusion reached seemed to be that progressive education had weakened the nation. The widespread criticism and early end of the Commission of Life Adjustment appointed by the United States Office of Education in the late forties exemplified the public mood.

Writing in 1950, Theodore Brameld summarized the criticism of education as the "New Reaction." He identified Robert M. Hutchins as the leading proponent of "perennialism," a retreat to the past, as reflected in the St. John's program of undergraduate education and in the Great Books program for adults. Brameld commented on the fact that "in at least one city, Hearst newspapers shout gleefully that school after school is returning to the 'three R's.'" [56] The city was undoubtedly Pasadena, California, where in midcentury the citizens rose up against the progressive superintendent of a system of progressive schools. Brameld, of course, felt that a reconstructionist approach to education was clearly indicated. In his preface he remarked: "The central theme is that education can and should dedicate itself centrally to the task of reconstructing a culture which, left unreconstructed, will almost certainly collapse of its own frustrations and conflicts." [57] The general criticism of education, which reached its climax as a result of the successful flight of the Soviet's Sputnik I in 1957, is part of contemporary perspective, which is discussed in Part 3.

PRINCIPLES

In a relatively short time the teaching-learning process has changed from the notion of a teacher and a group of students of varying

---

[55] Frederick S. Breed. *Education and the New Realism.* New York: Macmillan, 1939, pp. 225–226.
[56] Theodore Brameld. *Ends and Means in Education.* New York: Harper, 1950, p. 37.
[57] *Ibid.,* p. ix.

ages learning the three R's in a one-room schoolhouse to a vast enterprise with less clearly understood goals of "education for complete living." The principles underlying the relation of schools in the United States to society have persisted in spite of the lack of resemblance between the present school system and the common school. The society that first created a system of free and universal education has also changed drastically, and it may well be assumed that the American schools made a large contribution to many of the changes. Throughout the history of education in the United States the characteristic principles of the school as a social institution based on ideal value concepts and dedicated to the acculturation of the young have been recognizable aspects of the educative process.

1. *The first principle as an essential truth is that a change in society and social perception influences concepts of teaching and learning.* Concepts of the aim and character of education are based on the views that the people of a society hold about themselves. Changes in teaching and learning result from changes in social reality and the perception of that reality. But social perception does not always change readily. The United States had become an urban and corporate economy long before such changes were accepted as the character of the society. Wars, depressions, and other traumatic social events are important factors in changing social perceptions. Because of the complex and heterogeneous nature of American society, there are great differences in the beliefs and values that compose social perception, and many debates about education are the product of these differences.

Different groups in society may hold diverse views about the proper emphasis for American society and its education, and these views, too, give rise to differences of opinion about teaching and learning. The substance of some of them is examined within contemporary perspective in Part 3, but one example is the role of the adult members of society in relation to youth. A broad social perception of this role has strong influence on what happens in the teaching-learning process. In sum, educational content and method are dynamic outgrowths of social belief and values.

2. *The second principle recognizes the prime importance of philosophical and psychological views of such educational factors as the learner and learning, society and knowledge, and the schools as determinants in the planning of learning experiences.* It is obvious that the first step in planning to teach something is some kind of analysis of how it is learned. The child as a learner has been subject to

philosophical and psychological speculation throughout history, and it is not easy to separate the views of these two areas of knowledge. Is the mind a blank tablet to be written on? Is it muscle to be exercised? Are the mind, body, and spirit separate entities, and, if so, what is their order of importance or worth? Answers to these questions and to others that relate to man's ultimate purpose on earth, the history of life, or the cosmic organization of the universe affect concepts of learning and their aims and thus the methods of teaching.

The history of teaching and learning in the United States alone gives support to the importance of philosophical and scientific inquiry in the choice of direction and process. Beliefs and values in relation to every aspect of education are eventually expressed in both educational theory and practice. Indeed, the history of education can be analyzed in terms of its underlying rationale, composed as it is of a complex organization of facts, truth, evidence, and belief.

3. *The third principle implies that the determination of educational theory is in large measure a function of teacher-preparation institutions and professional organizations.* Public education in the early 1960s reached costs of more than $21 billion, involved more than 41.5 million students, and employed in excess of 1.5 million people as instructional staff members.[58] As the school system in the United States mushroomed, the problems of how to provide a unifying educational experience in the more than 150,000 individual schools became urgent. Though subject to criticism throughout its history, the National Education Association furnished one means. Other teaching associations, the United States Office of Education, state certification, departments of education, and national committees and studies have also contributed to shaping educational theory. By and large, however, educational theory has depended on the beliefs and values of the administrators and teachers within the school who are the direct agents for carrying on the educational process. Teacher preparation and organizations are the prime sources of these professional attitudes.

4. *The fourth principle is that the schools in the United States belong to the people and school policy is formulated by public support and lay control.* The tradition of public faith and support of education has never been subverted. At various times the public has exhibited different degrees of concern with the functions of its schools and has exerted its influence in several ways. Basically, however,

---

[58] *National Education Research Bulletin,* **40,** No. 2. Washington, D.C.: NEA Research Division, May 1962, p. 42.

educational structure and organization have remained rooted in their original principles of support and control.

Throughout the history of teaching and learning it is also apparent that the basic assumption of free and universal schooling has never been seriously challenged. Immigration, for instance, has consistently posed problems for education, but the solutions have always been sought in education, and the society of educational privilege is, at least, a classless one. All this has taken place in a setting in which local support and control is predominant. In fact, the intense commitment to local control of schools in a state system has been the crux of the argument over Federal aid to schools.

5. *The final principle establishes the fact that educational trends can be identified in the varied American educational scene.* The heterogeniety of educational opportunity and practice in the United States is well documented. Variations occur in a multitude of factors ranging from teachers' salaries to curricular offerings. The amount of money spent on each pupil varies greatly and attendance laws are not uniform in every state. Educational theory and philosophy differ from state to state and even from school to school. This may also be true of the classrooms of individual teachers within the same school.

Education in the United States is certainly complex and diverse, but it may be concluded that notwithstanding the wide variations major trends in theory and practice are identifiable. Trends toward consolidation of school districts, for instance, may not affect every school across the country, but they are significant in their all-pervading effect. The school with fewer than 50 pupils has probably changed from being the rule to being the exception. Similarly, many aspects of progressive education changed from being radical exceptions to accepted educational procedures. The testing movement, athletic programs, student activities, foreign languages, and so forth, are all examples of the kinds of change which have constituted educational trends. Moreover, trends are apparent in educational emphasis. American schools may be considered to have undergone transformations in their roles as "subject-matter centered," "child-centered," and "group or society centered." In all this diversity the trends stand out.

SUMMARY

The history of schools and society-established public education as a major social institution in the United States. Schools are rooted in a tradition of public faith and support and are charged with the primary task of youth acculturation within their dedication to the ideal social values of American society. On these basic assumptions an analysis of teaching and learning in historical perspective gives rise to the following principles:

1. Changes in society and social perceptions strongly influence views of the nature and aim of teaching and learning, and educational content and method are dynamic outgrowths of belief and value.
2. Philosophical and psychological views of educational factors are strong determinants in the planning for teaching and learning.
3. The increasing professionalization of teachers implies that educational theory is largely determined by teaching-preparation institutions and professional organizations.
4. Policies for the conduct of schools are determined by the enduring principles of public support and lay control.
5. Great variations in education exist in the United States, but major trends in theory and practice can be identified.

GUIDELINES FOR LEARNING EXPERIENCES IN DEVELOPING PRINCIPLES WITHIN THE HISTORICAL PERSPECTIVE OF TEACHING AND LEARNING

Foundations

1. *Compare* views of the nature of man's purpose on earth and try to identify implications for education in each view.
2. *Explore* such concepts as *tabula rasa, mens sana en corpore sano,* and ontogeny recapitulates phylogeny in terms of their meaning and the assumptions on which they are based.
3. *Discuss* how you think people learn and relate these concepts to psychological and philosophical theories.
4. *Analyze* what you have been taught in psychology or methods of teaching classes, or both, in terms of the underlying theories.

Principles

1. *List* the basic assumptions underlying the principles presented in the summary of this chapter; support or dispute them.
2. *Discuss* the advice often given to teachers: "Tighten the reins at first and it will be easier to loosen them later." State the basic assumptions underlying its meaning.

3. *Discuss* the theoretical framework for such practices as having slow students practice changing their clothes faster; giving merits and demerits; having students stand at attention during roll call; suggest the purposes implicit in these and similar practices.
4. *Analyze* the differences between progressive and traditional education; try to identify the principles implicit in the underlying beliefs.

5

PHYSICAL EDUCATION

Because physical education in the United States is part of the school curriculum, the ideas on which the subject is based arise out of concern for teaching and learning. How ramified these ideas may be depends on the way they are applied. Society's understanding of physical education reflects the image of the field created by members of the profession through their perceptions and interpretations. This image is part of the history of the *teaching* profession and is mirrored in efforts relating to physical education in the schools. Teachers of physical education have shown much interest in the cultural forms of sport and dance as learning experiences, in the results of research for their bearing on teaching or training methods, in the professional preparation of college majors at all levels, in school and service programs as vehicles for enhancing the welfare of individuals and groups, in physical education itself as an educational medium, and in its theory as a summation of educational purposes.[1]

Although it is possible, looking back over the history of physical education in the United States, to cite eras of emphasis, such time periods do not really begin or end with a specific event. From the vantage of the present it is easy to act as though we believed they

---

[1] Some of the ideas in this chapter were first presented at the Fortieth Annual Conference of Western Society for Physical Education of College Women, Squaw Valley, California, October 30, 1964. Some of the historical material appears in my doctoral dissertation, "Changing Conceptions of Purpose in Physical Education in the United States," University of California, Los Angeles, 1958.

did and to suggest that the "landmarks" of history really ushered eras in or out. Actually, one of the problems that has always plagued physical education has been a response to its own theory as though it were, by definition, an additive process. As a profession, physical education has hardly been able to reject an idea fully once it attained popularity or general acceptance. Most physical educators who decry the present theoretical confusion are really complaining about the irrationality of this practice. Conflicting ideas are allowed to exist not only in close association but also for some individuals in apparent harmony. It is only as we understand the sources of some of the ideas in physical education that we can examine them rationally.

Any historical view of physical education immediately implies that its influential ideas have related to its existence as part of the educational curriculum and as a profession devoted to that end. Both concerns were reflected in the two most important landmarks of the beginning of physical education as a school subject and a profession: the formation of the American Association for the Advancement of Physical Education and the Conference in the Interest of Physical Training.

The first of these events occurred on November 27, 1885, when about 60 people interested in physical education met at the Adelphi Academy, Brooklyn, in response to invitations they had received from William G. Anderson.[2] The topics considered by this group of physical educators reflected their concern. A discussion of measurement indicated the growing importance of tests. It was believed that averages obtained from measurements of many men would reflect the ideals in health and physical development. In his program at Amherst College Edward Hitchcock, Jr., included anthropometric measurements and strength testing, and Dudley Allen Sargent formulated a series of numerous measurements of the human body which he used at the Hemenway Gymnasium at Harvard. Hitchcock, the first president of the newly organized Association in 1885, was followed in that office by William Blaikie and Sargent, so that the influence of these men was significant in the early development of physical education.

The discussion of different systems of physical education at the first meeting of the Association marked a growing recognition of diversity of practice. In analyzing them Anderson wrote:

---

[2] *Proceedings of the Association for the Advancement of Physical Education at its Organization at Brooklyn, N.Y., November 27, 1885.* Brooklyn: Rome Brothers, Steam Printers, 1885, p. 3.

106   Historical Perspective: Principles as Essential Truths

"To summarize, we find that the objects of the different systems of physical training are: better health, better physique, grace, self-control, self-reliance, fortitude, courage, power of endurance, alertness of perception, quickness of action, higher degree of coordination, muscular development, will power, morals. While each school does not describe its object in the same words, it is plain that most of the results are common to each, in theory if not in practice. There is no American system of physical education, but if one is ever made it will be built upon sound principles, and its growth will be influenced by the experience of other schools." [3]

At the time of the 1885 meeting, however, the purposes of the different systems of physical training were not the main problem. The Association concerned itself with the advancement of physical education as a cause and, as such, in its early years, assumed that there was agreement on basic principles and that only the details needed attention.

At the second meeting of the organization in 1886 the most important papers presented covered such subjects as anthropometric measurements and testing refractive conditions of the eye.[4] The 1887 meeting considered military drill and engaged in further discussions of physical and anthropometric measurements.[5]

In 1888 Mary Taylor Bissell presented a paper before the Association in which she discussed the physical training of women:

"When we look for the harmonious and coincident development of mind and body, and for an improvement in the standard of health during the period of school-life, we need not turn our eyes to the schools of fashion or to the conventional seminary for girls, but to Vasser, Smith, Wellesley and Bryn Mawr, to the Harvard Annex and to kindred educational institutions of the country, where coincident with the intellectual standard is being developed a standard of health among women which can be demonstrated as *higher* than that of the uneducated girl. It is in these institutions alone that any adequate

---

[3] William Gilbert Anderson. *Methods of Teaching Gymnastics*. New York: Hinds, Noble & Eldredge, 1896, p. 47.
[4] *Proceedings of the American Association for the Advancement of Physical Education at its Second Annual Meeting at Brooklyn, New York, November 26, 1886*. Brooklyn: Rome Brothers, Steam Printers, 1886.
[5] *Proceedings of the American Association for the Advancement of Physical Education at its Third Annual Meeting at Brooklyn, N.Y., November 25, 1887*. Brooklyn: Rome Brothers, Steam Printers, 1887.

sense of the educator's responsibility for physical development is apparent."[6]

The work in physical training in these women's colleges, as had been true earlier in the men's university programs, had little effect on the public schools. It was also at the 1888 meeting that John S. White said:

"The fundamental principle, then, of the new physical education is this; aim not to produce great athletes, who can lift vast weights or hurl a ponderous hammer, while the multitude go untaught, but endeavor to train every individual to the highest symmetrical development, and the maximum of health and physical beauty of which nature has made him capable. Let Hercules stand aside for Apollo!"[7]

Part of White's argument was based on opinions prevalent at that time. Games and gymnastics had long been the basis of the English system of physical education. C. H. Ralfe summarized the English point of view when he said: "Gymnastics are useful substitutes when, from ill-health or other circumstances, natural exercise is not attainable."[8] Archibald MacLaren differentiated between recreative and educational exercise, holding that the object of educational exercise was to ensure the development of health, strength, and symmetrical development, whereas recreative exercise would maintain them once they had been developed.[9]

For the most part these theoretical considerations did not find their way into the early meetings of the American Association for the Advancement of Physical Education. The earliest efforts indicated that the members of the Association considered the advancement of physical education to be sufficient. At the same time it must be pointed out that they were concerned with what was happening in physical education, and many papers reflected the actual work being carried on in different situations.[10] In the 1880s most of the members

---

[6] *Proceedings of the American Association for the Advancement of Physical Education at its Fourth Annual Meeting at Berkeley Lyceum, New York, November 30, 1888.* New Haven: L. S. Punderson & Son, Printers, 1888, p. 9.
[7] *Ibid.*, p. 52.
[8] C. H. Ralfe. *Exercise and Training*, Health Primers No. 1. New York: D. Appleton and Company, 1887, p. 39.
[9] Archibald MacLaren. *A System of Physical Education Theoretical and Practical* (2nd ed.). Oxford: Clarendon, 1885, pp. 38–39.
[10] *Proceedings of the American Association for the Advancement of Physical Education . . . November 30, 1888.*

of the Association were teaching in colleges and universities, and programs in these institutions had been operative for a number of years. By 1890, for instance, Hitchcock was able to present to the Association a chart of the results of 15,000 examinations of college students, arranged by averages and showing anthropometric measurements.[11]

By the 1880s it seemed apparent that physical education, or physical training as it was more commonly called in light of the disciplinary theory of education, would be accorded more attention in schools. The *Report of the (United States) Commissioner of Education for the Year 1887–88* stated:

"More attention has been accorded this subject (physical training) than in previous years, and it cannot be doubted that the time is approaching when the full value of physical development will be universally realized." [12]

The next year Mary Hemenway and Amy Morris Homans, both of whom had been associated with educational philanthropies, called together a "Conference in the Interest of Physical Training," which was held in Boston on November 29 and 30, 1889. The ultimate purpose of this conference, which was the second landmark event of the 1880s, was to decide on a system of physical training for the school children of Boston. In the opening address of this conference William Torrey Harris, United States Commissioner of Education, declared:

"We open this morning a Conference devoted to the consideration of physical exercises for the development of the body. Physical training, I take it, is a part of the subject of hygiene in its largest compass, which includes dietary and digestive functions, and matters of rest and repose as well as matters of muscular training." [13]

Actually, the consideration of physical exercises at this conference was confined to muscular training and consisted of a presentation

---

[11] *Proceedings of the American Association for the Advancement of Physical Education at its Fifth Annual Meeting at Cambridge and Boston, Mass., April 4 and 5, 1890.* Ithaca: Andrus and Church, 1890.

[12] U.S. Department of the Interior, Bureau of Education. Discussion of Questions Relating to City School Systems, *Report of the Commissioner of Education for the Year 1887–88.* Washington, D.C.: U.S. Government Printing Office, 1889, pp. 211–213.

[13] Isabel C. Barrows (ed.). *Physical Training. A Full Report of the Papers and Discussions of the Conference Held in Boston in November, 1889.* Boston: Press of George H. Ellis, 1890, p. 1.

of the different systems of gymnastics. It was Mrs. Hemenway's intent that each system be presented by a leading advocate, that demonstrations of the work be shown, and that a decision be made regarding the system of physical training to be introduced into the public schools of Boston.

H. Metzner presented an address, "The German System of Gymnastics," and identified the purpose of these exercises when he said:

"The desire to improve or attain a higher standard in culture and civilization, natural to almost every human being, is the cause of all education, its aim is the perfection of mankind, and its means are the gradual development of all faculties, mental and physical, by instruction, example, and exercise." [14]

Metzner also said the German system aimed at general physical culture by selecting the exercises in classes according to age and ability and by starting instruction with simple exercises and proceeding to the more complex.[15]

The *Turners* had been making a definite effort to promote a German system of gymnastics for public school children before this conference was called, and members of the *Turnverein* had been attending meetings of the American Association for the Advancement of Physical Education since 1886.

The most important rival of the German system of gymnastics in the public schools was Ling's Swedish system. Edward Mussey Hartwell spoke of Ling as "a pioneer, but not the first or the last, in the modern development of physical education." Hartwell added that Ling deserved an honorable place in the annals of physical education because of "his endeavors to systematize and simplify the art of instruction in gymnastics and fencing." [16]

In writing of the history of Ling gymnastics in the United States, Fred E. Leonard distinguished between the Swedish Movement Cure and educational gymnastics. Leonard also credited Mary Hemenway, Amy Homans, and Nils Posse with bringing forward the claims of Swedish educational gymnastics.[17]

Speaking on the chief characteristics of the Swedish system at the

---

[14] *Ibid.*, p. 23.
[15] *Ibid.*, pp. 24–25.
[16] Edward M. Hartwell. Peter Henry Ling, the Swedish Gymnasiarch. *American Physical Education Review*, I, 1–13 (September–December 1896).
[17] Fred E. Leonard. *Pioneers of Modern Physical Training* (2nd ed., revised and enlarged). New York: Association Press, 1915, p. 137.

Boston Conference, Posse made the same distinction as Leonard, when he said:

"Before closing, I take occasion to warn you against confounding Swedish Educational Gymnastics with Medical Gymnastics, commonly known as 'Swedish Movement Cure'; although based on the same principles, the two are entirely different, not only as to their purposes, but in the exercises as well.' " [18]

Posse also pointed out that the Swedish system was based on progression and that the exercises began with the simplest and proceeded to the more complicated.

Claes J. Enesbuske, a Swedish physical educator, speaking on the subject of the place of physical training in a rational education, defined the Swedish object of physical training in schools: "The object of educational gymnastics is to train the pupil to make his body subservient to his own will." [19] He said further:

"*Physical Education* is not synonymous with Education. It is but *one* of the many departments of the whole province of education. *Education* has for its aim the highest development of the best possibilities of the individual. But the aim can be obtained only through the harmonious workings of the different departments." [20]

Hitchcock, who was the first physical educator to receive status as a professor, presented his view of the purpose of physical training at Amherst:

"Physical education, as the term is understood in Amherst College, is such a cultivation of the powers and capabilities of the student as will enable him to maintain his bodily conditions in the best working order, while providing at the same time for the greater efficiency of his intellectual and spiritual life." [21]

Sargent had become assistant professor of physical training and director of the new Hemenway Gymnasium at Harvard University in 1879. Speaking of the work at Harvard, he said:

"The great aim of the gymnasium is to improve the mass of our students, and to give them as much health, strength, and stamina as possible, to enable them to perform the duties that await them after leaving college.[22]

---

[18] Barrows, *op. cit.*, p. 51.
[20] *Ibid.*, p. 40.
[22] *Ibid.*, p. 68.
[19] *Ibid.*, p. 38.
[21] *Ibid.*, p. 57.

Sargent added that America needed a combination of European systems adapted to its own needs.

In writing of the Boston Conference, Leonard said, "It was peculiarly fitting that Dr. Edward Mussey Hartwell should be chosen to discuss 'The Nature of Physical Training, and the Best Means of Securing its Ends.' " [23]

Hartwell's remarks concerned the purposes of physical training:

"The aim of any and of all human training is to educe faculty, to develop power. As the means of developing power, certain actions are selected, taught, and practiced as exercises; and power when developed takes the form of some action or exercise due to muscular contractions. Viewed thus, muscular exercise is at once a means and an end of mental, and moral, as well as of physical training; since without bodily actions we have no means of giving expression to mental power, artistic feeling, or spiritual insight. Without muscular tissue we cannot live or move." [24]

Hartwell remarked that gymnastics, as compared with games, "are more comprehensive in their aims, more formal, elaborate, and systematic in their methods, and are productive of more solid and considerable results." [25]

Luther Halsey Gulick, Director of the Physical Department of the Young Men's Christian Association of Springfield, Massachusetts, offered a resolution of thanks to Mary Hemenway and Amy Homans at the close of the conference, noting

". . . that not only the Boston public schools, but the whole cause of physical education in America, has received a great impetus from this meeting, which is the result of their labors." [26]

In an address at memorial services for Mrs. Hemenway in 1894 James A. Page described some of the events leading up to the conference:

"In 1888 the co-operation of twenty-five teachers was secured, and the work was carried on for a considerable time in rooms at Boylston Place. After much experience had been gained and circumstances seemed to justify it, larger rooms were obtained. . . . It was in this year also, 1889, that the Conference on Physical Training took place,

---

[23] Leonard, *op. cit.*, p. 147.
[24] Barrows, *op. cit.*, p. 5.
[25] *Ibid.*, p. 20.
[26] *Ibid.*, p. 132.

112 Historical Perspective: Principles as Essential Truths

under the auspices of this school. . . . It was determined, I think, at this time, by a very general consensus of opinion, that for the public schools of this city as a whole, and with all their limitations, the Swedish system was the best adapted." [27]

On the same occasion Edwin P. Seaver, Superintendent of Public Schools in Boston, spoke of Mrs. Hemenway's having "persuaded the school authorities to adopt a system of physical training which will do much—nay, which has already done much—to give the next generation stronger and healthier bodies." [28]

The Boston School Committee had ordered that "the Ling or Swedish system of educational gymnastics be introduced into all the public schools of this city," and Edward Mussey Hartwell was elected Director of Physical Training as of January 1, 1891. [29]

The importance of the formation of the Association for the Advancement of Physical Education and the Conference in the Interest of Physical Training cannot be overemphasized in the history of physical education. They serve to remind us of the relative youth of physical education as a profession and as part of the school curriculum in the United States. These modest beginnings gave rise to a vast professional organization and to the inclusion of physical education in schools throughout the country at all levels. The detail in which the accounts of these events was presented makes explicit the fact that much of what obtained in the 1880s seems to be with us today. Indeed, both the principles and process with which these problems were identified and the way in which they were approached are familiar to many of us.

The prevalent educational view of the 1880s required that students be kept at intellectual tasks in an atmosphere of restraint for long periods of time, and the people who attended the Boston Conference were interested in short periods of calisthenics to combat the effects of the schoolroom, especially the resulting "schoolroom stoop," as it was then known. The educators in attendance were amenable to a corrective view of physical education but were firm in their commitment to an intellectual purpose. It was clear that any physical training would have to be carried on in the classroom; it would require

---

[27] Larkin Dunton (ed.). *Memorial Services in Honor of Mrs. Mary Hemenway by the Boston Public School Teachers.* Boston: George H. Ellis, Printer, 1894, p. 55.
[28] *Ibid.*, p. 10.
[29] Fred E. Leonard. *Pioneers of Modern Physical Training.* (2nd ed.). Revised and Enlarged. New York: Association Press, 1915, p. 143.

neither expensive equipment nor special teachers and would take little time from the "real" educative activities.

It is easy enough to criticize the limitations of the program the physical educators presented in light of what we know today, but the progress achieved at the time was nonetheless admirable. It does make us wonder, however, if the 10 minutes a day asked for calisthenics to correct the "schoolroom stoop" is so different from the 15 minutes a day being asked by some groups in the interests of developing "fitness."

The "battle of the systems" as a characterization of the theory of physical education in the United States persisted well into the twentieth century. The major systems seemed to be Swedish gymnastics, German gymnastics, English physical exercise or athletics, Delsarte culture, Sargent apparatus, the oratory of C. W. Emerson, the Young Men's Christian Association, and dancing.[30] The impetus for German gymnastics and the ideal of "symmetry" propounded by the Young Men's Christian Association was found outside the schools. By 1906 the North American Gymnastic Union or *Turnerbund* had a membership of 37,296 and 159 professional teachers, 79 of whom also gave instruction in public or other schools.[31]

Because both the North American Gymnastic Union and the Young Men's Christian Association, under the leadership of Luther Halsey Gulick, were preparing teachers for the public schools, the aims of both systems of gymnastics were inculcated into public school programs of physical training.

Dudley Allen Sargent was one of the first men to include athletics in what was called the "Sargent system." Actually, he advocated the systems of both Swedish and German gymnastics in addition to sports and his own ideas. Sargent also invented many machines and apparatus adaptable to the strength of the user as part of the complete physical training he favored. At the Harvard Summer School of Physical Education in 1887 Sargent conducted a practical course consisting of calisthenics, free exercise, tumbling, dancing dumbbells, wooden hands, Indian clubs, bars, vaulting horses, and rings.[32]

The inclusion of sports was a subject of controversy, partly because some of the evils attending athletic programs were already in evidence

---

[30] Luther Halsey Gulick. *Physical Education by Muscular Exercise*. Philadelphia: Blakiston's, 1904. pp. 54–63.
[31] Editorial Notes and Comment. *American Physical Education Review*, **11**, 282–289 (December 1906).
[32] Dudley Allen Sargent. *An Autobiography*, Ledyard Sargent (ed.). Philadelphia: Lea & Febiger, 1927, p. 209.

in the colleges and universities and partly because of considerations of contributions and purpose. Speaking as president of the American Association for the Advancement of Physical Education, Hartwell suggested that despite its valuable contributions, competition and cost precluded the general adoption of athletics as, "the principal means of securing the hygienic and educational ends of physical training for the mass of pupils . . ."[33]

Although "play" was reflected to some extent in programs, the corrective or defensive aim of physical training was the common element in all systems. In addition, there were secondary purposes. Delsarte culture, for instance, though never more than a vague set of principles and procedures, was based on devotion to a need for emotional expression. Emerson's theories regarding the relationship of oratory and the viscera showed some recognition of the importance of physiological considerations. Sargent, too, took cognizance of physiological bases in his system of exercise and demonstrated that women could engage in gymnastic exercises and sports without harm.

"The battle of the systems" was finally ended, not with a victory, but with a growing recognition that the greater purpose of the young profession of physical education was not being served and that education was changing. The professional association was growing stronger, especially with the publication of the *American Physical Education Review* in 1896 by the American Association for the Advancement of Physical Education, and today called *JOHPER*. It is only one of the publications of the American Association for Health, Physical Education, and Recreation. The school was taking cognizance of its wider purposes in relation to society, and physical education was seeking to unify the diversity of claims of various systems into some kind of guiding theory.

An important event in the development of a theory of physical education occurred in 1910 when T. D. Wood and Clark W. Hetherington conceived of "a new physical education." Hetherington first used the phrase in his writings which appeared in the proceedings of the National Education Association and in the *American Physical Education Review*. The first crystallized expression of Wood's ideas ap-

---

[33] Edward M. Hartwell. President's Address—the Conditions and Prospects of Physical Education in the United States. *Proceedings of the American Association for the Advancement of Physical Education at its Seventh Annual Meeting held in Philadelphia, Pa., 1892.* Springfield, Massachusetts: Press of Springfield Printing and Binding Co., 1893. pp. 13–40.

peared in *Health and Education,* Part I of the Ninth Yearbook of the National Society for the Study of Education.

The concepts of purpose in physical education held by these two men were broadened beyond the limitations of their field as it existed in 1910. Wood wrote:

"Not until the last few years has there been a practical recognition of the broader social scope of education with the implied obligation to the physical and social, as well as the intellectual and moral needs of the pupil. Beyond this it is but recently that modern psychology and physiology have proclaimed the scientific facts which have shown the more vital and intimate interdependence between the different aspects of life, which are called physical, intellectual, and moral." [34]

This view led Wood to conclude that physical education should occupy itself with a program of activities which would foster physical health, but they should be considered as by-products while the pupil was being guided toward the acquisition of mental, moral, or social benefits.[35]

Hetherington defined education as a lifelong process in which the individual's powers were developed "and adjusted to a social order for complete living." [36] He equated physical education with fundamental education and suggested that it provided the basis for all the rest of education.

A few years after 1910 many people were forced into the effort of preventing physical education from being interpreted with too much latitude. The advent of war in Europe, with the possible engagement of the United States, had a profound and almost devastating effect on physical education. Minnie Lynn wrote in her study of physical education:

"From 1914–1918 the mobilization of manpower introduced the more realistic criterion of fitness for service. Neither in education nor elsewhere was it necessary to justify physical sufficiency. The focus upon ways to secure it and both gymnastics and calisthenics returned as the most immediate processes for improving general

---

[34] National Society for the Study of Education. *Health and Education,* Ninth Yearbook, Part I. Washington, D.C.: National Society for the Study of Education, 1910, p. 80.
[35] Ibid., p. 81.
[36] Clark W. Hetherington. Fundamental Education. *American Physical Education Review,* **15,** 629–636 (December 1910).

strengths and endurance. Educational confusion stampeded school programs, for it seemed apparent that values suited to mind-education had not produced physical ends." [37]

In 1915 George W. Ehler wrote that "'Be Prepared,' the Scout watchword, should become the watchword of the nation." [38]

The fear was, however, that part of being prepared would include the replacement of physical education with some form of military drill. Ehler gave the examples of Annapolis and West Point, which both required four years of training in physical exercise. He also said:

"With more time given every day (no less than one hour) to fundamental education—vigorous physical activity, including athletics and games of every sort, supplemented by formal gymnastics where necessary . . . a new race of virile men and women will be developed, to whom the acquisition of military techniques will be simple and easy.[39]

An editorial in the *American Physical Education* Review said:

"The high schools have not yet accepted the rudiments of military preparedness which are *physical fitness*. The essentials of military preparedness are: first, physical fitness for a soldier; second, vocational skill in manufacturing the munitions of war. These ends may be secured first through as thorough courses in physical education as in intellectual education." [40]

It was also stated that formal calisthenics were not the only way to secure good posture and that perhaps the military ideal was responsible for the carriage of the West Pointer.[41]

In 1916 the American Physical Education Association held its twenty-third annual convention at which *preparedness* was the leading topic of discussion. The Association passed a number of resolutions to the effect that the requirements of preparedness were health and vigor, mental acumen and bodily and mental control, and a

---

[37] Minnie L. Lynn. *Major Emphases in Physical Education in the United States.* Unpublished doctoral dissertation, University of Pittsburgh, 1944, p. 97.
[38] George W. Ehler. Military Drill and Physical Education. *American Physical Education Review,* 20, 539–541 (November 1915).
[39] *Loc. cit.*
[40] Editorial, *American Physical Education Review,* 20, 535–537 (November 1915).
[41] George W. Ehler. The Place of Gymnastics and Athletics in the Program of the Department of Physical Education. *American Physical Education Review,* 21, 135–142 (March 1916).

courageous and generous spirit. The resolutions said that the people of the United States did not fulfill these conditions because of the lack of or weakness of physical education programs in schools. They further said

". . . that military drill in the public schools does not develop the necessary qualities in youth which prepare a nation for the struggles of war, to say nothing of those of peace, because: (a) It is not only very limited in its activities, but actually harmful in its effects on boys less than eighteen or twenty years of age. . . . (b) It cannot teach boys the real art of war, since they are too young to handle real weapons and undergo the rigors of adequate instruction. (c) It fosters a false sense of patriotism. . . . (d) Constant drill in a hall or on an athletic field is artificial, monotonous and wearisome, tending to produce an aversion for military training."

The Association concluded that military drill was less important than physical, mental, and moral preparedness which could be guaranteed by the adoption of state laws that would require a broad and flexible schedule of physical training with a generous time allotment.[42]

In February 1917 the Committee for Promoting Physical Education in Public Schools of the United States was formed. The slogan of this committee was a statement by President Wilson: "Physical training is needed but can be had without compulsory military service." The purpose of this new committee was

". . . to press for the adoption, in the various states, of a 'model' state bill, drafted by Dr. Dudley A. Sargent of Harvard, providing for the introduction of physical training, without military features, in the public schools.[43]

Earlier in 1917 the Regents of the University of the State of New York had approved a program of physical training for elementary and secondary schools. Clinton P. McCord, in discussing this program, which had been recommended to the Regents by the state military training commission, said:

"Thus it appears the requirements of the new program spell 'preparedness' in the fundamental sense—the only real 'preparedness' being

---

[42] News Notes. *American Physical Education Review.* 21, 428–444 (October 1916).
[43] News Notes. *American Physical Education Review,* 22, 113–120 (February 1917).

that which is based upon a clean, healthy, vigorous body. This is the 'preparedness' that physical educators have been preaching for the last decade; it is now given a great instrument for its effective realization—a mandatory law operating through the institution that holds in its keeping these future men and women for so great a portion of their waking time." [44]

The reaction expressed by McCord seemed to be the prevalent one. Physical educators acted as though they had been assured that by legislation their programs would gain status and recognition in the educational curriculum. That these programs were intended to serve military ends and were largely concerned with drill did not deter the physical educators.

A year after the formation of the Committee for Promoting Physical Education P. P. Claxton, United States Commissioner of Education, called a meeting of the representatives of 19 national organizations "to consider how in view of the proven lack of physical fitness on the part of our conscripted young men an adequate, successful system of physical education may become universal." [45] In 1918 a National Committee on Physical Education formed under the auspices of the Playground and Recreation Association became the National Physical Education Service. The efforts of this committee were directed toward securing legislation and aiding in the formulation of statewide programs of physical education. The work was undoubtedly successful. The United States Bureau of Education reported in 1929:

"Physical education may well be considered an important part of the curricula of the public elementary and secondary schools throughout the country. Not only have 35 states passed laws requiring that physical education be included in the school curricula, but in addition the majority of State departments of education have made very definite requirements regarding the training of teachers and supervisors of physical education." [46]

The Physical Education Law of California in 1917 stated the aims of physical education as the development of organic vigor, provision of neuromuscular training, promotion of bodily and mental poise,

---
[44] Clinton P. McCord. Statewide Physical Training. *American Physical Education Review*, 22, 1–6 (January 1917).
[45] News Notes. *American Physical Education Review*, 23, 179–193 (March 1918).
[46] Marie M. Ready. *Physical Education in City Public Schools*. Physical Education Series No. 10. Washington, D.C.: Department of the Interior, Bureau of Education, U.S. Government Printing Office, 1929, 1.

correction of postural defects, and coordination, self-subordination, obedience to authority, higher ideals, courage, and wholesome interest in recreation.[47]

The movements for legislation in the interests of improving physical fitness were a natural outgrowth of the war. It was not until after these movements had begun and the emergency was over that the battle cry of preparedness echoed more quietly in the schools.

As part of the aftermath of World War I physical educators began to conceive of the values of citizenship and social ideals as purposes of physical education. William Burdick stated the objective of good citizenship in his address as president of the American Physical Education Association in 1919.[48]

Dudley B. Reed, who followed Burdick as president, reaffirmed a belief in the purposes of citizenship in 1920.[49]

Part of the interest in social values and citizenship could be ascribed to the theories of John Dewey, made explicit in *Democracy and Education* in 1916. The democratic ideal was the framework for Dewey's whole conception of education.[50] Others noted that "it is not surprising that Dewey claims his educational ideal to be the protection, sustenance, and direction of growth." [51]

In regard to play, Dewey wrote:

"Modern psychology has substituted for the general, ready-made faculties of older theory a complex group of instinctive and impulsive tendencies. Experience has shown that when children have a chance at physical activities which bring their natural impulses into play, going to school is a joy, management is less of a burden, and learning is easier." [52]

The new concepts in physical education which Wood and Hetherington were developing as early as 1910 had not yet received a

---

[47] News Notes. *American Physical Education Review*, 22, 501–515 (November 1917).
[48] William Burdick. Presidential Address. *American Physical Education Review*, 24, 334 (June 1919).
[49] Dudley B. Reed. Presidential Address. *American Physical Education Review*, 25, 226 (June 1920).
[50] R. Freeman Butts and Lawrence A. Cremin. *A History of Education in American Culture*. New York: Holt, 1953, p. 347.
[51] S. J. Curtis and M. A. Boultwood. *A Short History of Educational Ideas*. London: University Tutorial Press, 1953, p. 466.
[52] John Dewey. *Democracy and Education. An Introduction to the Philosophy of Education*. New York: Macmillan, 1916, p. 228.

great deal of attention. As Dewey's theories began to have an effect and formalism began to fall into disrepute in educational conceptions, the popularity of gymnastic systems declined. The whole play movement consistently opposed programs of formal activities and flourished without the support of physical education. Henry S. Curtis continued to seek the recognition of physical educators for the importance of play. In 1917 he outlined the play movement in America. Curtis suggested that play was essential to the development of children and should be furnished to every child every day. This could be done only in school programs, he concluded.[53] Curtis referred to the work of Clark W. Hetherington at the experimental play schools of the Universities of California and Wisconsin as examples of education based on the natural activities of children.

Although physical educators were willing to recognize play and athletics, and indeed could hardly do otherwise because of their tremendous popularity, they were not willing to abandon a formal program. John P. Garber wrote:

"While play is necessary to satisfy natural, primal instincts, physical education in general has the broader problem of so caring for the body as to bring it up to its maximum efficiency in a well-proportioned, all-round development." [54]

Carl Schrader suggested that the Playground Association had been formed because the physical educators had effected a compromise at the Boston Conference in 1889 in accepting a limited program plan for the school classroom. Writing in 1924, Schrader said "Our poverty even today in school physical education equipment . . . dates back . . . to that dark spot in our history." [55]

In 1922 Hetherington expressed his ideas in a book that was considered an important work in the field of physical education. He suggested that four groups of social influences had inhibited the development of physical education programs to meet the growing demands of the times: public opinion about school functions, national

---

[53] Henry C. Curtis, *The Play Movement and its Significance*. New York: Macmillan, 1917, p. 19.

[54] John P. Garber. How to Organize and Plan for Physical Training and Give it its True Place in the General Scheme of Education. *American Physical Education Review*, 22, 401–408 (October 1917).

[55] Carl L. Schrader, President's Address. Objectives and Compromises, Past, Present, and Future. *American Physical Education Review*, 29, 279–281 (June 1924).

experience, powerful prejudices such as asceticism, scholasticism, and puritanism, and traditional educational thought. Hetherington conceived of physical education in terms of a program "which helps train children for the free, democratic and self-directing responsibilities of American citizenship." [56] Physical education, wrote Hetherington, "is a phase of general education, and its objectives should be interpreted in terms of the objectives of education as a whole." He concluded:

"Therefore, the objectives of physical education must be stated, on a background of education as a whole, from five standpoints:

"1. The immediate objectives in the organization and the leadership of child life as expressed in big muscle activities.

"2. The remote objectives in adult social adjustment and efficiency.

"3. The objectives in development or the changes in the activities, the development, and the adjustment.

"4. The objectives in social standards as applied to the activities, the development, and the adjustment.

"5. The objectives in the control of health conditions." [57]

Hetherington's work had been done as a subcommittee report for the National Education Association's Commission on Revision of Elementary Education. Actually, it applied to all levels of education and was drawn on by each of them.

Another report designed primarily to apply to the secondary school but which also found use at all educational levels was the report of the Commission on the Reorganization of Secondary Education. Published in 1918, this report, *Cardinal Principles of Secondary Education,* in acknowledging the conception of a democratic society, set forth seven objectives of education: health, command of fundamental processes, worthy home membership, vocation, citizenship, worthy use of leisure, and ethical character.[58] The Commission had redefined the role of

---

[56] Clark W. Hetherington. School Program in Physical Education. Prepared as a subcommittee report to the Commission on Revision of Elementary Education, National Education Association. Yonkers-on-Hudson, New York: World Book, 1922, p. 6–9.

[57] *Ibid.,* p. 21–22.

[58] U.S. Department of the Interior, Bureau of Education. *Cardinal Principles of Secondary Education. A Report of the Commission on the Reorganization of Secondary Education Appointed by the National Education Association.* Washington, D.C.: Superintendent of Documents, U.S. Government Printing Office, 1918, p. 22.

the secondary school in light of new forces in American life.[59] Its report had the effect of dignifying physical education, for health was listed as one of the objectives. Hetherington, in an article called, "Objectives of Physical Education," summarized them as follows:

"Physical education is that phase of education which is concerned first with the organization and the leadership of children in big-muscle activities, to gain the development and the adjustment inherent in the activities according to social standards; and, second, with the control of health or growth conditions naturally associated with the leadership of the activities, so the educational process may go on without growth handicaps." [60]

Hetherington also wrote the syllabus for physical education in the state of California. Its aims, he said, were the functional or developmental effects of the physical activity. To him this training provided the only means of developing organic power, which is the vitality or nervous capacity to stand the wear and tear of strenuous living. He also suggested that it developed the fundamental psychomotor strengths and skills and mental responses, and finally that it exercised the deeper instincts and emotions at the foundation of character.[61]

There is little doubt that the idea of physical education as a contribution to "education for complete living" has been the dominant theme of the field since the early years of the twentieth century. That idea in conjunction with the emphasis on physical fitness exemplifies physical education as a profession and a school subject. As new theories of culture and environmental effect developed, physical education seemed to assume an existence as a subculture with responsibility for every aspect of the growth and development of youth. To whatever educational theory recognized as important physical education gave emphasis, either by adding it to its long list of objectives or by underscoring it. This response is clearly evident in

---

[59] Lawrence A. Cremin. The Problem of Curriculum Making: An Historical Perspective. *What Shall the High Schools Teach?* 1956 Yearbook. Washington, D.C.: Association for Supervision and Curriculum Development. A Department of the National Education Association, 1956, p. 23.

[60] Clark W. Hetherington. The Objectives of Physical Education. *American Physical Education Review*, 27, 405–414 (November 1922).

[61] Clark W. Hetherington, *Manual in Physical Education for the Public Schools of the State of California. Part IV. Syllabus on Physical Training Activities with Methods of Management and Leadership.* (California State Board of Education Bulletin. Issued by the State Board of Education, 1918. Sacramento: California State Printing Office, 1919), p. 14.

such examples as a book by Agnes R. Wayman, *Education Through Physical Education,* in which she suggested that muscular development might be an end, ". . . but there is in addition a mental, moral and social education by means of physical tools." [62]

Physical education accepted its image as a medium of education and affirmed it as the means by which its academic worth was established. The oft-quoted statement made by Jesse Feiring Williams in 1923 that physical education should afford an opportunity ". . . for individuals to act in situations that are physically wholesome, mentally stimulating and satisfying, and socially desirable," sums up the history of modern physical education.

Because physical education depends on human interaction, social considerations have had an extremely important influence. The combined effects of John Dewey's theories and the stress on citizenship and social values that resulted from World War I heightened attention to democratic ideals and to the school as a social institution, and newer concepts finally brought an end to formalism in education and formal systems in physical education. Physical education has followed education through various periods of intense child-centeredness, group-centeredness, concern for the individual and his optimum development, and emphasis on democratic human relations. The stage for this kind of professional actualization was fully set by the significant work of Wood and Cassidy in their emphasis on a "naturalized activity program," designed to consider "factors for healthful physical, mental, moral, and social development" as they apply to youth and future adulthood.[63]

The "educational" scope of physical education has continued to receive a great deal of attention. As recently as 1964 the issues in physical education were identified as dealing with philosophy and purposes, social needs, sportsmanship, fitness, curricular requirement, the relationship to recreation, curriculum content, methods, student personnel, faculty personnel, boys' and men's athletics, and girls' and women's athletics.[64] These issues, suggested by professional leaders, would have been likely choices in any decade of the first half of

---

[62] Agnes R. Wayman. *Education Through Physical Education.* Philadelphia and New York: Lea & Febiger, 1925, p. 28.

[63] Thomas D. Wood and Rosalind Frances Cassidy, *The New Physical Education. A Program of Naturalized Activities for Education Toward Citizenship.* New York: Macmillan, 1927, p. v.

[64] Marion Alice Sanborn and Betty G. Hartman. *Issues in Physical Education.* Philadelphia: Lea & Febiger, 1964.

the twentieth century and would have been considered in a similar manner in terms of their implications.

The level of professional sophistication was, of course, increasing, and many fine attempts were made to deal with the assumed foundations of physical education insofar as they dealt with knowledge of human functions, development, and learning. The literature of the field, the expansion of professional preparation, and the growth of the American Association for Health, Physical Education and Recreation all served to define the force of the profession, which programs at every level served to give scope.

The forties and fifties in the United States were marked by the efforts of physical educators to utilize new evidence in psychology and educational concepts to define the commitments of their field and the recurrence of the physical fitness theme stimulated by World War II. The dualism inherent in these issues persists even today as a long-standing distortion of the situation. The attempt to displace the formalism of Swedish and German gymnastics was based on a newer recognition of the "whole man," on the integration of personality, and on acceptance of the individual, as well as on democratic tenets. The goal of physical fitness, on the other hand, seemed to presuppose a formalized drill situation.

The literature of this period is readily available, and professional periodicals such as the *Journal of the American Association for Health, Physical Education and Recreation, The Physical Educator,* and *The Progressive Physical Educator* contain what amounts almost to a running commentary on the dissent over the nature of physical education and its real contributions and purposes. This period also produced a number of books devoted to principles, interpretations, introductions, and methods in physical education, and theoretical bases were well explored by Jesse Feiring Williams, Jay B. Nash, Rosalind Cassidy, Hilda Clute Kozman, Eugene W. Nixon and Frederick N. Cozens, Delbert Oberteuffer, and many others.

The attention given to physical fitness during World War II is, of course, readily explainable. For the first time, however, it persisted after the war years, and in June 1956 President Eisenhower called a Conference on Fitness of American Youth. The President's Council on Youth Fitness was organized in September, and a week later the AAHPER Conference on Fitness was held. The AAHPER Research Council met in February 1957. After launching its youth-fitness program, which was based on a survey of 8500 boys and girls in grades 5 to 12, AAHPER in 1958 published the Youth Fitness Test Manual. This was followed by the AAHPER publications *Youth and*

Fitness (1959) and *Children and Fitness* (1960). In 1959 AAHPER announced its program "Operation Fitness—USA." In the meantime, spurred by President Eisenhower's Council, many states called governor's conferences on fitness, and various projects were underway.

On December 26, 1960, an article appeared in *Sports Illustrated* by President-elect John F. Kennedy, entitled "The Soft American," and in February 1961 President Kennedy called a Conference on Physical Fitness of Youth. In March he appointed Charles B. Wilkinson as Special Consultant on Fitness of Youth; the President's Council then prepared a series of publications, beginning with a test manual, commonly called the "blue book," which appeared in July 1961. In addition, the Council, under the leadership of "Bud" Wilkinson, utilized advertising media and personal appearances to promote a basic program of 15 minutes a day of vigorous physical activity in schools. In order to clarify its purposes, the title was changed to the President's Council on Youth *Physical* Fitness, and in 1963 Stan Musial replaced Wilkinson.

The decade during which it published its first yearbook, *Developing Democratic Human Relations through Health Education, Physical Education and Recreation* (1951), and launched Operation Fitness (1959) clearly reflected the problems of a dualistic emphasis on AAHPER. At its original conference on fitness the professional association attempted to incorporate President Eisenhower's concern with physical fitness into a deeper preoccupation with total fitness. By the 1960s this purpose had become somewhat obscured. The evidence presented and dealt with was solely concerned with physical abilities, such as strength.

The effect of the physical fitness movement on programs is difficult to estimate, but there is no doubt that it was profound. Physical educators committed to a broader purpose of their field, and unwilling wholly to accept the limited evidence on which many of the fitness tests and programs were based, were in a difficult position. It was not easy to point out that the real problem lay in confusing physical fitness with physical education.

In June 1962, however, many people found great reassurance of professional direction in the Conference on Values in Sports held in Interlocken, Michigan. The Division for Girls' and Women's Sports of AAHPER had been holding similar conferences—National Leadership Conference (1955), and Social Changes and Sports for Girls and Women (1958)—but in 1962 the conference was sponsored jointly by DGWS and the Division of Men's Athletics, which had been organized in 1958. The attention of the profession to personal-social values at this particular time was most encouraging to many physical educators who had wearied of the constant fitness theme. Emphasis on values was, however, only another reminder that the dominant theme in the history of physical education in the United States was its potential for educational gain.

SUMMARY

The challenges that have confronted physical education in the United States have been to the establishment of its position in the educational curriculum. The changing emphasis in physical education reflects the history of a young profession seeking to sustain itself and the history of a field of endeavor as molded by the educational milieu in which it has sought a place. Conclusions drawn from an analysis of the history of physical education in schools in the United States emerge as the following principles:

1. Conceptions of the role and purpose of physical education are primarily those of its educative function in terms of contributions to human development and well-being.

2. Theoretical emphasis in physical education is closely related to the prevailing view of the purpose of education; the history of theory in physical education is primarily one of justification of educational contribution.

3. Certain persistent themes in the theory of physical education can be identified; the most persistent is that of developing physiological fitness.

GUIDELINES FOR LEARNING EXPERIENCE IN DEVELOPING PRINCIPLES WITHIN THE HISTORICAL PERSPECTIVE OF PHYSICAL EDUCATION

Foundations

1. *Select* a year from each of three different decades in the twentieth century and read the issues of the AAHPER Journal for that year. Compare the difference in the apparent emphases reflected.
2. *Analyze* the works of a single author in physical education over a period of years and see if you can identify shifts in thought or emphasis.

3. *Compare* the ideas of different physical educators in a single historical period and identify the major assumptions underlying the ideas of each.

Principles

1. *Select* a practice in physical education; trace it historically and identify the underlying assumptions. Analyze these assumptions in terms of the principles involved and their validity.
2. *Discuss* the manifestation of an educational movement in physical education; analyze the principles involved in terms of their application.
3. *Analyze* the growth of professional associations in physical education and see if there are identifiable principles to account for the changes in their natures and functions.

PART THREE

Contemporary Perspective: Principles as Purposes

CONTEMPORARY PERSPECTIVE: PRINCIPLES AS PURPOSES

An important factor in the success of any undertaking is a clear conception and understanding of its purposes. When the goal is apparent and considered worthwhile, realistic means to attain it can be planned. Principles that are developed as concrete educational purposes serve as a philosophical framework and provide the foundation for a cohesive theory of physical education.

As discussed in Part 2, educational purposes are dynamic. They are based on man's interpretation of the knowledge available to him and on philosophical conceptions of human goals and destiny. Part 3 examines the contemporary basis for physical education, the problems that exist in the professional field, and the sources of purpose.

A statement of contemporary perspective is a reflection of ideas in process and is definitive only in its development of that process. The purpose of Part 3 is to demonstrate a problem-centered approach to the consideration of sources of purpose in physical education. The material available for such a study is limitless in that contemporary human experience and potential are limitless. The process is therefore based on selection and interpretation of materials with a view to understanding and developing purposes for the physical education school program.

6

THE PROBLEM OF PURPOSES

Because physical education has existed in the United States as part of the school program, the people who are physical educators are almost exclusively teachers. Physical education refers either to the profession or to the program at any educational level. All the literature, the research, the professional associations, the workshops, and conventions have been dedicated to the expansion and improvement of the school program. To study physical education means to prepare to teach it; and studying it in depth has traditionally meant pursuing advanced degrees designed to qualify the individual for teaching, especially at higher levels of education.

The fact that physical education exists as a curricular area means that it has been defined by its programs in the schools. It has been assumed that, essentially, physical education constitutes the activities in its programs, although definitions have frequently been based on the concomitant benefits believed to accrue from participation in these activities. The definition of physical education has broadened even more as programs have become more inclusive, and physical educator's claims of benefits to the student have become legion.

It is not difficult to understand the current problem. Physical education in this country was a stepchild of the educational curriculum, and throughout the last century it has fought for survival and expansion through more time and emphasis in the school program. Frequently, those who enter physical educational programs of professional preparation become militant partisans, ready to carry the banner before they understand the nature of the conflict. Indeed, we count as friends those who support us, no matter what their motives for providing support. There is little doubt that the profession has survived because of the faith and efforts of its exponents, but the victory of survival is at best a tenuous one, and our heritage of defensiveness is one of our problems. Physical education has been characterized by a "threatened" response; that is, it has fought to maintain the status quo in the face of challenge.

The defensive approach to challenges to the worth of physical education in schools has resulted in the use of a logical alliance with educational objectives as a guiding theory for the field. As recently as 1963 the physical education department of one eastern college prepared a document to show the seven cardinal principles of education and the contribution of their physical education program to each one. This was sent to every department in the college with the challenge, "Does your department do as well?" (In 1918, when these seven principles were formulated, the response of physical educators was similar.) Changing emphasis in physical education is reflected in the familiar list of accepted slogans: fitness, scientific method, education for complete living; fitness, group process, life adjustment; fitness, health, education for leisure; and so on. The process has been an additive one, until finally a reading of the literature of the field suggests that it is either everything or nothing.

Physical education has been defensive for many reasons. The long-accepted dualism of mind and body clearly implied the greater worth of mind. Our heritage of a work-and-play dichotomy perhaps still gives rise to feelings of guilt about play. In fact, this may explain why so many physical education teachers make every effort to structure the teaching-learning situation so that it is work rather than play. The teacher of physical education may not be clear about his own choice; after all, even though he found a way to make his play his work, others frequently view it as play and suspect it as an adult undertaking and life's work. The college student in the professional physical education curriculum spends a good deal of time attempting to convince his peers that his field of study is hard; and his professors join him in the attempt. Their efforts are not always successful, however, and the physical education major is considered "Mickey Mouse" on many campuses, though usually not by his fellow majors. Finally, it has never been fully determined whether physical education really does belong in the school program. Whether it does or not obviously depends on interpretations of the purposes of the school program and of physical education. Its long history is testimony to its effort to prove itself.

Accepted assumptions regarding the role of public education in the United States are subject to change within the social milieu. Major social events are echoed in the continuing debate about education. Because at least some educational experience is common to all citizens, national embarrassment can easily be laid at the door of the public school. The legislation that made physical education a school requirement in most states was a direct outgrowth of the widely publicized statistics gathered during World War I which seemed to indicate that many youths were physically unfit. Similarly, a statistical outgrowth of World War II resulted in a provision for physical fitness testing and programs which found its way into numerous state codes of education in the last two decades, along with tests that compared such things as the strength and flexibility of European and American children.

A significant social event of the late 1950s, the Russian Sputnik served to catapult American schools into the national spotlight. Americans not wanting to be second-class citizens of a Space Age set up a demand for heightened intellectual effort and emphasis to supply the leadership in scientific and mathematical fields which is vital to a nation firmly committed to competition in the race for space. This demand has become crystallized into a conception of basic education, or a return to the three R's. The psychological and emotional considerations that made the program of life-adjustment education broadly acceptable after World War II are being sharply rejected. That particular program is currently the public whipping boy of this generation of educational fundamentalists. California, long considered to have ideal programs of public education, and particularly physical education, saw fit in 1960 to elect Max Rafferty as State Superintendent of Schools on the basis of promises to return to a program of fundamental education and get rid of the frills and fads.

It may be presumed that the designational "frills and fads" includes physical education. Because its programs are usually the most costly and require the most space, many people question their worth even more intensely than if this were not the case. Vocational education, for instance, is expensive, and the importance of "homemaking" or "woodshop" to the space race is questionable, yet the attack on them is not so severe as it is on physical education. The reason might be the money contributed by the Federal government to support these programs.

Attempts to measure the value of physical education in a crisis of educational economy and direction have extended to athletic programs as well. Schools and colleges throughout the United States are confronted by attacks from segments of their communities on their programs of organized sport. At the same time, this country is extremely self-conscious about its standing in international sports competition, and Olympic gold medals have become symbols of a successful society.

CURRENT PROBLEMS

There is no reason to suppose that the need for a now or never alternative to physical education is more crucial now than it ever has been. It is unlikely that physical education will be outlawed overnight if it ignores or evades the present challenges to its existence or if it pretends or believes that they are of the same nature as past challenges. It is equally unrealistic to suppose that in the wake of the current controversies physical education will be able to maintain its status quo or simply continue to grow.

Many factors contribute to the syndrome of problems surrounding physical education today. Wartime statistics, which have been used to justify physical education programs in America for half a century, have finally been analyzed to show that the causes of draft rejection, except in a negligible percentage of cases, could not have been eliminated by programs of physical education or physical fitness. For the most part these rejections were made on the basis of medical or psychological inadequacies that were unrelated to the exercise history of the individual. It may even be that wide public attention to physical fitness has weakened programs of physical education by defining them as exercise programs. Communities could provide programs of mass exercise outside the school or for all pupils in the 15 minutes before school begins. Americans are already familiar with the image of a physical training instructor on a platform leading exercises in cadence, and they have been reminded of this image by current films promoting physical fitness for youth. Several states have begun calling their programs physical fitness rather than physical education, either because no physical educators were involved in a revision of the state code or because "the public understands what is meant." Physical education pioneers of the nineteenth century searched for a motor quotient which could be used to represent a generalized motor ability, much as the IQ score represented intellectual ability. It would be ironic if physical fitness test scores become some kind of

MQ at the very time that our knowledge has progressed to the point that we know generalized factors of intellectual and motor ability are hardly defensible theoretically.

The problem—and it has existed as long as the field itself—is "What is physical education?" The name itself is unfortunate, of course, because it explains nothing. We know—unless we wish to deny overwhelming evidence to the contrary and claim a dualism of mind and body—that the "physical" cannot be educated; and even if it could be, as programs of physical education have long seemed to suppose, what would such an education mean? We can assume that physical education as a designation replaced physical training on the basis of some recognition of the difference between training a body and educating an individual. The concepts and understanding underlying this difference must be developed beyond glib claims of contribution to educational purposes, though this approach has seemed to suffice.

The demand for more intelligent and insightful examination of physical education has been given impetus by the growing sophistication of introspective awareness concerning all human endeavor. Perhaps because we live with change as no generation before us ever has, we accept our Age of Analysis and try to understand ourselves as well as our world. Our cultural environment has become so vast and complex that it staggers the imagination to envision the knowledge that can never be mastered; perhaps, therefore, we are willing to exert greater effort toward planning our future. Because the potential of man for both good and evil has been glimpsed and the outcome of glory or horror is not yet known, perhaps our age is willing to commit itself to a greater responsibility for that future. Still heir to the insecurity of fear, we are caught in the self-doubt that made the characterization Age of Anxiety seem so acceptable. As citizens and physical educators, we want to look ahead; we prize courage and creativity but we also want to hold on to the familiar. We doubt the image of what we are but are not clear in the image of what we would like to be, and the fear of getting lost in the shuffle is ever present.

The status of physical education as measured by time and emphasis was hard won. It is not unusual today to find teachers who deal with classes of a hundred and who admit that it is impossible to teach effectively yet prefer it to making any concession to the amount of time required. Many physical education programs continue unchanged in the face of inadequate conditions. Regulations of showering and dress are enforced for 50 youngsters in a space designed for 25, and too many students emerge from our programs believing that there are

15 players on a volleyball team. Throughout the years physical educators have demonstrated a high degree of competence in the organization and administration of programs, even under adverse conditions; but this kind of competence is not an adequate answer to the contemporary challenge.

In answer to "What is physical education?" our answer would be our long-fostered ideal of a broad program of sports, games, dance, and aquatics, adequate facilities and equipment, and a required daily period of activity for all youngsters, with academic credit commensurate with other areas of the curriculum. It is possible to cite any number of purposes or potential benefits inherent in this program. A justification for it might well be compared to an explanation of the curriculum in English as the skills to be mastered and books to be read or in mathematics as numerical systems and processes. Of course, curriculum areas *are* often described and defined in just this way. The problem lies in the growing awareness that this is not enough in an age in which new knowledge, discovery, and invention are rendering the sum of human knowledge and culture incomprehensible.

Americans, confronted with change and discoveries of new knowledge they can never grasp, are looking to schools to provide their youth with the academic background and abilities now in demand. Older concepts of readiness having been discarded, children begin their learning tasks early. Preschoolers are taught to use typewriters; foreign languages are now the province of the primary grades; and parents frequently cannot understand the homework assignments of their youngsters. The demand for excellence in school programs is often translated into harder work, and the merit of the time spent in physical education classes is being seriously questioned.

PROBLEMS OF PURPOSE

It is recognized that physical education at any given time is the expression of a society's beliefs about man, his purpose, and, specifically, his body, whether considered a symbol of a self or an existent entity. One of the problems, of course, is that society rarely formulates and expresses agreed-upon views. More accurately, physical education is the expression of the physical educator's understanding and interpretation of the views of society, for school programs are usually developed and understood by their practitioners. These programs not only reflect society but seek to contribute to it, and because they are based on a selection of cultural materials some sort of contribution to societal change or development is ensured. It is also true—in the United States—that specialization is a recognized reality, and we look to the experts to provide leadership for developments in their own field. They must, of course, seek understanding and acceptance from their particular public, for no field of endeavor has absolute autonomy.

Physical education in America has not been clearly understood; there has been no general agreement on the understanding of what physical education is. Many times, in the search for professional acceptance, the physical educator has been willing to accept the interpretation of his field by those outside it. It is desirable for people within different disciplines to work together and share their knowledge, but in physical education it has more often taken the form of looking to those from other disciplines and areas of endeavor to provide the leadership for the field. The professional self-consciousness that allows this kind of theoretical approach has also made it difficult for physical educators to accept leadership from within their own field.

Because the answer to "What is physical education?" is reflected in statements of purpose as well as in descriptions of ideal programs, it is not surprising that many people feel the question has not been answered adequately. Each group of specialists who supported or examined physical education has left another imprint of potential purpose for the field. Anthropologists, psychologists, and medical personnel, as well as politicians, professional athletes, and recreation workers have contributed interpretations of the purposes of physical education, and physical educators have incorporated them into the field. There are few people involved in physical education who cannot recite statements of purpose for their programs which somehow involve the mental, moral, spiritual, emotional, and physical benefits that they provide.

The problem of purposes for physical education is compounded by the proliferation of aspects of the school program that are within its province. Purposes for varsity sports may not be the same as purposes for a daily program. Within these aspects there is also a diversity of view of purpose and function. In practice within the profession members of a special interest area frequently formulate their own purposes and ask themselves such questions as, "Is dance aesthetic or athletic?" or "Are health and physical education separate disciplines?" Sometimes the purposes formulated for boys and girls have been conceived separately, and the growth of coeducation programs inspired a host of newly formulated ideas. School level has presented still another problem in which purposes differ for the elementary, secondary, and higher areas of education.

The problems confronting physical education as it seeks to define itself and its purposes are not unique to that profession. They are made more complex, perhaps, by factors peculiar to the field. The most crucial is the almost exclusive organized existence of physical education as a school program. Certainly, what we call physical education in schools is extremely important—schools notwithstanding. Exercise in the United States involves an almost unbelievable emphasis on sports and recreational pursuits, but neither the proponents nor the participants in these pursuits are called physical educators. Traditionally, physical educators are teachers in educational institutions, and physical education is that which they teach. This means that too little effort has been devoted to defining physical education in substance; rather our definitions have been in terms of function. Physical education has been explained not as the "study of . . ." but as the "teaching of . . . ," which has resulted in the paradox of an academic discipline in colleges that is defined by curriculum in schools. As long as this is so, physical education will not have a substantive existence; therefore, its value, even in educational terms, is continually open to question.

Efforts to examine physical education conceptually have been limited. One of the most serious limitations has been the inability of physical educators to deal with the foundations of their field in great depth. The defensiveness of many physical educators has resulted merely in a study of foundations in search of justification for existing ideas and in a lack of critical examination. Thus ancient Greece is frequently cited as exemplifying a golden age of physical education, the importance of which was truly recognized in the harmonious development of man. The gymnastic systems of Ling and Bukh were readily accepted in their time because they were of European origin and seemed to be scientific. Just as popular educational theory influences physical education, social, psychological, and biophysical theories are frequently adopted by physical educators in diffuse and even contradictory terms. The recent attention of physical education to philosophy has been manifest in little more than the recognition that philosophical differences do exist. Although the history and philosophy section of the national association has presented several exciting and insightful considerations, for the most part physical educators have responded as though theory and practice were two different things—and philosophy, of course, interesting but irrelevant.

At the other extreme there are those who would initiate a somewhat pretentious philosophy of physical education.

The concern with programs in schools has meant that conferences, research, and literature of the field have been devoted primarily to educational problems and the processes of teaching. Until very recently almost all books published in physical education were geared to use in specific courses, and the accepted view was that general or reference books would be unmarketable. A very hopeful event was the initiation of *Quest,* a periodical published by the men's and women's associations of college teachers and obviously dedicated to discussion of ideas and issues on a level quite beyond the "how to do it" approach of some other journals. In late 1964 *JOHPER* also initiated a fine column under by-line of the National Kinesiology Council.

The problem of a clear identification of physical education and its purposes has persisted in spite of some very cogent efforts by physical educators to attack it. In view of the nature and focus of physical education, identification of leadership is not easy. In many fields leaders are those who are successful—the leading exponents. What would such a demarcation mean in physical education—the successful coach, the good teacher, the university professor, the Olympic champion, the president of the professional association? Certainly, members of the American Association for Health, Physical Education, and Recreation accept the leadership of officers in matters of practical procedure; but it would be difficult to exert much intellectual leadership during a term of office, and the association membership does not represent a high percentage of all physical educators. Coaching and athletics have long been considered different from physical education, and many of the coaches of sports in schools and colleges are not graduates of a program of professional preparation in physical education. Indeed, some schools do not allow an individual teacher to teach physical education and coach a major sport as well; and many coaches prefer to teach in the classroom in the belief that they will be fresher for their afternoon coaching duties. President Eisenhower chose a successful coach, "Bud" Wilkinson, to take charge of the fitness program; to succeed him, President Johnson chose a successful baseball player, Stan Musial, but physical educators have not accepted this leadership beyond a limited scope.

Teachers in programs of professional preparation have exerted a great deal of influence on physical education. By virtue of the numbers of students who graduate from professional curriculums and take their places in the profession there is the potentially great impact of a particular personality who teaches significant courses within a large department. The people who write, speak at conferences, and participate in organizations and workshops frequently become leaders within the profession, at least in that they and their ideas become widely known.

Agreeing on the leaders, however, does not mean accepting leadership. Physical education encourages disparity of view and open debate, but there has not been a cohesive effort to resolve the dichotomies of belief and ideas that typify the theoretical nature of the field. Because there have been so many claims of accomplishment by physical education, attempts to define it often meet with the comment, "that's been done before." Presentations of new ideas are often dismissed as "semantic" distinctions. New statements sound like restatements of something old, but the contextual understanding indicates a *real* difference. Only the naïve profess to have an understanding of intellectually complex philosophical views simply because they have used the same words before. Currently, the efforts of thoughtful physical educators to explore physical education's central concern with movement are dismissed summarily by a large segment of the profession on the basis that "we've always known that!" Interestingly enough, in the late 1950s when Eleanor Metheny and Lois Ellfeldt presented a movement theory that utilized new words, such as "kinestruct" and "kinecept," their work was rejected by many as pretentious in its use of these terms.

Perhaps because physical educators are game-centered, the search for understanding too often disintegrates into a contest in which individuals either choose or are assigned to a "team" and discussion becomes argument. Other professions have this problem, but physical education has become almost anti-intellectual in its continuing dichotomies of theory practice. A contributing factor to the problem is the inability of the profession to deal with its foundations in depth or with ideas that seem to challenge practice in any significant way. In other words, an idea that becomes popular and accepted is incorporated into programs or teaching methods in certain ways, but the understanding of the idea itself is often imperfect and the incorporation is usually vague enough to make it insignificant. Wide belief in the phrase "concomitant learnings" in physical education has meant that physical educators *assume* that a great many things happen in their programs, whether planned or not.

The examples that lead to this kind of indictment are countless. "Problem-solving" in physical education was translated to mean having basketball players make up their own plays; "self-direction" meant using squad leaders to take attendance; "democratic group process" was interpreted as occasionally taking a vote on some minor issue; and "developing responsibility" has sometimes meant giving out towels. In the same way, physical educators have avowed disbelief in a dichotomy of mind and body but continue to discuss motor learning. The dangers of mass exercise are well known, and physical educators have accepted a need for individualized screening of posture. Yet the boy with abducted scapulae must still perform the prescribed number of push-ups to pass his fitness test. Physical educators accept the idea that all movement is governed by certain underlying principles, but practice it almost solely in the reiteration of a few basic principles in the teaching of sports' movements. The recent spate of materials based on isometric exercise is also reflected in physical education programs, and the more zealous adherents of this procedure devote a great deal of time in their programs to the practice of silent muscular effort.

It is possible, of course, to find an example of almost anything within the vast system of physical education in the United States. The systems of physical education that were popular in the nineteenth century are still in evidence in some programs today, and there are undoubtedly many physical educators who accept only a physical premise as valid. This discussion is neither a plea for a single nationalized program of physical education nor for some statement of purposes for school programs that would be acceptable to all. On the other hand, the fact that there is diversity of views should not be used as a rationale for the acceptability of any and all of them.

SUMMARY

Physical educators must be able to answer the question "What is physical education?" in a way that leads to the formulation of clear purposes for school programs. It is hoped that the answer may also lead to the delineation of a substantive discipline of knowledge and inquiry, to research that will extend the frontiers of man's knowledge about himself, and to a material contribution to the good life which is an actualization of human potential in any philosophical view.

In an age beset by anxiety but focused toward the analysis and synthesis of knowledge the challenge of establishing purposes for physical education must be accepted. Our history of changing emphases and purposes would indicate that our approach to the problem must be more rational than it has been in the past. Public demand will not diminish simply because we claim a host of benefits that we cannot adequately explain. Until we examine our own expertise, we cannot provide the leadership expected of the proponents of a professional field. As long as we accept successful people in any field of endeavor as spokesmen for physical education, our leadership from within will not be accepted. We must learn to listen to those members of our profession who are expending effort to explore the understanding of physical education. It is difficult, especially for the long-term teacher, to face the unfulfilled responsibilities involved in new ideas. It is easier to insist that each new idea is just another "bandwagon" and that the enduring purposes of physical education, however understood by the individual, are the real ones. Although we accept the reality of a changing world, we have yet to learn how to deal with our own changing ideas. It must have been difficult for those who believed the world was flat, yet *knew* that it was round, for it is possible for us to accept new ideas but continue to act as though we still believed the old ones. It is more convenient for us in physical education to call our differences semantic—easier to force our thoughtful colleagues to become ideological adherents than to permit them freedom to explore new ideas.

The problem of purposes for physical education is a persistent one, but the following principles emerge to guide us in the process of their formulation:

1. Purposes for school programs of physical education are a reflection of theoretical understandings of the nature of the discipline and its educational function.

2. Purposes can and must be formulated as an outgrowth of a process of intelligent consideration of available knowledge.

3. It is the responsibility of physical educators to understand their field and its foundations and to express this understanding in purposeful undertaking.

4. Physical education is dynamic in its cultural and educational aspects, and its purposes should reflect developed processes of methods of inquiry as well as intelligent and open discussion by its professional members.

GUIDELINES FOR LEARNING EXPERIENCES IN UNDERSTANDING THE PROBLEM OF PURPOSES IN CONTEMPORARY PHYSICAL EDUCATION

1. *List* the titles of AAHPER Yearbooks and special association conference and workshops since 1950 to identify the major concerns of the profession.
2. *Examine* such publications as *JOHPER, The Physical Educator,* and *Quest*; select articles showing different conceptions of the problems and purposes confronting physical education.
3. *Select* one or two leaders in physical education for study. In each case try to identify the guiding beliefs of the individual as well as the kinds of professional activities in which he has engaged. If possible, analyze the influence the person has exerted on program changes and on other physical educators.
4. *Compile* a list of statements made by people who are not physical educators concerning the purpose and/or value of physical education. Try to identify the assumptions underlying these views.
5. *Survey* the book lists of various publishers and *identify* the probable purpose of recent publications in physical education—that is, the nature of the publication and its probable market.

7

THE PREMISE OF PURPOSES

It has been suggested that the organized educative process is a moral enterprise in that its goal is the modification of human behavior. Although the academic structure is compartmentalized, it does not include a curricular area called conscience that would be responsible for the development of ethical concepts and commitments. Those who call themselves teachers accept, in some measure, a commitment to a broad view of man in his world. Man, the rational animal, man, the symbolist, man, the energy system, or, man the player—all must be educated on a premise of man as human. A consideration of the meaning of the human potential is a philosophical concern, philosophy having been the area most clearly responsible for synthesis of knowledge. This concern has become the province of all educators. The search for meaningfulness—for the relation of knowledge to human meaning—characterizes the separate academic disciplines as well as the whole process of education.

It is not enough for a teacher to be soley a subject-matter specialist. The old plea for a general education for all teachers—instruction that would be humanistic as well as scientific—has grown to a clamor. The teacher must also be a *specialist* in his own area. James B. Conant, in *The Education of American Teachers* (New York: McGraw-Hill Book Company, 1963), took an eloquent stand for foundation courses that would be superior to the "pathetic" ones, currently available. He stressed, too, the need for academic preparation of teachers that would represent something more than the mere accumulation of credit hours.

The academicians seem willing, finally, to participate in the development of curricula in their areas of knowledge and in the revolution of conceptual schemata of various disciplines of knowledge, such as mathematics and physics, to be applied in the classroom. The Woods Hole conference called by the National Academy of Sciences in 1959 and devoted to education in science is one example of the joint attention of scientists, scholars, and educators to the problems of teaching and learning. Bruner, in his report of this conference, identifies the teacher not only as a "personal symbol" of the process of education, but as a competent person in his own area of scholarship.[1]

We should not be surprised to find an atmosphere of argument and confusion in educational discussion. American citizens as well as educators are seeking an objective view of their culture. Their efforts are an outgrowth of the cultural heritage they seek to understand and to shape and the transitional nature of social views in contemporary United States makes this difficult task even more complex. Conceptions of the role of the teacher depend on pertinent assumptions of the purpose of education in relation to the nature of the goals and processes of human existence and development. The task of trying to clarify this role seems—and is—monumental; but as long as teaching is a humanizing process education must seek its bases in a broad view of human purpose. The teacher, as both symbol and agent of the process of education, must conceive his own functional role within a framework of examined assumptions. In our dynamic society educational debate is here to stay. In the light of new understanding, new conceptions of the individual and society, social events and change, and the availability of a host of diverse processes of inquiry and analysis, we cannot plan the educational enterprise once and for all.

At the same time, arguments about education are essentially presentations of points of view. Unfortunately, they are not usually presented in cohesive theoretical perspective, with a clarification of basic assumptions and an analysis of emergent principles. Heated debates about whether schools should devote more curricular time to science and mathematics than to subjects such as physical education are not uncommon. The argument for greater emphasis on science is supported by the obvious need for scientists in the expansion of technology and by the current international competition for scientific advancement. Americans have placed their faith in education as the antidote and panacea for all national ills. Thoughtful people are

---

[1] Jerome S. Bruner. *The Process of Education*. Cambridge, Massachusetts: Harvard University Press, 1963, p. 90.

aghast at educational arguments that seem to be based on assumptions that have always been negated in the United States. People who decry the way of life in totalitarian countries are able to embrace educational theories that are outgrowths of the ideologies of these countries. Often we hear the youth of our country referred to as a natural resource, and some of the current support for educational programs for gifted students becomes, in its extreme forms, a negation of universal educational opportunity.

Education in the United States is an important social institution. As in all such major institutions, there exists a complex of ideas, traditions, hopes, fears, and realities. Many factors combine to produce a confused and controversial theory for the educational process and for its subject-matter areas: the dynamic nature of education in a changing society; the underlying devotion of the educative process to *potential*, whether clearly defined or not; and the vast, heterogeneous functional existence of the enterprise itself. Because Americans have thrived on controversy and an openness to discussion of ideas, it is unlikely that there will ever be a single educational theory that is imposed nationally. It is the contention here that each educator has a responsibility to understand the broad scope of educational events, to seek the development of his own theoretical understandings, and to provide leadership in the continuing debate that is the expression of the deep concern with which Americans view their educational system.

If those who strive to handle their educational roles intelligently are to avoid the obvious dangers of throwing out "the babies with the bath water" they must deal with the premises on which educational purposes are formulated, for they are the basic assumptions on which educational theory must be predicated. It is important to remember, however, that these assumptions are only a *part* of the whole theory. It is one thing to suggest that Americans are well mannered, even to imply that this quality is developed in schools; but it is quite another to advocate the teaching of good manners as the major purpose of education in this country. Indeed, one of the sources of confusion in the current debate about the role of schools is the failure to distinguish between premise and purpose in education. This confusion exists among teachers and students as well as their parents and results in the notion that every potential of educative enterprise can be considered a major purpose. Inevitably the arguments are couched in dogmatic terms about issues to which the "all or none" principle is hardly applicable.

An effort should be made to identify some of the premises on which

American education is predicated and to understand them as underlying assumptions of responsibility and purpose for all areas of the curriculum. The fact that education in the United States is free, universal, and compulsory is testimony to its own efficacy as a common socializing and humanizing institution for all Americans. Perhaps, as many argue, its role should be more clearly defined and its areas of responsibility curtailed, but in the final analysis these things can be done only when the responsibilities are assumed in some other area of social experience. Surely, there is no more practical undertaking than the school lunch program with its Federal support and tremendous commitment of time, facilities, and money; yet no one construes the purpose of education to be to provide lunch. The point is that the need is there, and at least in some cases the school cannot fulfill its role without concerning itself with this need. The school lunch program is one example of an underlying concern and commitment that became basic assumptions of educational responsibility. The full potential of the various subject-matter areas, as disciplines of knowledge and meaning, cannot be realized until these real concerns are understood and become basic assumptions of all curricula and all teaching. It may be, too, that as these premises of commitment become assumptions of educational purpose, physical education will find itself in the position of being able to contribute opportunities to their fulfillment—to an even greater degree than other subjects, but it will do so without mistaking such assumed purposes of education with its own distinctive purposes.

THE SOCIAL PREMISE

In a broad but incontestable sense the school has a responsibility to youth in their process of maturing. We expect somehow that their going to school and growing up will result in a nation of adult citizens, complete with all the rational and ethical qualities and personal skills and abilities deemed desirable in the United States. It is also characteristic of our society, or at least of the majority of its citizens, to view the future with hope and faith, to want more for our children than we ourselves had. These expectations for our youth therefore represent the most idealistic projection of our potential rather than the reality of the adulthood we know. It may be that the violent rejection of life adjustment as an educational characterization stemmed from an unfortunate disregard of this vision in the use of the word adjustment, with its connotation of dealing with what already exists. At any rate, the relationship of school and society, previously explored, is the critical premise of education in America. Schools exist as part of the social scene and they are expected to reflect the society and contribute to it. The implication is that in reflecting society's ideal view of itself education will facilitate progress toward that ideal.

The contribution of schools to society is manifest in the development of the individuals under their care. The national concept of education devoted to the "optimum development of the individual" has long been accepted and can be defined as a major premise of the educational system. Americans are characterized by their almost boundless faith in the future and in their youth, and optimum development is an expression of that faith. This may not be true of all Americans or of all socioeconomic groups, but this faith is strong enough to be a major force in educational commitment. It is interesting, too, that recent developments in psychology and education seem to support this open-ended view of the individual. Not too long ago it was possible and popular to try to establish a finite picture of individual abilities and potential through psychological and intelligence tests. It was believed by many that the abilities, values, and responses of early youth, whether inherited or not, were more or less fixed; and education could, indeed, be considered a process of helping the individual adjust to his own defined potential. These assumptions have been reexamined and for the most part discarded. Subsequent research indicated that this position was not tenable.[2] The result has been a greater effort than ever to take cognizance of every group. Social and educational semantics now include such terms as disaffected youth, culturally deprived, slow learners, gifted, underachievers, and overachievers. Have we come full circle? Perhaps our old naïve faith in the individual is now being reasserted with the backing of the same science that made it seem so naïve.

It would be foolhardy to try to chronicle the values, beliefs, and attitudes of a whole society. Certainly in the complex and heterogeneous society of the United States it is possible to identify as many negations as assertions. We can examine the evidence on a broad scale, however, and come to certain conclusions which seem to be true in that they are trends of thought or ideal commitments that have endured. It is important to avoid the snare of what Galbraith has identified as conventional wisdom, which makes the familiar

---

[2] Gardner Murphy. *Human Potentialities.* New York: Basic Books, 1958. R. F. Peck, R. J. Havighurst, and others. *The Psychology of Character Development.* New York: Wiley, 1960.

the most acceptable and leads us to approve of what we want to hear, usually because we have heard it before.[3] This is especially crucial as we seek to identify our educational premises with our society's democratic commitments. It is a truism that democracy is a social as well as a political ideal and that it is both the characterization and expression of our essential national philosophy. Until recently, however, the conventional wisdom in education depended on a recognition of the social aspects of democracy. Progressive educators, in battling the isolation of education from society, actually employed principles of democracy and human interaction and interdependence as arguments for change. In fact, as schools became humanized, the radical became the moderate. In no sense was the end of the progressive education movement an ideological defeat; rather what had been dynamic new conceptions of the role of education became basic assumptions of the educative enterprise and part of the acceptable and conventional wisdom.

Democracy as social interaction is not fostered in every classroom, but it is certainly accepted as a major premise of educational purpose. No matter what educational issue may be in the spotlight, Americans assume that their youngsters nevertheless will learn to respect the rights of others and the dignity of man in their schools. No matter how strongly this society or any segment of it wants winning football teams or superior Olympic contenders, the assumption is that our young people have learned to play by the rules and respect the spirit of sport as an important aspect of the life of democratic America. These basic assumptions of educational responsibility need constant reaffirmation and attention; there are no premises of American education more important than the democratic tenets on which society is based. In educational theory social democracy must take its conceptual place as a major premise and not as the major purpose.

Society and education have come to realize lately that faith in rationality is also a basic principle of democracy, and the dynamic nature of society today seems to demand rational process and ability as never before. Society in this country has been described as anti-intellectual—for example, use of the word "egghead"—but it is reasonable to assume that there is more involved than derision. Although the idea of an intellectual elite is repugnant to Americans, they have always admired knowledge and intellection. In some ways, the common man with common sense has been considered the most competent in

---

[3] John Kenneth Galbraith. *The Affluent Society*. Boston: Houghton Mifflin, 1958, pp. 9–11.

practical affairs, and ivory tower theorists somewhat suspect. But recent years have produced monumental evidence that the intellectual may serve as a desirable adjunct to the realm of social practicality. In the emergence of a highly technological society there remains little that can be called common or uneducated. As technology and automation advances, rationality may become the one sphere in which man's influence will be exercised. It is said that we are capable now of producing large numbers of machines that could perform on a level equal to that of men with high school educations. The importance of rationality, then, is a social premise with vast implications for education. In 1961 the Educational Policies Commission cited this, with attendant meanings of thoughtfulness and creativeness, as the central and all-pervasive purpose of education.[4] In the years since 1961 these concepts have included meaning as basic to the motivation of man.

It would follow that as society becomes highly technological, as it has in the United States, creativity and innovation become highly prized. In recent years democratic and educational commitment to the highest development of individual potential has been popularly interpreted to mean development of the creative and unique abilities of the individual. This does not suggest that all indictments of conformity are no longer justified; but the approval of others, so closely linked to conforming responses, depends in some measure now on individualization. If, in America, there is no true renaissance at least in aesthetic values, there is more emphasis than ever on the performing and the fine arts. The growth of foundations, centers, and schools devoted to the arts has great social and educational implications.

All societies, of course, exist in transition because of the nature of social growth and change. It might be said that the United States in the twentieth century has existed in revolution rather than transition. The fact of change has become a social premise, and there is now a growing insight into the relationship between the choices we make today and the social and cultural revolutions we expect tomorrow. Adult Americans do not have to turn to comparative anthropology to know that mores are not fixed; an abundance of evidence has been available in any decade of their lives. We know that our world and time will make demands on qualities of adaptability and flexibility in understanding and functioning—demands that we can hardly envision. We have become acclimated to the revolution in availability of new

---

[4] Educational Policies Commission. *The Central Purpose of American Education.* Washington, D.C.: National Education Association of the United States, 1961.

things. In an age of rockets and missiles and proposed trips to the moon we can look back and identify with those who witnessed the invention of automobiles, telephones, radio, and television. We listen with comparative equanimity and a kind of accepting wonder to predictions of the technological conveniences that will be available to the next generations. Revolutions in social patterns and mores are more difficult to understand and to accept. It is easier to envision oneself living in a world in which all communication is televised than in one in which executives are obsolete at thirty-five. The changes themselves and the predictive statistical trends seem staggering. Can it be that today's average twenty-year old can anticipate having six different careers during his lifetime and that more than one per cent of the presently employed workers will have to be retrained annually?[5] If so, what does it mean to us and to education? One analysis of our current economic revolution has led to the conclusion that it is time for a guaranteed income for all citizens in the United States. Under this plan, an income of 3000 dollars a year would be available to all, and the individual could choose to work or not.[6]

Whether or not a guaranteed income becomes a reality, Americans are faced with a changing image of themselves as a hard-working nation. They have more leisure time, for certain segments of the population work only 30, even 25, hour weeks, and several million high school dropouts are not working at all. At the same time, this century has seen women join the labor force in large numbers. It has been estimated that the number of women who work during their lives has increased by more than 90 per cent in the twentieth century. Women, too, have become part of the dramatic movement toward civil rights in this country, and all Americans look forward to a future in which equal opportunity for all will be a social reality. Equal opportunity for all, unlike a guaranteed income for all, encourages competition. Americans accept competition in every sphere, and Commager has identified it as one important aspect of the American way of life.[7] Commager has also suggested that if there is an American philosophy it is pragmatism, with its accompanying faith in processes and functions and the use of a problem method for the study of most things.

---

[5] Edward T. Chase. The Job Finding Machine, *Harper's Magazine,* **229,** No. 1370, 31–36 (July 1964).

[6] Michael D. Reagan. For a Guaranteed Income, *The New York Times Magazine,* 20 (June 7, 1964).

[7] Henry Steele Commager. The Ambiguous American, *The New York Times Magazine,* 16 (May 3, 1964).

Our age is too sophisticated to employ concepts of the average American without a hint of facetiousness. Competition implies evaluation, and the motivation in the United States seems to be to prove that one can excel or at least measure up to the best in whatever sphere the evaluation takes place. The values involved may differ. For instance, a father may consider it better for his son to be the best athlete rather than the best scholar; but being best is still a value in itself. Excellence as an educational concept was immediately understood and well received by the American public because it was based on a value already held. It is not worthy that excellence was much more acceptable than its forerunner competence. It would seem, once more, that excellence implies the greatest potential development and is therefore more consonant with American ideals.

The social premise of purposes in education is the development of an adequate and excellent citizenry, with all the attributes of personal ability needed to enhance the individual and his society. The reality of the educational process as it exists and is maintained in the United States is an expression of the charge to educators to analyze what this premise means and translate it into goals and programs. No other course is acceptable and no other premise must be allowed. The dichotomy of theory and practice which accepts this premise in theorety but denies that it can be achieved must be recognized as a failure to achieve and does not belie the importance of the goals or the continuing efforts that must be made to reach them. The social premise provides assumptions of the value of the individual in a dynamic, competitive setting in which the achievement of personal goals will benefit the whole society. This premise can be proved only if the ideal assumptions of that society reside in the individual, and society expects that it will be as a result of the educative process.

THE HUMAN PREMISE

The limitations of education in its contribution to the ideals and goals of society, are, logically enough, attributed to the limited potential of certain individuals and incomplete knowledge of the processes on which education depends. For many years arguments about the importance of heredity versus environment were rampant; but an emergent view has emphasized the potential of individual development. In the face of limited knowledge about heredity it would be foolish to deny its effects, but there is little doubt that the nation's present philosophy focuses mainly on the human environment. Commager is certainly correct in identifying pragmatism as a distinctly American philosophy existing in a pervasive form that transcends all other existing philosophical beliefs. Despite the social and individual inequalities that exist, it can be concluded that equality of opportunity stands as an ideal value of major importance in this society. The availability of education is the greatest insurance of this equality.

The United States by choice and tradition is a classless society in which the individual, regardless of his socioeconomic background or position, may rise to any height in the realization of his abilities. "Democracy might be called the political aspect of the assertion of the supreme importance of the individual." The nation's history and its documents attest to the importance of this basic tenet, and there have been many fine discussions of this concept of the history of America and its fabric of life.[8] One important work identified the realization of individual potentialities as a major goal of this nation and suggested that concern for individual and human excellence is a reflection of the ideal "of the overriding importance of human dignity."[9] The ideal of human dignity gives rise to objections by most Americans to a view of themselves as social units or manpower or their youth as a natural resource. An important aspect of education in America is that each individual has worth and an equal right to opportunities for self-realization. Furthermore, this right is not to be denied easily at any developmental point simply because the individual does not show great promise. Reluctance to accept individual inability to utilize opportunity may have led to the recent and promising efforts to help those whose potential seemed impoverished.

Recognition of individual worth and dignity is also an important basis for rejecting mechanistic and dualistic concepts of personality in the United States. The premise of man as human, with corollary concepts of wholeness, rationality, and civilized processes, must serve as the basic tenet of school and society. Man's inhumanity to man is seen and deplored, but it cannot be tolerated in the organized institutions of a society committed to ideals of human promise. Respect is a crucial component of a free society and must exist without reference

---

[8] Henry M. Wriston. The Individual, chapter submitted for the consideration of the President's Commission on National Goals, *Goals for Americans*, administered by the American Assembly, Columbia University. Englewood Cliffs, New Jersey: Prentice-Hall, a Spectrum Book, 1960.

[9] The Rockefeller Panel Reports. *Prospect for America*. Garden City, New York: Doubleday, 1961, p. 341.

to the descriptive facts of an individual's life; they express his human rights and cannot be corrupted by such distortions as status and snobbery.

It would be unrealistic, however, not to take cognizance of the values-reality in America that engenders a concept such as status to measure individual worth. The United States is a mass culture in the sense that it makes available the means to the generally conceived good life. If material values seem to dominate the society, at least there is some equality of opportunity to share in this material well-being. The search for status as measured by the acquisition of material goods is further complicated by its continual redefinition in terms of quality of taste. Concepts of "U" and "Non-U," "in" and "out," and others are expressions of the American's search for identity and his changing value-orientation. The importance of this social and individual phenomenon cannot be denied, especially as it seems to obtain in the world of children as well as adults.[10]

Although status seeking, like conformity, has come to represent a distorted scheme of values in individual motivation, the premise it represents cannot be ignored. The individual in a diverse and mass culture seeks enhancement of his identity in the recognition and approval of others. Individual worth, dignity, and respect demand recognition if they are to be meaningful, and the diverse nature of society and its values does not readily indicate the means for their attainment. The individual is surely aware of the tenuousness of his human importance, and the increasing emphasis on technology in almost every sphere of living in the United States has increased this feeling. Recent humorous situations depict the evaluation of human achievement in the number of digits that must be used to express individual identity. But this is more frightening than amusing in a world in which machines are infinitely better than people at dealing with numbers.

It can be said that the human premise in this country is both the ability and nobility of man. In science, economics, and politics current views embrace excellence and prosperity with surety. We have faith in our war on poverty; we have made incalculable progress in wars against disease, inequality, and ignorance. There are many problems, of course; some are of long standing, and some are created by the times in which we live, but in the face of all of them we are sometimes confronted by a growing sense of meaninglessness in human motiva-

---

[10] Mary Anne Guitar. Status Seekers, Junior Grade, *The New York Times Magazine*, 47–48 (August 16, 1964).

tion. Meaning is the premise of life simply because it is synonymous with the motivation to live.

Our age has been charged with failure to deal with transformations in values and technology. We deplore the growing realities in our society that confuse moral norms with statistical norms and lead to the evaluation of morality in terms of central tendency; that is, the moral response becomes what others think is moral.[11] Yet we recognize that in our society there is no clearer evaluation of human behavior or pertinent motivation for human choice than the rationale of what others will think. A view of life without meaning is part of the loss of identity of man in an age of radical change, threatened extinction, and the crumbling of older faiths and values. Countless individual and social examples continue to be chronicled as thoughtful people are brought to the realization that the individual's view of his own identity is probably central to all other considerations. The development of an adequate, if not excellent, self-concept becomes a critical human premise; for surely both the ability and nobility of man depend on it.

As a nation, we know that faith in the individual has little meaning unless the individual has faith in himself. All of the hopes for human achievement and self-development depend on the individual's enthusiasm for his own achievement and his belief in his own ability. Youth is often accused of being without ambition and drive, unwilling to risk personal sacrifice or even time in the pursuit of long-range goals. A society that still cherishes an image of its own individualism and sense of adventure cannot understand what impels a twenty-year-old to accept employment on the basis of the fringe benefits it offers. On the other hand, our notion of ambition once meant selecting a life's vocation with a willingness to prepare and work toward that goal—a notion almost obsolete today, when life changes radically in a very short time. If America's prevalent philosophy is pragmatic, youth can readily understand it as a philosophy of expedience because of its tendency to give greater weight to immediacy than to any other concept of time.

Although we can understand the factors that contribute to acceptance of a rationale of expedience as a philosophical and personal premise, it must still stand as the antithesis of every assumption of human purpose on which this society depends. The United States has

---

[11] Kenneth D. Benne. *Education in the Quest for Identity and Community.* Columbus, Ohio: The College of Education, The Ohio State University, 1961, p. 11.

been highly successful in its efforts toward social democracy, but underlying concepts have sometimes become distorted. It is not democratic to be equally accepting about all events, behavior, or production —that is, to lend them equal credence. That kind of attitude can lead only to a society without standards of value or judgment. Many Americans believe the damage has already been done. The kind of statistical morality referred to is a natural outgrowth of a social environment in which the majority rules in all matters. The problem confronting the schools and society today is a redefining of the areas in which majority opinion should properly rule and those in which it should not. The process of popularizing the many areas commonly associated with notions of the good life has resulted in a radical transformation of the values associated with those areas. It is no wonder that our youth express a view of the world, including its institutions and people, as one large cafeteria-style setting in which their whim of self-selection is the most important guide and one that cannot be challenged.

In general terms, the basic human premise is that of developmental man actualizing human attributes of rationality and value in community with his fellows. This presumes a highly developed value system and the possession of intelligent ability. It also presumes a self-view that will permit the individual to function in a dynamic and effective manner within the human community. The world as we know it, existing in commonplace crisis, must have these kinds of individual, and it looks to education to accept the creative and exciting task of helping to foster these human qualities.

THE CURRICULAR PREMISE

Like the society it serves, America's educational enterprise is vast, diverse, and heterogeneous. The pragmatic philosophy that prizes a problem method in planning policy continues to approve principles of local control of schools and educational change geared to the solution of specific problems or the resolution of particular issues. Eventually, of course, this will lead to a situation in which educational ideas or theories will be accounted for in some way and educational conflicts or problems handled in many ways. New ideas, new educational plans, and innovation in general are becoming more and more commonplace in schools. It can be fairly estimated that the rate of educational change is increasing and that the time that must be allotted to an educational lag is shorter now than it ever has been. The futility of trying to encompass changing educational demands and needs within the old structures is finally being recognized. The *Los Angeles Times* of August 23, 1964, reported that abolition of grades was being practiced on a limited basis in some California school districts—Sacramento, Barstow, San Mateo, and Torrance. This is occurring throughout the country. Educational theory has recognized for some time that age has little to do with level of ability. Ungraded schools in which students can progress in terms of subject-matter groupings may make better sense than those in which each grade level is aimed at a particular age.

Recent innovations in education have resulted in the appearance of television, tape recorders, and teaching machines as commonplace classroom appurtenances. Soon the traditional time span of the academic year may become obscured by extended days, summer sessions, and quarter systems and trimesters. Team teaching, flexible scheduling, and multisized, multipurpose classrooms are educational realities. All of these things are eloquent testimony to a changing curricular concept and a more functional and experimental premise of educational concern. The recent availability of Federal funds to support educational research and experimental projects may become a significant force in hastening change.

The once-radical view of the curriculum as a representation of all planned and guided school experiences is now a premise for the planning of school experience. The dimly understood concept of subject-matter integration, usually translated into contrived relationships between subjects, has been supplanted by new attempts to understand the essential nature of knowledge in synthesis and analysis. In fact, the traditional categories of the curriculum and as they have existed may disappear.

Progress is not measured simply by change, and the current educational premise of intelligent guidance of curriculum change is basic. It is also important to avoid the pitfall of evaluating current educational debate in terms of the new and the old. True, the arguments for a return to the three R's suggest a traditionalist point of view, but they also represent a position of philosophical realism with a well-conceived theory of evaluating knowledge. Surely no one advocates the sole use of teaching machines to replace traditional concepts of teaching and learning. Actually, those who endorse the old educational fundamentals of subject matter as the most important curricular concept are more likely to approve of the new teaching machines, which are based on behavioristic principles of learning and retention.

The premise of the current educational problem seems to be the acceptance of ideals of excellence, both human and educational, within a democratic framework of educating the individual to full potential. The problem is compounded by the far-reaching implications of changing knowledge in a changing world—implications that impose a complex challenge to the application of creative intelligence. Further complications lie in the ever-increasing size, heterogeneity, and cost of the American system of schools. The educational lag, or the dichotomy that exists between theory and practice, is an outgrowth of the operational situation. Schools continue to function, controversial policies or practices notwithstanding, and changes can only be functionally incorporated into the existent structure. This is not to suggest that structures are not changing radically, but it does mean that the process of change is evolutionary in nature. It also means that the problem approach can be applied to a variety of aspects of education at the same time.

The educational curriculum, insofar as it represents planned educational experience, is the expression of theoretical commitments in every aspect of rationalized human premises. That is to say, whatever is taught in schools is a reflection of choices based on some rational process. These choices are an outgrowth of commitments—whether of value, belief, or both—to conceptions of human nature, purpose, and destiny, as understood in a framework of society and civilization. The curricular premise is that plans will be made and problems solved in such a way that whatever is taught in schools will represent the most rationally valid commitments to premises of society and humanity. The corollary premise is that curricular experiences will be effective in translating these assumptions into educational accomplishment as applied to the individual and to society.

PHYSICAL EDUCATION AND ITS PREMISES

Although educational progress and curriculum change usually result from the pressures of specific problems or insights, there are certain basic assumptions of the nature of curricular purpose that need clarification. The history of the school curriculum in America indicates the presence of underlying values in commitments to knowledge, as it has been continually developed and understood, as well as to the individual in relation to his needs and role in society. Each subject-matter area in the curriculum is an expression of these values. Mathematics, for instance, may be considered as a structure or area of knowledge and at the same time understood as a school subject intended to help the individual develop skills he will need to function in society. Arithmetic has often been cited as obviously important in view of our need to cipher, count change, and so on. There has been a revolution, however, in the teaching of arithmetic and mathematics. The subject is now being taught in its theoretical structures so that many adults are aghast at their own inadequate understanding of the subject as their children are learning it. Surely this is related to the revolution in our understanding of our changing world; the functions of arithmetic might well be meaningless in the future of today's children, but understanding a theoretical structure and the process of learning to understand it have continued significance.

Another underlying value of curricula arises from a recognition that our schools provide a common experience for all youth. They are in a position, therefore, to apply certain societal standards to individual development. Children learn ways of living at school; they brush their teeth, wash their hands, and have lunch whenever it is necessary for them to learn to do these things in accordance with social demands. Schools ensure that youth will have the opportunity for medical and dental attention, personal health and cleanliness, and remedial experiences, when necessary, for all aspects of individual development.

This area has provided the most important rationale for the inclusion of physical education in schools. The concept of school responsibility is reflected, for instance, in the 10 minutes a day of calisthenics required by Boston's public schools to combat "schoolroom stoop"; in the common observance of a recess period for games; in the passing of state laws requiring physical education; and in the recent efforts of the President's Council for Physical Fitness. From primary grades to university educators accept the responsibility of providing experiences that will help the individual develop as a healthy organism, best able to perform his adult roles.

Physical education programs are also based on a concept of the commitment of education to help youth learn those skills that will enable him to participate in his culture. Being able to dance, swim, and play tennis or baseball is no less important in our society than being able to drive a car, write a business letter, or read and understand directions. In a simple analysis these abilities are necessary in order for the individual to feel adequate in his world. They are requisite means in the pursuit of the good life. The advantage of the movement activities is that they represent important areas of cultural emphasis while contributing to the participating individual's health and well-being.

Physical education has also been committed to a goal of helping to achieve maximum individual ability in movement activities. Programs of competitive athletics exist in almost all schools and youngsters are encouraged to seek excellence in athletic performance. It has long been recognized that people pursue excellence according to their interests, and schools have tried to provide the means for development in a wide variety of areas with an impressive array of athletic opportunities.

Practically, curricular emphasis is evaluated by the time, money, and effort accorded an area. This means, in many states, that physical education is one of the major areas of emphasis and value within the schools. At the same time it is based on premises of educational purpose that are viewed as supplementary. The crush and complexity of new knowledge, the new ways of looking at knowledge, and the urgency of the search for self-identity are the bases of the character of the challenge to subject-matter areas in education. As long as physical education is based solely on premises of individual development in health or fitness and skills for cultural participation and leisure-time use it is in danger of being classified as a "frill" and given less and less curricular emphasis. The point may be that school subjects of such limited premise *are* frills in a world in which there is so much to learn and so little time in which to learn it.

This in no way means that schools will not be concerned for individual well-being, but like the school lunch program physical education could become another service area. Questions have already been raised whether physical education really requires professionally trained teachers, should be accorded academic units, or can be considered educational at all. Many feel that the contributions of physical education, though desirable, can be achieved in settings other than educational. In most communities now athletic activities for all age levels as well as recreational opportunities to learn and participate in sports and other movement activities are available. Certain communities responded to the presidential pleas for youth fitness by organizing youth exercise programs, either as adjuncts of the school day or in the school setting.

It is paradoxical, too, that although physical education accepted a major responsibility for fulfilling the social and human premises of our society in its programs these premises have been neglected in the face of current emphasis on physical fitness. These concerns may not be issues in the educational debate, but they stand as educational premises, and physical education is in a good position to enhance them in its programs. The development of the values categorized in the concept of sportsmanship is an undeniable premise of physical education, for these values apply to both sports and society.

Current demands for rationality and meaning in education will undoubtedly persist as the major themes of curriculum. They are not satisfied by the claim of physical education that it contributes to intellectual development by having students learn strategy and rules and even do homework. In fact, these demands are being made on a level of sophisticated awareness that reduces to absurdity the traditional response of physical education in chronicling its contributions to the physical, mental, emotional, social, and moral aspects of the individual. Physical education is faced with the task of defining its premise as a discipline of knowledge or recognizing its limitations in the educational curriculum. The pretentiousness of present-day programs in their struggle for academic status is becoming an educational anachronism that will not be tolerated for long. The premise of purpose in physical education, as in every area of the curriculum, must be one of structure and process of knowledge within the boundaries of human significance.

SUMMARY

The premise of purpose in education in the United States includes the assumptions underlying the concept of universal, free, and compulsory school experience. It represents the ideals of a society committed to a belief in its youth and the future, and the important role of education in their development. These assumptions are purposes of education; purposes for which every aspect of the curriculum must assume responsibility. Furthermore, they must be given a high priority of importance, and all teachers and others involved in the processes of education must find better and more pervasive ways of contributing to their fulfillment. The categories used to express these concerns in this chapter are (a) social premises and (b) human premises. No matter how they are considered, they must be understood in relation to the fabric of society; its enduring faiths and ideals, its conflicts and realities, its changing nature and image, and its values. The school curriculum—in content, scope, and process—represents value and beliefs and is the experience-expression of human and individual goals. The simplest premise of educational purpose is that these goals are worthwhile and that all youth must attend school as a necessary part of the process of attaining the mature self-identity that incorporates these goals into individual value-structure.

It has been suggested, however, that the premise of individual development is a basic assumption of purpose for all educational effort and is not to be confused with the major purposes of specific areas of the curriculum. Society assumes that rationality and knowledge are primary concerns of education. If they are to be developed in any meaningful way, each area of the curriculum must assume the responsibility for analysis and synthesis of a discipline of knowledge, and the structure and meaning of each discipline must be understood in itself and in its relation to human existence. Each curricular area must be based on a cohesive theoretical understanding of a field of knowledge; without it, cogent purposes of education cannot be formulated in terms of that knowledge. It is simply and obviously impossible for the school curriculum to maintain a random additive development in the current context of exploding knowledge and radical change. It is not defensible to retain curricula that do not absolutely require organized education for the fulfillment of its purposes or are wasteful in that they are not developing the kinds of learning with immediate value.

The notion of an enduring traditional educational structure or curriculum is obsolete. Education, like society, is recognizing that a changing world demands the highest degree of adaptability, flexibility, and creative response and initiative. It is recognizing, too, that urgent demand requires urgent response, and educational evolution will not be allowed its old leisurely pace.

If this is the premise of purpose in education, its promise lies in the exciting and creative ways in which many proponents of curricular and academic disciplines have responded and will respond in formulating the major purposes of their areas. We in physical education are confronted with an urgent challenge in this task. It must be undertaken with the realization that the rug of complacent reiteration of time-worn clichés has already been pulled from beneath our feet.

GUIDELINES FOR LEARNING EXPERIENCES IN UNDERSTANDING THE PREMISE OF PURPOSES IN CONTEMPORARY PHYSICAL EDUCATION

1. *Compile* a list of values that you think are widely held in the United States. Try to relate them to their sources, especially to such documents as the Constitution and the Bill of Rights.
2. *List* the most important realities about life in American society. Discuss them in terms of the underlying values involved and their educational implications.

3. *Select* articles or advertisements from popular magazines and try to analyze them in terms of what they signify about attitudes toward the American way of life. Discuss general implications of the images of people and society as projected by the communications media.
4. *Discuss* current ethical issues presented by TV shows, novels, or in the newspapers in terms of the value implications you and those involved perceive.
5. *Formulate* purposes of physical education based on the social and human premises you identify as important and examine the implications of your purposes for the process of teaching and learning.
6. *Examine* textbook statements of purpose in physical education and try to analyze them in terms of the nature of the underlying premise; that is, whether they are geared to individual development, social development, and so on.

8

THE PROMISE OF PURPOSES

~~~~~~~~~~~~~~~~~~~~~~~~~~~~~~~~~~

The purposes of school programs are formulated and understood as desired individual achievement and effect. As soon as ideas or knowledge are discussed in relation to the school setting, they are considered within a program of teaching and learning and their implied results. This fact has contributed to the continuing preoccupation of physical education with concerns for individual development and fitness, socialization and character-formation, and other needs related to human well-being. Physical education, as a field of study, has never been truly differentiated from physical education as a desirable school and life experience. When asked to describe the nature of physical education, those involved usually offer a confusion of stated aims, supposed contributions, and popular activities.

The attacks on physical education began, understandably, in higher education. Colleges and universities, faced with pressures of new knowledge and growing student populations, sought to clarify their functional roles as academic institutions. If the traditional conception of higher education was to be fulfilled, each area of the curriculum had to be defined as a unique academic discipline—that is, as a developed body of knowledge with its own structure of related questions and an evolved mode of inquiry. The nonacademic needs of students were seen as a lesser area of responsibility in higher education, and the service of these needs, a function separate from the curriculum. Beyond its role as a service area physical education in higher education had been concerned with professional preparation;

but the place of fields that might be considered only as applied in their manner of dealing with knowledge, only vocational in their intent, is questionable. There is little doubt that many attacks on existing physical education programs in higher education were well justified on the grounds of insufficient academic standards, as well as inadequate, if not downright ridiculous, research efforts, and a "how we do it" curriculum not even appropriate to elementary levels of education. Physical education has been forced to accept changes from a required to an elective program in many colleges and universities, and it is faced as well with seemingly never-ending questions about its credits, grades, and general academic worthiness.

These questions, however, are no longer restricted to the college level. The challenge of academic value, well-defined and unique contributions to rationality, and a substantive existence as a field of knowledge must be faced by physical education at all school levels. The choice to be made in the near future will be based on the alternatives of physical education as an academic discipline or rationally understood field and physical education as a program devoted to the serving of nonacademic or personal needs. Those physical educators who deny the existence of these alternatives are lending support to the definition of physical education as activity programs, their purposes the fulfillment of the premises of education, and therefore able to serve only a limited role. Fortunately, a great number of physical educators are firmly dedicated to the belief that there is indeed significant knowledge in all that we have known as physical education. Many are excited by the prospect of the imminent development of a theoretical rationale for the analysis, synthesis, and exploration of ideas and consider this process and its results the premise of purposes in physical education.

It must be clear that purposes as part of a discussion of education can relate only to desired effects. A discipline or body of knowledge has no purpose, but it provides the major source of purpose for the curricular idea that is based on it. A great deal of worthwhile research has been done in physical education in areas such as human performance, physiology of exercise, the performance of motor tasks, and training. The use of the conceptual data that grew out of these ideas and research efforts, however, has been conceived in relation to facilitating learning or understanding the participant and his responses. Because these concepts developed no commanding form of their own, they did not lead to the initiation of a discipline in which knowledge itself was formulated to be transmitted to students. Indeed, the relation and significance of these concepts have not been fully examined.

(Many of these ideas were formulated by Edrie M. Ferdun of the Ohio State University. Some were expressed in a speech that she presented on tape at the Conference of the Mid-West Association of Physical Education for College Women, Fall, 1964.) In view of the fact that the field of physical education evolved as an outgrowth of the identification of basic needs and remedial effects rather than as an expression of a formalized discipline of knowledge, it is logical that its concepts and ideas have been considered in terms of application alone. Physical education has done a rather good job in terms of such sources of the curriculum as the needs and nature of the individual, the ideal premises of society and social reality, and education itself. The major area of neglect has been its own body of knowledge. Its consideration of its own subject-matter as a source of purpose has been largely restricted to a survey of activities, in which curriculum choices depended on such bases as which sports were more widely played in the culture and which activities provided the greatest amount of exercise in the shortest amount of time.

THE CHALLENGE OF THE DISCIPLINE

Physical education, because of the nature of its activities and its history as an area of the curriculum, has reached a point of broadly conceived concern with total fitness. Numerous contributions to the individual have been made through experiences in physical education in the potential anhancement of all the educational premises. As recognition of changing educational demands is translated into a changing emphasis, however, subject-matter areas are being called on to clarify their own distinct bodies of knowledge as well as their unique and primary contributions to education. Those aspects of educational purpose that have been identified as the premises of education in the United States are responsibilities of *all* areas of the curriculum and presumably can be fulfilled in many situations in which engrossing activities are carried on in a social context. Parenthetically, it might be added that the demand for a clarification of the *unique* role of physical education provided the impetus that finally dispelled the notion that education through the physical was an adequate rationale for the field. Although a popular concept for some years, the reasonable outgrowth of that theme is a characterization of physical education as a method of education rather than an as area of subject-matter with any kind of intrinsic value of its own.

Physical educators have responded to the demand for a clarification of their contributions to education with the identification of two major organizing ideas, the first of which has been physical fitness. Though this is, indeed, a unique contribution, it is not a facilitating theme in educational terms because it is still based on a framework of the nonacademic needs of students and a consideration of physical education programs in the service area. Justification for a professionally trained staff, college majors, graduate degrees, and even school credit and grades cannot be found in a concept of physical fitness as the basis of the subject-matter area of physical education. It is true that the designing of effective programs to develop physical fitness requires a great deal of professional knowledge; but the question remains whether the teachers or practitioners who would carry out these programs could be adequately trained without a long period of professional preparation in the context of higher education. In discussing the need for physical education to define its field of knowledge as an academic discipline in the college degree program, Franklin Henry suggests that one of the characteristics of a discipline is that the acquisition of such knowledge is a worthy purpose apart from considerations of its practical application.[1] Obviously physical fitness is not adequate as an organizing theme for physical education; its attention is on individual effect, apart from academic concerns (except in a highly specific and limited way).

In the 1950s movement as a unifying conceptual base for physical education began to gain recognition. Because a consideration of movement leads outside the framework of individual effect, the pursuit of it as an organizing idea for physical education can lead to the identification of a body of knowledge and the structuring of a discipline. Once physical education identifies its concern with ideas rather than well-being, further efforts can be made in developing a body of knowledge. The consideration of movement in terms of its nature, meaning, forms, and so on holds promise in giving direction to the expansion and development of knowledge. The promise is negated, however, if the consideration implies movement *education.*

Movement as an organizing concept for physical education is still not wholly accepted by physical educators. Perhaps the first definitive statement of physical education as a school program based on a body of knowledge conceived as the art and science of human move-

---

[1] Franklin M. Henry. Physical Education an Academic Discipline. *JOHPER*, 35, No. 7, 32–33 (September 1964).

ment was made by Camille Brown and Rosalind Cassidy in 1963.[2] In their Preface the authors state that they began work on the book in 1958 and proceeded in their own department at UCLA in the development of a functional description of a body of knowledge that could be used as a basis for a new curriculum. The revised curriculum at UCLA, where kinesiology is used to describe the field of inquiry, contains provision for the student in physical education to prepare for a career other than teaching. It is believed that there will be career opportunities in research and consultant work in human movement, but this, of course, depends on the development of an adequate body of knowledge. The curriculum also provides for the study of an allied discipline, which should be significant in future research interests and endeavor.

Although Brown and Cassidy first presented a cohesive theory of physical education as a school program based on the discipline of human movement, many other efforts have been applied to the understanding and acceptance of movement as the underlying theoretical essence of physical education. Eleanor Metheny, working alone and with Lois Ellfeldt, has given cogent expression to the need for a meaning-centered emphasis in curriculum in physical education. In the 1950s and 1960s she delivered major speeches at numerous conferences of professional groups, and her articles have appeared in such publications as *The Physical Educator,* the *Research Quarterly,* and *Quest.* Throughout these years Eleanor Metheny's work has reflected the highest degree of sophisticated awareness and pioneer development of physical education as a meaning-centered discipline of knowledge with attendant philosophical bases. Her *Connotations of Movement in Sport and Dance* (1965) provides a significant expression of ideas and a valuable contribution to the literature.

The April 1964 issue of *Quest* was devoted to the art and science of human movement. Because this publication is sponsored by the National Association for Physical Education of College Women and the National College Physical Education Association for Men, extensive influence can be assumed. In 1965 Lawrence F. Locke spoke on "The Movement Movement" at the AAHPER national convention in Dallas; his article, titled the same, was published *JOHPER* (January 1966). Locke, in his position as Editorial Chairman of the National Kinesiology Council of AAHPER, is also responsible for a continuing kinesiology column in *JOHPER* which presents relevant ideas.

---

[2] Camille Brown and Rosalind Cassidy. *Theory in Physical Education: A Guide to Program Change.* Philadelphia: Lea & Febriger, 1963.

The literature of physical education reflects concern with the theme of movement. Bryant J. Cratty's *Movement Behavior and Motor Learning* (1964) provided an excellent summary of research findings in these areas and also indicated needed directions for research. Other books and articles have attempted to deal directly with knowledge of human movement as a departure from the traditional approach of physical education to knowledge considered only in its implications for teaching and learning.

It is understandable that when the profession of physical education accepted the validity of a concern with movement immediate attempts were made to translate it into program experiences. This has occurred most frequently in relation to elementary school children, partly because a great deal of pioneer work in the area of movement with young children was done in England before a general professional response developed in the United States. In 1960 Gladys Andrews, Jeannette Saurborn, and Elsa Schneider published *Physical Education for Today's Boys and Girls;* its first chapter is entitled, "Movement as a basis for physical education." Development of this theme is reflected in elementary school programs with such titles as "basic movement," "basic skills," or "fundamental movement." Janet A. Wessel's *Movement Fundamentals—Figure, Form, Fun,* published in 1957, has been revised and reprinted and attests to the popularity of a whole range of activities centered around the theme of movement applicable to secondary school programs.

The problem lies in the confusion about the nature of a discipline of knowledge and the development of a field of inquiry. Unfortunately, the activities that center around movement frequently parallel the focus of those centering around physical fitness. In both cases the focus has been developed on the basis of incomplete understanding and may serve only to provide another rationale for activity programs already in existence or slightly modified. These programs are a simpler answer to a complex problem. Surely the use of movement experiences to teach principles of physics is a distortion of both disciplines.

It seems fairly apparent that the challenge confronting physical education is one that must be met by cohesive and rational processes in developing or identifying its body of knowledge and formulating a structured discipline of knowledge. Imperfect understanding of the nature of this challenge has led some physical educators to add courses or units devoted to some aspect of movement or to change their teaching a bit by throwing in a few principles of movement in their presentation of skills. The use of such terms as human movement or kinesiology to designate the discipline is considered by many physical educators to be a feminine response. Fortunately enough thoughtful male physical educators realize the essential validity of these concepts. As contributions of original thinking and insightful analysis are identified with men as well as women, it is hoped that this last-ditch effort to reject the ideas that must indeed cause a revolution in curriculum and teaching will fail.

It is difficult to accept the fact that in the professional lifetime of most people in physical education the underlying assumptions about society, humanity, and education have changed so radically that answers once learned must be consigned to the realm of obsolescence; the questions have changed. This problem is intensified because few people in physical education ever made an initial effort to identify their field as anything but an educational process. In fact, as Franklin Henry pointed out, many physical educators were actually in programs of professional preparation so closely geared to the profession of education that they have accepted the paradox of teacher-education programs in an area not even recognized as a subject-matter field in many colleges.

Clearly, the character of today's attempts to identify a body of knowledge and conceptualize an academic discipline in that area of study known as physical education is quite different from that in the past. To dismiss the current concern with movement as a restatement of an old theme, to consider it—as many do—another bandwagon in the physical education parade of pretentiousness, is to miss the point of academic alternatives. It is true that in recent years there has been a greater effort to examine the scientific bases of physical education activities and programs. Research has become a highly regarded undertaking and in many instances has been conducted in accordance with the highest standards of method and procedure. Many physical educators are conversant with knowledge in such fields as physiology, psychology, and sociology as they provide foundations for physical education. Efforts toward greater intellectual sophistication among physical educators, however, have been carried on within the framework of assumptions about physical education as it exists. This means that these efforts have not led to a cohesive theory of physical education as an academic discipline, although they have led to extremely effective programs that contribute to the growth and development of the individuals in them. The challenge now is to transcend the existing notion of physical education as myriad experimental and affective activities and examine it as a field of study with potential validity and worth in the education and life of man.

THE NATURE OF THE DISCIPLINE

One characteristic of an academic discipline is the structure of concepts which leads to an interlocking of ideas in their relationship to the field of knowledge. Because an academic discipline is the study of some fundamental grouping of ideas, things, functions, or expressions, the process of construction must proceed from related questions of significance. As these areas of significance are explored, a logical structure of concepts emerges, and this structure gives rise to further theoretical and research implications.

The essential concerns of the field of knowledge obviously warrant first consideration. The study of movement as a statement of the underlying theme in physical education arises from the recognition of man in motion as the all-pervasive concern of the field. This study would include inquiry into the nature and meaning of human movement, its function in terms of the individual and society, its relationship to other variables, and the cultural and aesthetic significance of its game and art forms. The traditional interpretation of physical education has implied that it is a body of knowledge comprised solely of the effects of participation in organized movement *forms*. Further restriction to forms which involved gross motor tasks or large-muscle activity has meant an extremely limited view of the subject-matter of physical education. Within this view attention has been paid to a conceptual base of man in motion, but the theoretical considerations have been sporadic and the results little understood in their logical relationships.

If we assume the study of human movement to be the underlying concern of physical education, the task of identifying the body of knowledge would lie within a context of information about man in motion. We would want to understand human performance, to be able to develop methods for analyzing it, recording it in symbols, and relating it to the other processes and products of man. We would want all the information available on movement forms in this and other cultures, and we would want to understand their development, existence, and utilization in human history and endeavor. We would want to understand game theory, game construction, choreography, natography, and related processes. It would be important to understand outstanding performance, its development and evaluation. We would want to understand the various purposes of movement, its human meanings and motivations as well as its individual and social effect. Knowing all this, we would hope to be able to program movement according to purpose and use it effectively in education.

Physical education programs have been concerned with many aspects of man in motion. Attention has been given to movement in its cultural forms as sport and dance, in its expressive forms, and in its personal application and effect. One rationale of physical education has always been the recognition of movement as basic to life and as expressive of the self in personal and social development. Fields of study such as psychology, physiology, and sociology have been utilized as foundations for physical education, and sometimes it has seemed as though physical education existed as the application of these fields in the medium of movement. The body of knowledge in physical education must be considered as more than a collection of data from all the disciplines of knowledge that seem to affect its concerns, and human movement, as a field of study and an academic area, must evolve its own discipline of knowledge. To conceive of movement as a medium, whether for the application of knowledge or the enhancement of individual benefit, is to belie the existence of physical education as anything but a process or method of education. It is true that disciplines of knowledge are applied in education and result in the development of skills and personal growth, but this application must not represent the sum of an academic area's concern.

In its concern with man in motion the body of knowledge in physical education necessarily includes information deriving from data assigned to the fields of anthropology, psychology, physiology, and others, but this does not preclude the development of a separate discipline of human movement. The physiologist uses data that are chemical in nature without being accused of infringing on the field of chemistry. The task is not only to employ data from other fields but to seek them within the unique consideration of motor response and behavior. No other field of study is *primarily* concerned with understanding the nature of human movement, and physical education cannot rely on other disciplines to provide the knowledge or the theoretical framework for its efforts.

The key to the development of a discipline of knowledge in physical education probably lies in the consideration of human movement as a significant process. Its significance is a basic assumption of all its existing and potential reality: its place in play or art; its structured forms; its expressive and creative uses; its relationship to man's behavior, environmental interaction, and scientific and social motivation and actualization. The phenomena involved in the study of the process of human movement exist as both science and art, rich in conceptual materials. The development of physical education as a discipline of knowledge would lead to logically related understanding and methods of dealing with the conceptual and study implications of the concerns of the field.

Certainly the body of knowledge, rather than teacher preparation alone, should be the basis of the curriculum in higher education. Although teaching might continue as the motivation for most people in physical education, the development of a body of knowledge might also lead people into journalism, composing, criticism, performance, and research, all within a frame of reference of human movement. At least the attraction of physical education as a professional field might be heightened by the promise of a field that would deal with potential interests and goals from a perspective that would have depth, breadth, and cognizance of fundamental relationships with other disciplines. This attraction might extend to students in other disciplines—students whose professional goals are not in physical education. College majors, however, are not our only concern. Disciplines of knowledge are still the cornerstone of curriculum sources at all levels of education. They have always been considered in curricular reality, but the history of education in America is one of changing emphasis, and at different times both the individual and society have been accorded greatest recognition as a source of the curriculum. It is only now that the subject-centered curriculum is gaining prominence in the newly conceived light of consideration of the essential realms of knowledge and meaning in each discipline. This is not to presume a return to older notions of subject-centered versus child-centered versus group-centered curricula; rather the purposes of education emerging from considerations of the individual and society as curricular sources have become educational premises of great importance. With these premises as assumptions, education is free to accept the challenge of knowledge to conceptions of purposes of developing rationality within the meaning of various disciplines of knowledge.

Jerome S. Bruner identified his own statement that ". . . any subject can be taught effectively in some intellectually honest form to any child at any stage of development," as a bold hypothesis, but he added that it was an essential one in considering the nature of the curriculum.[3] The disciplines themselves and the nature of education and the learning process are being examined and reinterpreted. The

---

[3] Jerome S. Bruner, *The Process of Education*. Cambridge, Massachusetts: Harvard University Press, 1963, p. 33.

emerging curriculum is primarily based on the "inner logic and relationships peculiar to each branch of learning." This approach will surely lead to revolutionary changes in our school systems, because the experiments "directly challenge education's 'conventional wisdom.'"[4] The educational problem of what should be transmitted at what school levels can be dealt with more easily if the area of knowledge is examined in terms of its generalized principles and clarified in terms of its bases and direction. Before physical education can presume to teach its subject matter in some intellectually honest form, it must deal with its body of knowledge in an intellectually honest way.

The discipline of knowledge with which we are concerned, the verifiable facts underlying our field, and the theoretical consideration of conceptual relationships will remain in dispute and jeopardy as long as we maintain the fiction of designating our field of study as physical education. The semantic challenge to define a subject area dedicated to the intellectually untenable task of educating the physical continues to deter honest efforts to clarify the principles and nature of the field. In the course of this century physical educators who have attempted to deal with their field in its theoretical implications have continually decried the use of physical education as both a misnomer and an intellectual stumbling block. Jerry Barham used the term kinesiology to represent the whole of the discipline of man's knowledge about human motion and suggested *general kinesiology* as the area concerned with general motor performance, *applied kinesiology* as the study of specific performance areas, and *clinical kinesiology* as the scientific investigation of the problems of motor activities in relation to education and recreation.[5] Brown and Cassidy used physical education to represent the school program while identifying "the art and science of human movement" as the essential concern of the body of knowledge. Perhaps this approach is adequate; at least it provides for separate considerations of the discipline of knowledge and the programs based on it. Whether the term physical education persists as a designation of the subject-matter field in schools, it cannot be used to represent the field of study. Some more acceptable designation must be found and agreed on, whether it be human movement or homokinetics; kinesiology or anthrokinetics. Hopefully, these changes will be brought about in the near future—initiated, most

---

[4] Ronald Gross. Two-Year-Olds Are Very Smart. *The New York Times Magazine*, 10–11 (September 6, 1964).

[5] Jerry Barham. Organizational Structure of Kinesiology. *The Physical Educator*, 20, No. 3, 120–121 (October 1963).

appropriately, by major departments in institutions of higher learning whose faculties recognize the great importance of clear semantic expression of their real concern and knowledge.

PRINCIPLES AND PROMISE

The problem of purposes in physical education arises in large measure from the diversity of answers to "What is physical education?" Confusion is compounded by the diffuse and vague consideration given to the formulation of acceptable educational assumptions. As long as the educative process is thought of as a generalized enterprise devoted to doing its best to help all children develop, physical education experiences are of unquestionable value. If life were more leisurely and the skills and understandings required by that life more simply identified, perhaps unexamined notions of the value of experiences such as play would be more acceptable; but the principles of the necessity of a rationalized focus and cohesive effort for education in our complex, dynamic, and demanding society emerges as an essential truth underlying present-day considerations. This principle exists, however, in relation to the equally important assumption that our ideal and philosophical commitments to the individual and all humanity provide the all-pervasive premise of education in the United States and should be reflected in every aspect of the educational situation.

The history of physical education is replete with evidence of its concern and contribution to the premise of individual well-being. Few would dispute the value of exercise and sports in personal experience; many fully recognize the social development fostered by physical education programs. The purposes of physical education, as defined in terms of remedial and developmental effect, are understood and effectively realized in many programs and by many physical educators. If we recognize a discipline of knowledge as a formalized area of study, a structure of related questions with an evolved mode of inquiry, *we must also recognize that physical education as it is now is not a discipline in that it has not formalized its area of study or developed a clear structure emanating from key questions.* It is possible that as physical education clarifies its body of knowledge more than one discipline will emerge.

The record of physical education reflects an earnest effort to find acceptance in the school curriculum on the basis of educational contribution. As long as the purposes of education were conceived in terms of complete living and all aspects of individual betterment and development given equal value, physical education could be justified as a worthy program area; but educational conceptions change, and the pervading purpose of education—to foster rationality, discover meaning, deal creatively with intellectual process, and equip individuals with the means of functioning in a world of exploding knowledge and heightened complexity in every sphere—must be recognized as the criterion of curriculum excellence. There is every indication that this purpose will be given more weight in the selection of curriculum content, and an understanding of the accepted guideline of excellence will mean excellence of conceptual bases for all fields.

Present evidence suggests that physical education is on the verge of being defined as a discipline of knowledge. It could be transformed, in the near future, from its vague and diffuse conceptual state to a cohesive and directing form. Physical education must develop a theoretical structure apart from its wholly educative aspects; it must give definition to a significant and developed body of knowledge in which its nature can be clarified. The evidence is given support by the fact that physical education has devoted a great deal of effort to certain kinds of study. Perhaps the clues to its nature emerge from the study of its concerns as being representational of notions held by physical educators to what physical education is or should be. The human body has been studied in its external form by measurement and structure and its performance capacities under a variety of conditions. Exercise has been studied in relation to the human body itself and to future and past performance. Physical educators have considered the mechanical aspects of exercise and performance. Physical education has studied learning skills and performance and has tried to determine the nature of skill, its relationship to performance, and the elements of success and effectiveness in learning and performance. It has been concerned with the relation of skilled motor performance to other manifest human abilities and conditions and with unskilled performance and overt inability to learn in relation to other factors. The school program has been studied with great attention to curriculum, organization, administration, and methods of teaching, and physical education has been studied in relation to the history and philosophy of education and school programs. Physical education has been concerned with health itself and its relation to physical education activities, and it has studied the recreative uses of physical training and the recreational pursuits and needs of man.

Before the results of study and theoretical examination of concerns can be understood and employed by physical education, they must be considered in relation to knowledge-themes rather than individual learning. The usefulness of applying knowledge is limited by the status of those to whom it is being applied, but the development of further understanding depends on theoretical structures of knowledge that give insight into the logic of the data as both process and product. If we consider the concerns of physical education as manifested in the kinds of study undertaken and the content of physical education as the activities with which we are familiar, it becomes apparent that some ideational theme must be identified in order to establish direction. The identification of human movement and man in motion as the essential focus of physical education provides an organizing theme for the knowledge of the field and gives rise to principles of theoretical assumption and potential actualization.

Once the focus of a field is defined in terms of specific knowledge, the study of that field can be defined as the study of (that specific knowledge). This in itself is an important step for physical education, which has usually been defined only as a process or a medium. On the other hand, if we consider man in motion to be the art and science of human movement, we are still concerned with that movement as a significant process. We are concerned with process, however, as an assumption of the substantive existence of the knowledge of movement. Physical education is the study of movement as an art, a science, and a significant human process. The foundations for this study and for physical education as a discipline of knowledge lie in the scientific data and understanding of human movement in initiation and effect, in the aesthetic understandings of human endeavor as process and product, and in the realm of knowledge about human motivation and behavior in which movement is considered as a significant human process.

Before physical education can be justified in terms of its worth physical educators must translate their intense convictions into an articulate expression of a discipline of significant knowledge. To most of us in physical education the "exercise boys" approach (as Delbert Oberteuffer calls it)—which we have come to recognize as the "physical fitness kick"—has a stultifying effect on the potential role of physical education in human life. Oberteuffer suggests that many physical educators approach their field in the same manner as the exercise boys responsible for training race horses and that the world of drills and workouts, as imposed on a horse or a student, is a world of physical training or physical fitness. It is not a world of physical *education*.[6] Parenthetically, it is interesting to note that whereas each race horse probably has his own exercise boy 50 children must share one in the schools, and therefore we can assume that a horse receives a much more individualized exercise program than any youngster. A point well taken is that education must represent a great deal more than programs devoted wholly to the development of individual skills, whether in movement, language, or laboratory. Education represents principles of human knowledge and human good that must be inherent in every curricular area. Education must define and plan its contributions to them.

SUMMARY

In the process of becoming a discipline of knowledge, whether academic or educational, physical education can identify its major organizing theme as a concern with man's movement as a scientific, aesthetic, and human phenomenon. Educational purposes are derived from the nature of the body of knowledge in a subject-matter area. This means that in physical education purposes are to be found in the understanding related to man in motion. The purposes of education, based on premises of humanity, are basic to all areas of the curriculum, but they should not be confused with the purposes arising from the nature of each discipline of knowledge.

GUIDELINES FOR LEARNING EXPERIENCES IN UNDERSTANDING THE PROMISE OF PURPOSES IN CONTEMPORARY PHYSICAL EDUCATION

1. *Define* different academic areas such as psychology, physics, and sociology and compare the definitions with those of physical education—definitions as stated by you or by others you may ask.
2. *Justify* physical education as a worthwhile subject in schools; analyze your justifications as academic or nonacademic or in terms of whether they are on the basis of effects on the individual or development of his knowledge or understanding.

---

[6] Delbert Oberteuffer. Confederation and Mutual Assistance. Report of the WCOTP Committee on Health, Physical Education, and Recreation, International Conference, July 29–31, 1959, Washington, D.C. Washington, D.C.: International Council on Health Physical Education, and Recreation, 1960, p. 9.

3. *Discuss* the nature of physical education in schools as a required and/or elective subject. Determine the purposes of physical education implied by its curricular existence.
4. *Examine* the implications of physical education as a college major and a career. Direct your attention to such matters as the courses included. What are the goals of those people selecting the major? How is the curriculum determined?
5. *List* the things you would have to know in order to understand human movement as a science, an art, and a significant human process.

PART FOUR

Projected Perspective: Principles as Guidelines for Action

PROJECTED PERSPECTIVE: PRINCIPLES AS GUIDELINES FOR ACTION

The key to the development of a theoretical framework for school programs lies in application. Concepts are explored and theory formulated in a rational and intelligent approach to the problem of selecting and devising effective practices whose goal is the realization of valid purposes that are understood.

The theoretical factors affecting any aspect of education are dynamic and complex, and the task of intelligent conceptualization is a never-ending one. Educational practice, as program, method, and organization, must be conceived as a process with its bases in a variety of complicated views of value, ideal, and commitment. Ultimately, however, all aspects of education are largely determined by the understanding of those responsible for carrying them out.

The purpose of Part 4 is to clarify the relationship between principles emerging from considerations of the various perspectives of physical education and those that can be identified as guides to practice. Principles as guidelines for action are valid only when they are related to principles in their foundational context. As such, they represent hypotheses based on critical examination and should provide clear insights into practical decisions.

Within a theoretical framework any problem can be considered critically and guidelines firmly based in principle can be established. Part 4 treats major aspects of the educational process in physical education as an application of the materials contained in the foregoing presentation of perspectives.

9

THE PRACTICE OF THEORY

It cannot be emphasized too strongly that the first assumption of the nature of the educational enterprise in the United States lies in the reflection of intelligent and considered analysis. Educational existence involves a necessity for continual choices from myriad alternatives of program, content, method and organization, and the process of developing rational methods of choosing is the most important task. These choices are delegated to a variety of sources and influenced by many more. Ultimately they express individual perceptions of premise and promise as shaped by special-interest groups, organizations, and society itself and as modified by experience and interaction. No educational choice can guarantee the achievement of a desired effect, nor can it be assumed to reflect an enduring certainty. We must accept the dynamic nature of educational purposes and theory and of our own underlying assumptions of truth or value. The world changes; people change; and the relative truth of our perceptions of goals and values depends on the insightful intelligence we bring to the refinement of information and understanding that provide the bases for our beliefs. The task is difficult and complex, but it is the contention here that anything less than full devotion to it by those involved in education is an immoral approach to the responsibility educators accept for human development.

GUIDELINES FOR PROCESS

Everything that we know about the complexity and importance of the educative process leads to the conclusion that the program of teacher preparation and the practice of teaching as a profession should be devoted to individual attention to rationality in the consideration of theory. The rationale for every teacher must lie in an understanding of his own field of study and its relationship to the needs and goals of education in America. It is not enough to equip the prospective teacher with a set of generalized attitudes toward education or to allow the practicing teacher to operate within a theoretical framework of unwarranted assumptions. Students, teachers, administrators, school staffs, and professional groups representing subject-matter areas as well as school boards, state legislatures, and the public all have an obligation to intelligence as the principal guideline for action in every sphere of decision-making in today's world. It is true that there are some educators whose limited rational powers or distorted motivations render them unable to apply a guideline of intelligence to their endeavors. Such application in no way lessens the importance of the process of developing theory in education. In a profession responsible for youth in so many ways, to lack ability or to be inadequate to the challenge of rationality is unfortunate, but to be unwilling is immoral.

One of the factors contributing to inadequacy in dealing with problems is failure to recognize the importance of continuing to examine underlying assumptions in the interest of correctly identifying and dealing with problems. It can be assumed, too, that many physical educators possess the required knowledge for an analysis of a problem, yet wait to be told. Through local statutes affecting school programs, many communities finally outlawed deep-knee bends after being shown the extent of knee injury that seemed to be directly attributable to these exercises in physical education classes. Even now many thousands of young boys whose major postural defect consist of forward shoulders and abducted scapulae are performing 25 to 50 push-ups daily without other exercises to counteract the effects. If we cannot assume that physical education teachers have learned enough about exercise to develop programs that at least do not directly violate the principles of recognized effect, how can we expect them to give insightful examination to their bases for other aspects of their programs? The grim humor in this particular example is that probably the same physical educators who guidelessly and indescriminately administer programs of push-ups to all students would be quite capable of a kinesiological analysis of the push-up in action and effect. The problem seems to be the failure of physical education and other professional fields to foster a teaching approach whose essential characteristic is a critical examination of the assumptions of knowledge and purpose and their relation to practices.

The basic assumptions of educational practice should be determined by a critical examination of the nature and purposes of the undertaking and the most valid principles of knowledge pertinent to its scope and process. Validity, as it is used in relation to knowledge commitment, demands continuous re-examination and re-evaluation. It means that we can never adopt a relaxed attitude toward what we know and believe. We cannot assume that once we reach a conclusion or develop some insight we can act on it securely forever after. We must come to regard our knowledge and beliefs as precious commodities—never fixed, yet never modified without adequate evidence. The necessary commitment of education to constant investigation is clear. Research effort should cover every aspect of education, and the values of pursuing and utilizing research results should be fostered by all educators. For the teacher, who is really a clinician, this means wide reading in his own and related fields so that he can understand the research reports he reads and develop a teaching approach that expresses the application of a method of intelligence to solving problems and developing practices.

Every aspect of the teaching-learning process is the expression of a set of hypotheses: about how people learn, about what is important, and about the human and social and educative context. The implicit charge to all educators is that these hypotheses be grounded in the finest concern for a rational consideration of relevant factors and a dedication to the highest ideals of humanity. All educators must accept the responsibility for fulfilling this charge. In ideal and tradition, the teacher is accorded an important role in the formulation of his responsibility and in sharing the charge of leadership. Schools are not always organized in wholly democratic ways; neither do they employ total concepts of line and staff organizations. The problems of bureaucracy exist in schools, but there is also an underlying democratic approach to school policy and problems that involves wide participation in decision-making. Ultimately, the teacher makes the final decisions in the privacy of the classroom relationship, and a wise administrator recognizes the desirability of involving teachers in policy making at all levels so that these final decisions will be good ones. Without a true understanding of the bases on which an hypothesis is developed, we cannot predict how it will be applied. If school staffs value a cohesive effort toward clear and examined goals, the first guideline for process indicates that it should be shared in rationality.

Educational hypotheses rest on complex bases; therefore a guideline for process in formulating them is the participation of everyone involved in continual and insightful examination. Miel suggests that the weakness of curriculum that involves the issuance of courses of study, centralized textbook selection, and other practices not resulting in individual teacher effectiveness is caused by the ". . . lack of faith in the ability of teachers and principals to plan appropriate experiences for learners in their own schools with the help of the adults most closely concerned and with the help of the learners themselves." [1]

We know too much about human motivation and behavior to go on fostering situations in which people are asked to act with no understanding of the nature of what they are supposed to be doing. We can be effective only when we understand the goal and it has value or significance for us; and to accept anything less, especially of teachers, is untenable in the light of that knowledge. The goal of earning a salary which usually involves great personal meaning is certainly important; but if we want effective and dedicated teachers the goal of teaching must be far more inclusive than the simple fulfillment of assigned tasks requisite to receiving a paycheck. Even without considerations of ethics or effectiveness in terms of valid goals, a wise administrator recognizes that people in general will exert greater effort in tasks they helped define and will carry out decisions they helped to formulate. There is even more importance in the recognition that every choice and every action reflects a basic belief and value; however, unless those involved have the opportunity to examine these beliefs their efforts are not likely to be cohesive ones directed toward valid goals. The guideline for process in education as the expression of democratic values and methods is one that must be applied in every sphere.

The use of democratic processes formulating educational theory and practice implies an ability to participate with intelligence and effectiveness. A recognition of the equal importance of means and ends—that is, process and product, in the development and application of theory—is basic to those involved in the task. This kind of involvement presupposes a professional background and dedication grounded in

---

[1] Alice Miel. *Changing the Curriculum: A Social Process.* New York: Appleton-Century-Crofts, 1946, p. 53.

an understanding of the nature of theoretical considerations of educational aims and practices, especially as they relate to one's own field. The basic assumption of teacher preparation and teacher actualization is the development of a valid and understood theoretical framework within which to operate and also considering and ultimately making decisions. With the development of the complexity of knowledge, the teacher's task may become more specialized. Philip Phenix suggested a more limited role for the teacher when he said, ". . . While he should seek to make the disciplined materials his own, he should not presume to originate the knowledge to be taught, nor should he expect the fruits of learning to come forth as if by miracle from the shared experience of the students or as the products of common sense . . ."[2]

At present, however, the scholar in physical education is the teacher, and the following diagram helps make the process clear.

PERSPECTIVE FOR ACTION

Physical Education Experiences
are based on
Principles as Guidelines for Action
which are expressions of rationalized belief that
indicate application and arise from
Principles as Purposes

by the teacher as a theorist and clinician; his understanding and interpretation of relevant knowledge and his ideals, beliefs, and values	formulated and modified	by physical education as a subject-field and a profession; its scope, ideals and values

based on a conceptualization of

Principles as Essential Truths

which are statements of belief arising from an examination of the historical and contemporary perspectives of physical education in the

---

[2] Philip Phenix. *Realms of Meaning: A Philosophy of the Curriculum for General Education.* New York: McGraw Hill, 1964, p. 10.

context of its sources; that is, the areas of belief and value on which education depends, which influence it, and which can be designated as

Society	School	Students
forces and realities	educational reality	growth and development
ideals and values	educational philosophy	personality and learning

Body of Knowledge of Physical Education

scientific and aesthetic, conceptualization of man's movement as science, art, and a significant human process

As the diagram illustrates, the framework for theory and action in physical education is outlined in terms of elements of the conditions under which the field exists. In the consideration of physical education in schools it is assumed that attention will be paid to all the affective factors, for valid theory cannot be developed on the basis of only some. Teachers of physical education—or any other subject—are expected to understand the nature of their roles with all their attendant responsibilities. They are expected to be able to make wise choices in the face of many possible alternatives and to make them on the basis of a clear understanding of task and purpose.

Perspective for action in physical education includes rational investigation of the sources of knowledge affecting the purposes, plans, and application of the teaching-learning process. The development of principles as guidelines for action presupposes this investigation and a formulation of principles as essential truths, valid in their assumptions, and understood in their implications. The teacher is, indeed, a clinician and a practitioner, but the assumption of practice as the testing and application of theoretical hypotheses must not be negated. Somehow, all teachers must come to recognize their responsibility to examine their roles and the knowledge on which they depend as critically as possible. The challenge of teaching must be recognized as a challenge in the highest degree to the exercise of critical and rational abilities. The guides to action for each teacher can be creative and dynamic expressions of his response to that challenge—expressions of intellectualized knowledge and understanding inspired by vital concern for youth and for physical education.

GUIDELINES FOR TEACHING AND LEARNING

Each teacher develops beliefs and guidelines to action within a framework of understanding the foundations and principles of knowledge relevant to his teaching. Obviously, these guides should be clear and explicit, for only when we subject our assumptions to critical review can we be sure we are identifying and using them correctly. We must also recognize that the application will vary from teacher to teacher in view of Comb's suggested definition of the effective teacher ". . . as a unique human being who has learned to use his self effectively and efficiently for carrying out his own and society's purposes." [3]

In a definition such as this it is impossible to spell out good teaching in terms of either teacher-held traits or specific teacher behaviors. It does not, however, imply that there are no standards for goodness in teaching or that whatever the individual teacher chooses to do is acceptable.

A basic guideline for the teaching-learning process is a commitment to the premises of education in principle and practice and to their fulfillment in ways that are theoretically defensible in the light of knowledge of society, the individual, and his learning. Problems relating to development of this guideline in teaching are not usually identified on the philosophical level. Most teachers in America readily accept the school as responsible for preparing youth for adulthood in a democratic society and would generally agree on the nature of the desired human and social products of education. It seems difficult to understand, then, why there is such general disagreement as on methods of accomplishment. One problem is that although teachers agree that it is an educational task, the responsibility of *each* teacher, regardless of subject-matter area, to contribute to it has not been established clearly. Somehow the traditional assumptions of education have been typified by compartmentalization, and the common roles and responsibilities of teachers have not been given sufficient emphasis. In addition, many teachers assume that there is no need to incorporate these goals into their planning and teaching—that somehow they will be realized in the process of going to school and learning. Unfortunately, this is not valid; but many teachers cling to this naïve assumption while negating in actuality the potential development of those qualities they identify as desirable. Finally, the major deterrents to the fulfillment of these educational premises are based in failure to understand either the requisite abilities of the individual or the processes by which he develops these abilities.

Physical educators have had a great deal of difficulty in dealing

---

[3] Arthur W. Combs. The Personal Approach to Good Teaching. *Educational Leadership*, 21, No. 6, 369–377 (March 1964).

with their commitment to educational premises of individual development. On the one hand, many have recognized the unique opportunities inherent in the structure of activities and classes for dealing with individuals and groups on the basis of personal and social development. This insight has led to popular claims that physical education is, indeed, a human relations laboratory. On the other hand, in view of the great number of students and a traditional emphasis of organization and hard work, physical education is often a dehumanized experience; classes are work- and teacher-centered, so that little attention is paid to other aspects of youth development. The solution, of course, lies in purposes that fulfill educational premises within the nature of the subject field. This approach is especially appropriate for physical education insofar as the tenants of democracy and fair play are closely allied. It cannot be assumed that good sportsmanship is a direct outgrowth of participation in sport. If the attitudes and qualities that comprise our understanding of sportsmanship are to be developed, they must be planned for as part of the teaching-learning process. The humorous concept of "gamesmanship" as winning by taking legal but unfair advantage of an opponent should help us to understand that fair play is not necessarily a built-in aspect of all sport. In order to develop values of sportsmanship youngsters must have experience in which these values are made explicit and viewed in a larger context of human behavior.

The development of a value-system consistent with the ideals of society and education is the purpose of all school experience. The school program must not only exemplify those values held to be most worthy but must also provide direct experience in which youngsters examine values and are helped to understand them as they exist in motivating human choice and behavior. This means that the physical education program itself must be based on notions of human worth and dignity and must also apply such values consistently as part of the teaching-learning process. As long as our society prizes individual qualities of self-direction, rational thinking, and human decency, every school subject has a responsibility to foster them by the program experience it provides.

The assumption of the importance values and beliefs as basic factors in influencing behavior is a central guideline of understanding the process of teaching and learning. Learning itself must be considered to be behavior and must be understood within the individual framework of the student. We have always known that learning takes place more easily and effectively when there is interest in what is being learned—that is, that the learning has some personal meaning or significance and the individual sees the necessity, desirability, or usefulness of it because of the relevant values and beliefs he holds. The task of teaching effectively, then, involves helping students to find personal relevance in the subject matter to be learned and in the experiences provided, to identify underlying principles of learning, and to apply them to the structuring of learning experience. There are several such principles that should become guidelines for action, although it is understood that they may be modified by research and theoretical investigation. It must also be understood that learning and personality theory go through such modification, and we should use these theories on a pragmatic level to seek the best available hypotheses on which to base our efforts. As such, the following might be principles that could be used effectively in the teaching-learning process:

1. *Students learn best when the goal is clearly perceived and understood.* This is true in terms of the long-range goals of a program and the specific goals of learning skills or performing patterns. As a guideline for action, it means that students must be provided with opportunities to envision the projection of their undertakings, whether this is understood as whole-part method or pupil-teacher goal setting. It means that when a teacher says "I want you to . . ." he is obliged to add "because . . ." In other words, although students at all levels have learned to follow directions and to be cooperative, they will learn *best* if they understand the purpose of their activities.

2. *Students learn best when the goal has meaning.* It is not enough for students to understand only the purpose of an activity; to learn it they must also *want* to learn it. Meaning implies that there is some personal significance involved, and we know that the nature of such significance varies. Some students find motivation (or meaning) in the need to accomplish and excel; others, find it in doing what everyone else is doing; and some are challenged by all learning activities. Meaning is involvement. If the goal is considered worthwhile, great effort may be expended toward attaining it. Sometimes the real goal of an experience may not have significance for the individual and he must find other goals within the experience that have meaning. For instance, a girl playing softball may run around the bases with great energy—not in the urgent need to score a run but in the hope that this will lead to a better figure. Perhaps initial meaning is lacking because the unfamiliar is simply not meaningful, but a significant goal of some kind must be found if learning is to be pursued at all. When something has meaning, we pursue it with eagerness; when it has not,

we forget our necessary preparation and find many reasons why we cannot participate. The greatest justification of pupil-teacher planning and goal setting is the knowledge that if students are allowed to express themselves, to be involved in some way in the process of selection, there is greater likelihood that their values will become apparent and can be used as a basis for making the goal meaningful. It is generally true, of course, that grades have great meaning to students and can always be used as the goal for all learning; realization of that goal, however, cannot be considered a worthy contribution of physical education to the lives of its students.

3. *Learning tends to be most effective and permanent when it is actually put to use.* This principle is being recognized whenever we test learning; for even that is putting it to use. It is employed in most physical education activities in the attention given to practice, game situations, and the like, but it applies to other kinds of learning as well—learning to make decisions, to become self-directed, to solve problems, and to remember the correct time periods in which games are played. This is not quite the same as saying that repetition is requisite to learning. It is a broader concept of perceiving the goal clearly and accepting its meaning. In that sense, and if the goal is important and understood, learning is used because it is relevant to the activity. These several principles of learning are related. For instance, in teaching the spike in a unit of volleyball care is taken to point out its importance in the game and the desirability of developing it. Practice time is provided and students attempt to master it. The game situation that day might include the awarding of extra points for the performance of the spike. All of the principles have been employed. The *goal* is clear and understood, its *meaning* should be clear, and if it includes playing well learning the spike can be assumed to be meaningful and opportunity for the use of learning has been provided. Why, then, is the spike so poorly learned by most students? Perhaps, we must understand that the use of learning implies development in depth; that a skill which is difficult to acquire and not really necessary to the conduct of the game must be fully used by the learner before it is effective and permanent. Too often in physical education it is assumed that once something has been taught it has been learned, when in actuality there has not been sufficient encouragement of use. If this were not so, it would not be necessary to teach the same skills so often to the same students.

4. *Learning tends to be most effective and permanent when it is related to a history of success.* No matter in what framework of personality or learning theory is considered, success as a concept of

reinforcement is recognized as an important factor in learning. We may no longer agree with James's notion of "stamping in the S-R bonds through reward," but as teachers we do recognize that people tend to repeat those responses that have proved effective. Most teachers understand that one application of this principle is to provide initial experience in which the individual has great prospect of success. In the teaching-learning process short-term goals are set, complex patterns are broken down into smaller, more easily accomplished units, and students are encouraged and praised at every level of their learning. Some teachers and athletic coaches still do not use this approach; in fact, they withhold praise and use constant criticism as a spur to learning. This approach might work with the student or player who has already experienced a history of success in the activity and therefore continues to learn even in the absence of a feeling of accomplishment in present efforts. Success is related to another principle underlying learning—the importance of self-perception.

5. *Learning and performance are related to self-perception.* The importance of a history of success in the pursuit and achievement of learning activities is explained perhaps by the fact that a feeling of adequacy is a determining factor in the kind and amount of effort that will be made. The suggestion that we can accomplish anything we put our minds to does not take into account that we must also feel confident of succeeding. If we accept the assumption that the individual's behavior is a functioning of his perceptions, his perception of himself in relation to learning as desired behavior must be a central aspect of his performance. The research that has been done since the thirties on levels of aspiration is based on recognition of the effect of the student's perception of his *possible* performance on his *actual* performance. Current efforts to understand the motivations of learners who are overachievers or underachievers are based on a like assumption of the importance of the perceptual determinants of value and history in the individual's approach to learning. Some of the research conclusions have broadened the scope of the application of this principle as part of the teaching-learning process. Child and Whiting concluded that shifts in level of aspiration are partly a function of changes in the subject's confidence in his ability to attain his goals.[4]

Rotter identified the level of aspiration score as a demonstration of

---

[4] I. L. Child and J. W. M. Whiting. Determinants of Level of Aspiration; Evidence from Everyday Life. *Journal of Abnormal and Social Psychology,* 44, 303–314 (1949).

the degree of feelings of inferiority or inadequacy and the nature of the defenses or compensation with which the subject attempts to meet feelings of inadequacy.[5]

After comparing the results of projective tests and the level of aspiration scores, Cohen concluded that very high and very low goal settings were related to self-rejection and that only those who could accept themselves were able to use low positive goal settings.[6]

Martire suggested that although self-concept and level of aspiration measures were meaningfully related to projective measures of achievement motivation, they could not be readily related to each other.[7]

Within the scope of physical education, Cornie Smith studied the ultimate and immediate aspiration levels of members of the freshman football squad as determined by the number of minutes they thought they might play in each weekly game and the number of minutes they thought they might play in some game during the season. The players were asked to indicate these minutes of play aspiration each week, and records of actual playing time were kept but not made available to the players. The following conclusions were reached:

"1. There is a tendency for successful individuals to raise their levels of aspiration and for those experiencing failure to lower them.

"2. Individuals with extremely low levels of aspiration tend to escape from failure-producing situations after having failed objectively.

"3. Individuals with somewhat higher levels of aspiration maintain some hope of success by repeatedly experiencing failure.

"4. Individuals with highest levels of aspiration tend to exceed their aspiration levels repeatedly and experience success, even though this success has caused them to raise their aspiration level.

"5. Ultimate aspiration is not correlated with ultimate accomplishment.

"6. Immediate level of aspiration is definitely correlated with immediate accomplishment related to toleration of or escape from failure-producing situations.

---

[5] J. G. Rotter. Level of Aspiration as a Method of Studying Personality; the Analysis of Patterns of Response. *Journal of Social Psychology*, 21, 159–177 (1945).

[6] L. D. Cohen. Level of Aspiration Behavior and Feelings of Adequacy and Self-Acceptance. *Journal of Abnormal and Social Psychology*, 49, 34–36 (1954).

[7] John G. Martire. Relationships between the Self-Concept and Differences in the Strength and Generality of Achievement Motivation. *Journal of Personality*, 24, 364–375 (1956).

"7. These facts suggest that in actuality a number of players are forced to experience failure repeatedly and consistently." [8]

Numerous research efforts have shown the effects of renewed striving as an outgrowth of goal attainment and the relationship of self-conceptualization to performance. Schilder and Herod have dealt with body image and support the idea that by continual acceptance and rejection of perceptions the individual selects those that are compatible to his body image and self-structure and new movements or equipment must be incorporated into the image in order to be utilized.[9]

Fisher and Cleveland also cite the body image as a factor that influences the ability to perform certain skills.[10]

A study done by Clifton and Smith showed that viewing oneself in motion affected perceptions of performance in certain skills and viewing alone, rather than in groups, effected more positive change.[11]

Physical educators have employed this principle in providing encouragement to students and in their own approach to the mastery of movement skills as being within the scope of the ability of all learners. Even more specifically, in order to understand and deal with a student's self-perceptions as a factor influencing his attitude and effort, the learner must be given opportunities to see the activities as relevant to himself. This concept relates to the principle of finding personal significance in activity, but it also involves (a) providing models with which students can identify, (b) helping students to perceive the demands of an activity realistically (in terms of movements and principles rather than as a gross complex pattern), and (c) helping students to develop knowledge of themselves and of movement so that they can understand the demands of motor tasks and relate their own abilities to them. We do not yet fully understand this process of perceiving movement.

There are dangers, however, in any extreme application of this

---

[8] Cornie N. Smith. Inference of Athletic Success and Failure on the Level of Aspiration. *Research Quarterly*, 20, 196–208 (1949).
[9] Paul Schilder. *The Image and Appearance of the Human Body.* New York: International Universities Press, 1950. Joyzelle Herod. *Implications for Physical Education from the Body Image Concept.* Unpublished master's thesis, University of California, Los Angeles, 1961.
[10] Seymour Fisher and Sidney E. Cleveland. *Body Image and Personality.* Princeton, New Jersey: Van Nostrand, 1958.
[11] Marguerite A. Clifton and Hope M. Smith. Viewing Oneself Performing Selected Motor Skills in Motion Pictures and its Effect upon Expressed Concept in Self in Performance. *Research Quarterly*, 33, 369–375 (1962).

principle. If motor tasks are presented in an oversimplified context, the learner may respond with effort but he may be satisfied at too elementary a level. On the other hand, if they appear too difficult and complex to him, he may not put forth any effort at all in the belief that he cannot succeed.

Teaching methods, of course, are selected, whether consciously or not, on the basis of beliefs in purpose, human personality, the nature of schools and physical education, and the learning process itself. Because everything the teacher does is an outgrowth of these beliefs, the strong contention here is that this process should be one of rational consideration of the bases of belief and their relation to actual teaching practices. Chapter 10 considers the role of the teacher specifically, but certain guidelines for action as implications of principles of learning and behavior can be identified as part of this examination of the teaching-learning process.

1. The atmosphere or climate in which the teaching-learning process is carried on is extremely influential in the response of individuals and groups and in the degree and kind of learning that will result. Many studies have been devoted to the differences in various learning climates, describing them, for example, as authoritarian, laissez-faire, or democratic. Unfortunately, there is a great deal of confusion about what these terms actually mean in their implications for teacher behavior. In physical education classes at one time or another anyone of these atmospheres may exist—that is, some times the teacher may direct the learning in an authoritative if not authoritarian manner, and some times the student may play and experiment in ways that *seem* random and undirected. The overt response of students in liking a teacher or the way he teaches sometimes indicates that the strong teacher is the most respected and admired. We have all listened to countless cases involving a harsh teacher, who puts up with no nonsense, does not concern himself with the feelings of students, but later comes to be well loved and deeply appreciated. We have also heard lurid recitations of experiences in which a teacher's efforts to be democratic resulted in a class experience of endless conversation which was really an exchange of ignorance in which nothing at all was learned. Individual distortions of the application of principles as guidelines for action must not be allowed to be the standard by which a principle is judged. Just as theories of progressive education were misused and misapplied, any theory can be maligned and rejected on the wrong basis. Fortunately, the truth of progressive notions, in terms of understanding the learner and providing real and meaningful learn-

ing experiences, has been ultimately recognized, with evidence that the radical idea becomes a basic assumption if it is based in valid theory.

In its simplest aspect the learning situation or climate must be one in which the greatest opportunities for learning are fostered. This means that youngsters must be free to experiment and to make mistakes, for if the consequences of trying and failing are too great students will not try, and they can hardly learn the complex motor patterns with which physical education is concerned without a great many fruitless and unsuccessful efforts. This type of free climate presupposes teacher–student rapport based on the understanding that each has dignity, ability, and limitation. It also presupposes that the goals of learning are worth seeking with effort; that there will be differences in the degree of attainment of those goals, and that individual dignity will not suffer if the effort is not successful. Dignity is in no way served by everyone's receiving good grades but rather by the appreciation of course objectives—and an evaluation of individual progress toward them—as an overt expression of the *learning* process, which is one sphere of actualization of the *human* process.

2. Learning activities should be well planned and carried out in relation to purposes in such a way that accomplishment represents a challenge and the student can become self-reinforcing in relation to his progress. We recognize that in most situations some kind of learning takes place, whether planned or not. Students are continually learning new attitudes toward school, programs, activities, and themselves and their abilities. They are learning to consider teachers and others either as allies in the complex business of living and learning or as enemies concerned only with a process of self-enhancement and unaware of its effect on others. They are learning to feel adequate or inadequate in relation to the demands of specific subject fields and to the whole process of learning and performance itself. Unfortunately, in many school situations they are learning to rely on others for an evaluation of themselves and their learning.

Most teachers agree that the most desirable approach to the teaching-learning process is one in which students understand what they are supposed to be doing, pursue it with enthusiasm, and know when they have accomplished the goals. In the characteristic school situation, however, this approach is not employed to its fullest degree. The goals are not made sufficiently explicit; youngsters are more often threatened than challenged, and the evaluation of learning or progress is often a surprise to the student. To foster a more desirable learning situation the goals must be clear and meaningful, standards of performance must be made explicit, students must be encouraged to feel adequate, and such things as correction, individual guidance, and evaluation must be intrinsic. Physical educators are frequently amused by evidence of a student's misunderstanding of the games taught or the terminology used, but this means that the situation was not clarified enough for learning to take place.

The teacher must become an expert at seeing students clearly enough to evaluate their response and their learning. The word feedback is most appropriate in terms of the teacher's gathering of evidence of clarity of presentation and the student's knowing whether his efforts are likely to be fruitful. One important need for ensuring student familiarity with some principles of movement and their description lies in the usefulness of such words as flexion and extension, contract and relax.

Many teachers use these words because they are meaningful to them, but often they are not clearly understood by students. Currently, with increased recognition of the importance of clear perception in learning, much more attention is being given to techniques of gathering feedback. The result has been a startled recognition by many teachers that the students who cannot perform such skills as a handspring or a back dive, or even a free throw or a spike, cannot explain these skills either; that is, they do not really see the relation between force and direction and sometimes their perception if so distorted that performance continues to be impossible. It is important in every single aspect of the teaching-learning process to gather data regarding the perceptions of students. What they see as goals, values, demands, and potential will become the notions that are responsible for their behavior, and the wise teacher makes every effort to find out what they are so that planning can be made meaningful and rational in realistic terms.

3. Evaluation is the means by which the effectiveness of the teaching-learning process is refined and by which students are helped to develop realistic perceptions of self and ability and goals of learning. Fortunately, there are few teachers remaining who construe evaluation and grading to mean the same. It is understandable that grading—an assigned and therefore meaningful responsibility and goal—has great significance in the teaching-learning process. Evaluation, however, implies much more than concern with student achievement. It implies the means for planning and improving the learning activities and experiences and for increasing the probability of student progress. The rational person evaluates his experiences critically so that he can improve or change certain factors in the future. His

evaluation is not simply an unexamined judgment but an attempt at insight into causes and effects and critical relationships, with a view to understanding situations and his behavior within them. The teacher, too, needs to understand what really happened in the learning experiences that were provided. In evaluating his own planning and teaching, the teacher must know how the students perceived the experience, how they felt about it and about the teacher himself. The purpose in gathering these kinds of data is that they can be used by the teacher to refine the teaching-learning process; it does not imply that the students' opinions and reactions become the sole basis for choosing or structuring experiences.

The teacher evaluates whatever he considers important; therefore we can conclude that the teacher who uses evaluative procedures to determine skill alone considers them to be the primary if not the only goal of the teaching-learning process. The reason that concomitant benefits of physical education cannot be considered actual purposes of most programs is that they are not usually planned as experiences and are rarely evaluated by effect. This means, of course, that the teacher may be assuming incorrectly that some kind of attitude change has occurred but that he will never really know whether it has. Evaluation can be applied only to behavior, whether considered in its verbal or motor expression. The implication for the teacher is the necessity of translating program objectives into descriptions of student learning as behavior. This is not an easy process, but if our purposes are to be real ones and we are to understand the teaching-learning process well enough to provide opportunities and experiences that contain the greatest potential for the realization of those purposes it must be done. This process also provides evaluative guidelines by the nature of the clarified goals; that is, once an objective has been stated, such as to be able to perform a lay-up shot successfully from various positions on the court, it becomes much easier to determine whether this particular skill has been developed. In fact, as the teacher clarifies the goal, he might eventually include the evaluative criterion in a statement of the objective. For instance, one objective of the basketball unit might be to be able to perform 10 lay-up shots consecutively with success from the right side, left side, and center of the court. A specific objective such as this would provide guidelines for teaching and evaluation. In addition to the actual presentation and individual coaching of lay-up shots, the teacher would provide opportunities in which the skill might be practiced in relation to the clear goal of developing enough skill to make 10 baskets in a row from each angle of the court. It would also be necessary to provide the means for recording progress toward the goal; but the criteria for good evaluative techniques would be fulfilled as follows: (a) the goal is clear and understood; (b) opportunities for meaningful practice in relation to the goal are provided; (c) students can be self-reinforcing in terms of progress because the evaluation of their performance is readily obvious; (d) the teacher can evaluate individual progress immediately; and (3) the evaluative tool is not only a test but contains provision for challenging students to increase their learning accomplishments. The use of this kind of technique, which leans heavily on students accepting the responsibility for their own learning, presupposes that the goal has been really clarified. We know that making 10 baskets may not be an adequate test of the skilled movement requisite to shooting good lay-ups; therefore the teacher must structure the use of the tool itself, with the understanding that no rules be violated. Furthermore, the dimension of excellence as related to the performance must be clear. One drill or evaluative tool may not be able to accomplish all of this. The teacher may find that a subjective estimate of form, as well as the goal of making the baskets within the defined structure, is necessary.

It cannot be emphasized too strongly that evaluation should characterize the teaching-learning process. First, it is well known that learning proceeds most effectively when the learner has knowledge of the results of his efforts in relation to the goals. Second, it is apparent that selecting the focus or emphasis of the teaching effort depends on knowing the status and needs of the learners as related to the goals. Many experienced teachers believe they can do this simply by observing their students. It is difficult, however, especially in dealing with great numbers of students. Specific evaluative planning is one way in which valid evidence is gathered and the margin of error diminished.

SUMMARY OF THE TEACHING-LEARNING PROCESS IN PHYSICAL EDUCATION

Planning

1. As related to the development of guidelines, planning refers to the process of selecting experiences.

2. Once selected in nature and scope, experiences must be planned and structured with the highest promise of fulfilling the purposes and guidelines established.

Presentation and Procedures

1. The teaching-learning process includes the presentation of material to be learned, but it must be considered in whole terms with the focus on mastery of learning.
2. The teacher is applying the process in all actions and words; they must be carefully developed as most likely to enhance learning.
3. Procedures do not always reflect exact planning; many modifications are necessary on-the-spot in order to promote desired learning.
4. Presentation and procedures must be developed according to guidelines and defined with logic; essential ingredients of good procedure include clear understanding of the purpose and nature of learning and of *all* related factors, as well as the ability to provide experiences that will promote the learning.

Evaluation

1. Any valid purpose must be evaluated regarding student progress and teaching effectiveness.
2. Evaluation must be a continuous process designed to improve program and learning. It must bear a close relationship to the purposes of the experiences and have the dimension of contributing to those purposes.

Grading

The policy of grading should bear an honest relationship to the purposes of the learning and adequately reflect its underlying values.

GUIDELINES FOR PROGRAM

Program or curriculum in physical education represents the sum of learning experiences that best provides the means of fulfilling established purposes and objectives. This describes the process of selecting experiences and product and represents a plan for any unit of work, whether for weeks, semesters, or years. In general, a program should be planned in relation to the broad purpose of physical education in schools: the development of understanding and ability that will lead to effective adult individual and social functioning. Because it is so broad and equally applicable to all school subjects, this purpose must be understood by physical educators in regard to specific qualities and ability requisite to such effectiveness. Physical educators have examined and come to understand this broad purpose to mean those objectives of physical education that are derived from its educational nature. The focus of physical education for many years has been on developing social attributes and understanding. Although it has not been reflected in the nature of physical education programs, this focus has characterized them as part of the teaching-learning process. Physical education has reflected a confusion of focus, particularly in the area of program purposes derived from the body of knowledge. Programs obviously reflect the body of knowledge in that they consist of learning experiences that are logical in terms of physical education. As long as the field of knowledge is dimly understood there is the danger of activities becoming both the program and the body of knowledge and to be considered as such. This has led to the paradox of physical education activities becoming media for the development of educational objectives only.

Sports and dance, as movement forms and cultural products, provide a vast body of knowledge in themselves. Understanding the nature of these forms, their structures, and their meaning in relation to culture is a large task. It is made even larger when the development of ability to participate and appreciate are added, and it is conceivable that physical education in schools could devote itself to this area of concern alone. Certainly in physical education the structure and relation of movement patterns and activities and their roles in community, school, and culture are very important aspects of the body of knowledge. It is primarily through this aspect of the field that such educational concerns as human relations and interaction, human and social values and behavior, and individual awareness and responsibility have the most obvious relations to the learning situation.

Physical education has been concerned with the effect of its experiences on the individual not only as a player or participant but as a person. This has led to programs of body mechanics, fitness testing and development, and the basic movement or basic skill units of learning. Some physical education programs are devoted entirely to this area, and if they include sports or dance at all it is as an adjunct to the real focus of the program.

The basic guideline for program in physical education is that they should be organized on the basis of their contribution to purposes—those that reflect the educational aspect of all school programs and those that have been rationally derived from the field's body of knowledge. This means that programs will not be conceived as sports and dance alone nor as experiences geared only to their effect on the individual. It means that program planning is the rational expression of understanding of the whole field of knowledge and is designed to promote purposes that have been derived from that understanding. The focus for curriculum in physical education must transcend experiences in which students are encouraged to action or activity without understanding the rational implications of what they are doing.

Experiences in physical education must be organized around knowledge themes related to its discipline of knowledge. Though not yet wholly articulated, that discipline incorporates the knowledge and understanding of man in motion, basic concepts of human movement as a process of learning and actualization, and a product that is the evidence of that learning. The focus of physical education must be the transmission of knowledge, organization of themes, and the techniques and processes of developing ideas within its area of study. Programs must ultimately reflect the development of that discipline of knowledge in experiences designed to help students understand the conceptual ideas and their application in movement activities and forms.

Programs in physical education should reflect a considered approach to the sources of purpose for curriculum and a rational investigation of the bases. It is easy to make hasty program decisions based on incomplete considerations. One of the seven cardinal principles, for instance, was worthy use of leisure time, and we are constantly bombarded with information on the increasing amounts becoming available. Obviously, if future use of leisure in activity is to be a consideration, individual sports have greater usefulness than team sports for most people. Recognition of this point has led many physical educators to abandon team sports whenever possible and to emphasize those activities that have carry-over value. Many of us change our programs reluctantly, for we love team games and, for some of us, badminton will never be so exciting or challenging as basketball. The time has come for more than a cursory investigation of these concepts. Are there more meanings in basketball that more truly reflect our discipline than there are in individual sports alone? Is the worthy use of leisure a more complex notion than merely being able to participate in an available sport? Perhaps the real purpose is one derived from understanding that aspect of the body of knowledge which suggest that sports and dance are movement forms that are products of cultural meaning. This might imply that becoming a fully participating member of the culture is one goal in movement forms and that another is understanding the social reality in which leisure time is spent in watching and reading about sports and dance as well as in participating in it actively. Surely this is worthy if we believe that the appreciation and understanding of movement forms are valid aspects of human actualization for the person as an individual as well as a member of society.

A summary of guidelines for programs would have to include every commitment or belief about students, schools, and physical education, for ultimately each becomes a guideline for the provision of experiences designed to fulfill their purposes. In the pages that follow, examples of the way in which specific units of work can be planned are presented. The Physical Education Unit is planned for use in the classroom but could be developed as an activity unit as well. The important point is that two important or key ideas that are representative of physical education's body of knowledge have been kept separate. If our theoretical considerations lead us to consider the understanding of movement important, curriculum must reflect it with integrity. This means that we must not confuse such knowledge with the playing of basketball. The purpose of knowledge of human movement is not simply to increase skill at basketball, and the purpose of basketball is not simply to learn principles of movement.

PHYSICAL EDUCATION UNIT: A STUDY OF MOVEMENT BEHAVIOR [*]

STATEMENT OF CONTEXTUAL POINT OF VIEW

Physical education has existed as an integral aspect of school programs since the latter part of the nineteenth century. In general, its purposes have been conceived in relation to the needs of youth and the goals of effective adulthood in the United States and its programs have been focused toward individual development in activity-experiences. The importance of the contribution of exercise and physical education activities to the health and welfare of youth is continually supported by evidence from such research sources as medicine, physiology, psychology, and interpersonal sociology. School programs as

---

[*] Prepared for use at Earl Wooster Senior High School, Reno, Nevada, Fall, 1964 by Carolyn Bell, Joan Maguire, and Wendy Rupp (Wooster High School), Joe Barrett (student-teacher), and Jan Felshin and Edrie Ferdun (University of Nevada).

general education, however, are currently being re-examined in terms of their conceptual implications. More and more recognition is being given to the importance of rationality as a pervasive factor influencing the quality of individual actualization in a complex cultural milieu. Each subject matter area therefore is committed to the task of refining its body of knowledge and related intellectual processes and translating them into school experiences. Physical education recognizes its responsibility to foster the understanding needed by today's youth in regard to knowledge as well as experiences in the important area of human endeavor and significance that the field represents.

BASIC ASSUMPTIONS OF THE UNIT

1. Physical education is a subject-matter field concerned with the art and science of human movement and human behavior as they concern the individual in his cultural setting.

2. The individual must be able to use movement effectively to express himself and to increase his understanding of himself, others, and his environment, to solve the motor tasks with which he is confronted, and to help him become a fully participating member of his culture.

3. Sports and dance are significant cultural forms in America, symbolic of the goals and values of the culture. Their importance is manifest in the vast numbers who participate, whether in spirit as spectators and supporters or as actual participants in recreational or professional pursuit, and by the attention given these activities in commercial enterprise, community support, and the public relations media.

4. Movement existing within an environmental context depends on the individual for initiation. Anything that affects the individual or the environment will be influential in terms of his movement. These variables may be categorized as on p. 210.

5. Effective use of movement implies the ability to analyze and to solve movement problems as well as to use movement in experimental and creative ways.

6. Fitness as a desired goal implies the ability of the individual to identify his status as it relates to the demands of living and his ability to provide means for the fulfillment of appropriate goals.

7. A satisfying participation in movement activities depends on the understanding and use of principles of good human relations as they function in a competitive as well as a cooperative framework.

Human Movement

Individual Variables	*Environmental Variables*
Physiological-Anatomical	Physical-Mechanical
age	space, force, time
body structure	physical laws and principles
strength	weather
flexibility	surface and topography
endurance	equipment
balance	apparel
perceptual acuity	
Psychological-Philosophical	Social-Cultural
self-concept; body image	groups
beliefs, values	social values
attitudes	beliefs
needs	attitudes
goals	traditions
perceptual range	heritage

Purpose:
Functional
Expressive

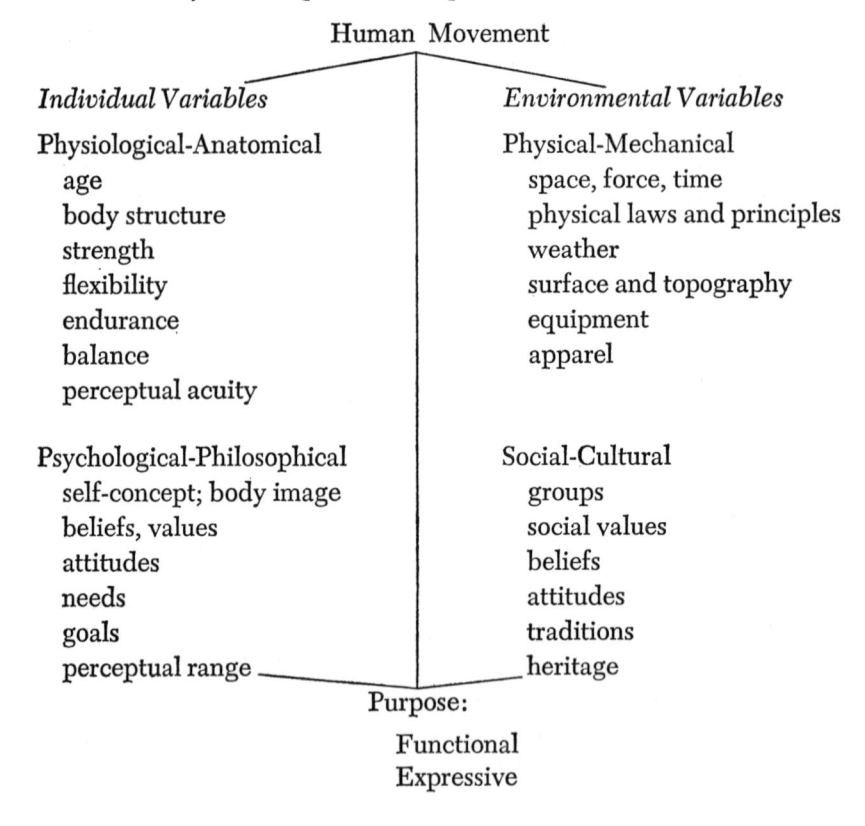

OBJECTIVES OF THE UNIT

1. To understand physical education as a subject-matter field.
    (a) Movement as an individual phenomenon.
    (b) Movement in terms of the factors which influence it.
    (c) Movement as a means of cultural expression.
2. To apply knowledge of physical education to the understanding of the needs and goals of the individual as a person and member of society.

CONCEPTUAL GUIDELINES FOR THE UNIT

Human Movement

"... human movement is the change in position of man in time-space as a result of his own energy system interacting within an environment. Human movement is expressive and communicative, and in the interactive process changes both the individual and the environment."[12]

1. Movement as a process, a method by which (a) contact is made with the environment, (b) the individual distinguishes himself as a distinct unit in the environment, (c) adaptation and accomplishment take place in relation to the environment, (d) anatomical structure is defined, and (e) perceptions and experiences, as related to self and reality, are extended.

2. Movement as a human product is the observable evidence of (a) feeling, (b) understanding, (c) accomplishment, and (d) past movement experience.

Variables Which Influence Movement

1. The individual is an interrelated and dependent system with (a) a structure of a certain age and dimension, with capabilities of strength, flexibility, endurance, and balance, and (b) a personality and system of beliefs, values, attitudes, needs, and goals concerning himself and the world.

2. The environment (a) a perceived physical universe governed by laws and principles (of gravity, motion, force, and leverage), and (b) social environment made up of groups and societies, their beliefs, values, traditions, and heritage.

Movement Forms as Products of the Culture

Like other aspects of culture, movement forms such as active games, sports, and dance develop out of human needs, purposes, and values and survive as long as they have meaning in the culture.

1. Sports and games reflect the application of social phenomena in that they (a) conform to structure in the pursuit of goals deemed worthy, (b) define their purposes as division of responsibility, best use of abilities, and the use of strategy and specialization, (c) provide penalties for infringements of the structure, and (d) reflect cultural meanings and personal significance attached to the concepts related to them.

2. Dance reflects the values of the culture in that it (a) is used as expressive and creative movement, (b) is considered in terms of the

---

[12] Camille Brown and Rosalind Cassidy. *Theory in Physical Education: A Guide to Program Change.* Philadelphia: Lea & Febiger, 1963, p. 54.

individual and an audience, (c) consists of structured and non-structured forms, and (d) expresses cultural meanings in organization, use, and form.

SEQUENCE AND EXPERIENCES

The sequence reflects the outline of conceptual guidelines in the development of subject-matter.

Following the development of the concepts, a short unit of work is devoted to applications, in which students are helped to apply their understanding (a) to their own movement abilities and limitations, (b) to the setting of desirable goals in relevant life-tasks, and (c) to planning the use of conceptual data in future movement experiences and fitness goals.

The learning experiences includes lecture and presentation, discussion, individual assignments, self-tests of movement attitudes and abilities, self-inventories, and individual planning.

Evaluation includes many of the results of specific learning experiences as well as other techniques specifically planned to evaluate the progress of students toward the unit's objectives.

UNIVERSITY OF NEVADA

Department of Health, Physical Education, and Recreation

BASKETBALL
J. Felshin

BASKETBALL UNIT

Context

The unit is planned to develop the competence and understanding of professional physical education students at the freshman level. Although a diverse background in understanding of the game and skill development can be assumed, there is a generally enthusiastic response to the game that implies a history of successful participation in classes and extracurricular events. In addition, the level of the group's movement ability is fairly high, and the majority of the class displays a willing response to the challenge of sports.

Purposes

1. To develop understanding and ability in terms of effective performance as players in the game of basketball.
   - (a) Development of requisite skills at an intermediate level of performance.
   - (b) Ability to use skills effectively and intelligently.
   - (c) Ability to apply knowledge of the rules of basketball to conduct of the game and to development of good strategy.

2. To develop understanding and ability in terms of competence as prospective physical education teachers.
   - (a) Understanding of developed structure of the elements of basketball; their relationship to the sources and variables that affect and modify movement activities.
   - (b) Ability to participate in the conduct of the game in various roles.
   - (c) Ability to make actual and verbal discriminations between correct performance, use of strategy, and rules of the game.

3. To develop realistic and positive concepts of self and ability as a performer, team member, and prospective teacher.
   - (a) Understanding the significance of goal-setting and evaluative procedures.
   - (b) Appreciation of the processes of human interaction and the development of abilities such as self-direction, leadership, and class and team membership.
   - (c) Ability to demonstrate competence in and understanding of the processes of decision-making, skill, and knowledge development and competition and cooperation as relevant to the group and the game.

Guidelines for Experiences

Classification	Performance Standards
SKILLS	
Passing and Catching	Ability to perform a variety of passes; selection of appropriate pass, use of pass with accuracy and control (stationary and moving) to players in a variety of situations (stationary and moving).
Drills that emphasize use of passing and catching in stationary and movement situations.	
Catching and passing in relation to patterns of movement on the	

Classification

SKILLS (Cont.)

court; other techniques of ball handling and evasion maneuvers.

Attention to use of skills in game situations; principles of use of space, selection of pass, accuracy, control, and following the techniques for handling the ball.

SHOOTING

Proficiency in performing any shot close to the basket; use of lay-ups, moving into basket from a range of positions and in response to various ball receptions.

Set shots, especially in relation to free-throw; use of shot in position beyond normal range of zone; jump shots.

DRIBBLING

Understanding use of force and angles of impetus and reception.

Use of dribble to cover space.

BODY CONTROL

Guarding, taking jump balls, and rebounding, require an understanding of principles and physical laws affecting the movement situation.

Importance of these skills and use of good mechanics in maintaining balance and ensuring possession of the ball; avoiding fouls.

GAME INTELLIGENCE

Use of skills; application of strategy; zone defense; fast break; shooting.

Performance Standards

Ball control as evidenced by ability to catch passes in a variety of situations (stationary moving); in relation to force differences and situations on court and in relation to other players, teammates and opponents.

Ability to be effective in performing lay-ups; failure to perform effectively only in terms of other factors affecting situation.

Skill in set-shots requires a great deal of practice; evidenced in use of shot at appropriate time, success in more than 50 per cent of attempted shots.

Development of jump shot to be used as a maneuver to throw opponent off-balance and heighten probability of success in getting off the shot.

Perform easily, rhythmically, low to ground to ensure keeping control of the ball.

Sufficient skill so that dribble can be used appropriately and ball control retained.

Ability to stop, change direction, evade an opponent, guard, jump, and get rebounds.

Skilled movement as evidenced by balance, control, avoidance of fouls resulting from lack of controlled movement.

Performance in relation to others; choice of maneuvers; perceptual acuity in terms of possibilities.

Classification	Performance Standards
GAME INTELLIGENCE (Cont.) Knowledge of rules and insight into structure of the game in terms of strategy.	Selection of appropriate decisions within structure and conduct of game.
Effective use of positions, tactics, and techniques in relation to game structure.	Use of abilities and use of plays, either in generalized principle or as specific tactics.
Use of plays in relation to other players.	
CONCEPTUAL UNDERSTANDING Development of knowledge of the game and its rules; application to the game of principles of skill and movement development.	Ability to respond verbally to situational problems in basketball. Decision-making as a team and class function.
Attention to human relations as a generalized factor in team play.	Selection of teams; appropriate experiences; analysis of learning.
Attention to the nature of basketball and other sports; purposes of physical education and cultural significance.	Verbal analysis of affect in basketball; self-perceptions, feelings, and responses.

Role of the Teacher

1. To provide learning opportunities designed to fulfill purposes and guidelines for experiences.

   (a) Providing practice and drill experiences to help students develop important skill and knowledge.
   (b) Setting clear standards for performance and accomplishment; using circuits, practice drills, and evaluative experiences.
   (c) Keeping accurate records of individual progress toward identified goals; making provision for individual variations in interest and ability within the framework of the game and class.

2. To set a climate and establish policies and relationships that enhance development of the purposes.

   (a) Establishing personal and group relationships; providing specific guided observation and individual correction.
   (b) Providing for understanding of the goals, continuity, and evaluation.

Evaluation Experiences

1. Evaluative standards of performance; that is, 10 lay-up shots performed successfully and consecutively from each of the three major shooting directions; 10 successful free-throws performed consecutively; performance of circuit requirements correctly and within specified time limits.
2. Officiating experience with observation by teacher; use of score sheets and timing procedures.
3. Team rosters, shooting and playing records,
4. Written quizzes and final examination.
5. Team selection and positioning; play and tournament records.
6. Sociometric techniques; evaluation of experiences, teaching.

Sequence and Responsibility (specific objectives of daily lessons)

GUIDELINES FOR LEARNING EXPERIENCES IN UNDERSTANDING THE PRACTICE OF THEORY IN PHYSICAL EDUCATION

1. *Analyze* the relationship of theory to practice in terms of (a) what makes theory adequate and valid, (b) how theory is developed, and (c) how it is applied, that is, the way in which practices are chosen or structured.
2. *Discuss* the teaching-learning process. Give examples of various aspects of it as carried on in schools and identify the categories of choices or decisions made.
3. *Determine* the nature of program planning and the teaching-learning process as carried on in your institution; identify responsibility and process as handled in relation to (a) developing philosophy or purposes in physical education, (b) policies that affect program and students, (c) program opportunities and structure, and (d) evaluation.
4. *Examine* the units presented and try to design a sequence of experiences that might be used for developing the unit.
5. *Organize* a unit of work that you might use with high school students in a selected activity and show the experiences you would plan for fulfilling purposes derived from the nature of education and the nature of physical education.

10

THE PRACTICE OF PROFESSION

"The vital force of this profession is its worthy intent."[1] Most physical educators would agree that this is an accurate definition of their motivations. From the beginning, the focus of physical education and its practitioners has been a concern for human welfare and well-being —a concern that has influenced the life-view of those who chose the field as a profession. At times there is doubt regarding the authenticity and multiplicity of claims that physical education experiences benefit the individual in many ways; it must be recognized nonetheless that good intentions have always been implicit. If this concern for human welfare has not been translated consistently into positive experiences, we can assume that failure was the result of imperfect understanding of the nature of the task and not willful neglect. The teacher accused of throwing out the ball, rather than teaching his classes, was probably motivated by a sincere belief that his method was desirable.

The worthy intent that typifies physical educators is based to some degree on a pervasive and personal commitment to their field of endeavor. It is not surprising to find teachers in physical education who seem to deal with their field on a naïve level of understanding and expression, for their understandcng of its benefits is highly emotionalized and nonverbal. The experience of participation, especially on levels of excellence in activities, results in a kind of *knowing*, a kind

---

[1] Catherine L. Allen. Introduction, The Significance of the Profession in American Culture. *JOHPER*, 35, No. 9, 37–42 (November–December 1964).

217

of sure commitment that does not demand intellectualization. The time of life at which an individual chooses his professional field is a time in which sports and ability to perform well have great significance as a value in the realm of school or college and in relation to the peer group. For men perhaps more than for women there is little doubt that the selection of physical education as a profession is motivated by a desire to maintain symbolic status of excellence and accomplishment as well as to pursue personal satisfactions. The old saw, "those who can, do, and those who can't, teach," cannot be applied to the superior athlete-turned-coach and that is a continuing source of satisfaction to those who have performed well. Logical application of personal experience in sports lies in competition and athletics, and there is little reason to wonder why these areas are emphasized in programs for men and boys.

Many girls choose physical education as a career, even though they are not skilled and have not had a background of participation at high levels of competition in sports. The reason, perhaps, is that these young women see in the field a rich opportunity to actualize their concern for youth. The application of this professional rationale becomes a climate of acceptance and of concern for the individual that frequently results in little or no emphasis on performing excellence. This is not to suggest that there are only a few qualified women in physical education whose backgrounds and understanding of activities enable them to deal with students in developing high levels of skill, but it is true that men in physical education seem to be more commonly qualified in this respect. Many older women in physical education who despise the appellation coach consider its connotations most undesirable. The informality of the word may be considered objectionable because many women insist on physical education as the proper description of their subject field rather than the more casual "PE." In fact, it is an interesting phenomenon that women in physical education usually structure experiences in more formal ways, whereas men emphasize development of skilled performance in the program itself. Methods of teaching and policies of organization depend on underlying assumptions of belief and attitude, yet these assumptions remain unexamined by physical educators.

GUIDELINES FOR COMPETENCE AND EXCELLENCE

As has been pointed out, the focus for developing theory in physical education is application in school programs, the realm in which the subject area now exists. This means that the teacher is ultimately responsible for the actualization of theoretical knowledge and belief in the choices he makes, in the programs and experiences he plans, and in everything he does in his various school and professional roles. It has always been difficult to describe the essence of good teaching or the necessary attributes of a good teacher. It is the contention here that good teaching should contribute to excellence by a clarification of theoretical aspects and related abilities. Two major theoretical areas that might be clarified are (a) the role of physical education, with its attendant considerations of educational premises, and (b) the discipline of physical education, with its concern for understanding and purpose as derived from the body of knowledge. The following statement of guidelines for competence and excellence was developed by a physical education staff for use in a professional program; it applies to the teacher as well as to the student.

DESIRABLE COMPETENCIES FOR PROFESSIONAL STUDENTS IN PHYSICAL EDUCATION [*]

THE ROLE OF PHYSICAL EDUCATION

A. Ability to analyze and support the role of physical education in school and society.

1. Knowledge of American society; understanding of the ideal principles and goals upon which it is based.
2. Knowledge of social structure and sociological phenomena, especially as they operate in the United States.
3. Understanding of the role and demands of adulthood in this country.
4. Understanding of the relationship of American schools and society, now in the past.
5. Understanding of the goals of education in the United States.
6. Awareness of the potential contribution of this field and related professional fields to the goals of education.
7. Ability to analyze the relationship of physical education in schools to broad educational goals and problems.

---

[*] Developed by the Curriculum Committee of the Women's Section, Department of Physical Education, University of Nevada, March, 1963, by Janis Crooks, Edrie Ferdun, Iona Mowrer, Ruth Russell, and Jan Felshin, Coordinator.

8. Understanding of the field's unique contributions to the goals of education.

B. Ability to synthesize knowledge into a cohesive philosophical framework for teaching physical education.

1. Understanding of validity as a criterion of the consistency of values and beliefs.
2. Ability to identify principles and evaluate their validity.
3. Knowledge of the bases on which a philosophy of the field is founded.
4. Development of personal commitments to valid principles of educational purpose and process.
5. Ability to apply principles to the solution of problems, formulate plans and decisions, and evaluate practices.

C. Ability to apply the teaching-learning process effectively and assume the roles of a physical education teacher.

1. Ability to identify the purposes of the field in general and to establish specific objectives for experiences within the program.
2. Understanding learning and the relationship of guided experiences to desired outcomes.
3. Ability to plan, organize, and administer all aspects of a program with the greatest enhancement of the individual as a pervading goal.
4. Understanding the growth and development of the human being as a sociobiopsychological organism.
5. Understanding individual differences and the ability to provide for them in the learning situation.
6. Ability to understand and deal effectively with the behavior and problems of students.
7. Willingness and ability to work constructively as a member of the school staff, the community, and the profession.

THE DISCIPLINE OF PHYSICAL EDUCATION

A. Understanding the nature of human movement as a biophysical phenomenon.

1. Ability to identify motions that occur at the various joints.
2. Ability to identify muscles that produce motion.
3. Ability to identify most efficient muscle use for tasks.

4. Ability to identify, analyze, and apply mechanical principles.
5. Ability to identify the ingredients of successful performance of specific motor tasks.
6. Ability to identify biophysical adequacies and inadequacies.
7. Ability to program movement to enhance physiological functioning.
8. Ability to identify and apply space, force, and time relations in movement.
9. Ability to notate or describe movement patterns.
10. Ability to identify the biophysical variables that affect movement.
11. Ability to exemplify efficient movements.

B. Understanding the nature of human movement as a psychosocial phenomenon.

1. Ability to recognize the effects of psychological variables on performance.
2. Ability to program movement to enhance psychological and social functioning.
3. Ability to apply psychological and sociological principles to individual movement patterning and to structured movement activities.
4. Ability to identify the psychological and sociological demands inherent in specific movement activities.
5. Ability to identify adequacy and inadequacy in terms of psychological and sociological variables necessary for success in particular movement activities.
6. Ability to identify cultural attitudes, beliefs, and values that affect motivation and participation in movement activities.
7. Ability to identify the role movement plays in the peer culture.
8. Ability to identify and appreciate the role movement plays in this culture and in other cultures, now and in the past.
9. Ability to understand the factors contributing to cultural differences in unstructured and structured movement activities.
10. Familiarity to a high degree with the major movement activities of the culture and the ability to perform the basic skills of these activities.

This kind of statement, of course, provides only broad guidelines for the development of understanding and ability and assumes a logical relationship between theory and practice. All of these guidelines can be used by the teacher as a basis for self-evaluation, but each one presupposes further development and requires the setting up of evaluative guidelines. Each provides some theoretical insight into the nature of the two primary demands for good teaching: (a) knowledge and understanding of the subject-matter field, and (b) a frame of reference within which to consider the field. Specifically, of course, it would be necessary to establish guidelines for the kinds of perceptions that good teaching demands in relation to the subject field, to self and others, to the nature and purpose of the teaching-learning process, and to the actual role of the teacher.

GUIDELINES FOR PERCEPTION AND PERSON

It has been said that youth has the need to and does identify with successful and attractive adults. Certainly, teachers should fulfill a desirable image of adulthood and provide a model on which youth can pattern itself. Not only does some learning take place by example, but the teacher as a person and on his behavior clearly indicates and communicates his own underlying beliefs and values. The importance of the teacher's understanding behavior as an expression of value cannot be emphasized too strongly. The teacher must have confidence as an outcome of his faith in his own choices and ability. Somehow the teacher must develop a secure system of values so that he can teach and deal with youth in a positive and confident manner.

Some attempts have been made to analyze self-perceptions as part of physical education's recruitment problem, but they have dealt only with the most obvious categories of positive or negative feelings about stereotyped images. The negation of a pejorative image of physical education ultimately depends on a healthy professional climate in schools, colleges, and universities and within the profession itself. The first step in achieving such a climate is to accept the necessity for rational consideration of the field. As physical educators come to understand the nature of their field in its knowledge-concerns and significance in human life, they will be less defensive in their attitudes and have less concern for what others think of them. If present attempts to evolve a discipline of knowledge succeed, the whole syndrome of self-perceptions common to people in physical education should change. Many of the current professional problems will no longer exist in the evolution of these changes. In a healthy climate important matters are given consideration. In physical education this means that more attention may be paid to theory and scholarship than to the personal skills of the teacher.

The second step in developing a desirable state in physical education concerns the people involved in it. The teacher must recognize his role as an important one, feel adequate to it, and know that his effect on others is all-pervasive. This can happen only in situations in which the standards of achievement are explicit and maintained. A profession cannot afford to be ashamed of its members, nor can a school be ashamed of its graduates. This is illustrated by AAHPER's setting up of standards of accreditation concerning degrees as requirements for members. That is only a start, however, and it remains for the profession of physical education to upgrade itself in all aspects. Preparing institutions have a great responsibility to select and retain qualified students and to design curricula that reflect the best available knowledge. The process of preparation in physical education now and in the future must evolve from a theoretical framework rather than from a response to existing job demands. Those who become teachers must be clearly aware of their responsibility for knowledge about the field and the context within which it operates. Attainment of these ideals—or any one of them—is not possible without a free and open approach to knowledge and its exchange. This exchange must exist at all levels in the profession.

A final requirement for physical education, implied by the need for rationality and the development of adequate professional self-perception, is the establishment of clear personal goals in regard to it. Each physical educator must make every effort to assess strengths and limitations, to acquire needed knowledge and understanding, to plan realistically and continually for growth, and to free himself from bias and prejudice in his own development of theory.

Personal growth of the teacher as an attractive and successful adult is a relatively new concept. It means, in part, that the student's perceptual field must be expanded to include a view of himself as such an adult. This is accomplished by his experience in understanding such models. The teacher as a paragon of virtue is no longer an acceptable image, for if we expect students to develop meaningful concepts of maturity we cannot provide methods so far removed from real life that they have no relevance to his perceptions. At this level maturity may simply mean the acceptance of a older self as a competent adult.

The teacher must hold a perceptual view that permits an understanding of behavior—his own and that of others—in order to lead to the greatest possible individual development. This presumes an openness of perceptions, emphasis on the positive nature of human action, and a belief in the potential perfectability of human motivation and behavior. This view also assumes a relationship between positive perception and experiences that enhance an individual's view of himself and others. The teacher must become secure in the acceptability of his perceptions so that he can actualize them in ways most likely to result in individual enhancement and learning within a climate that challenges rather than threatens—a climate that permits freedom and experimentation and the willingness to risk error or failure. Such a climate is based, of course, in concepts of individual worth and dignity and importance of goals and activities. It also implies great faith in the human dialogue and in creative and intuitive approaches to knowledge. Analysis is part of the rational process, but it does not represent the whole of reason.

GUIDELINES FOR ACTUALIZATION

"If this study has been of value, the crucial relationships of means and ends are seen, not as vague theory, but as a conviction in your heart and a tool to your hand."[2] This statement expresses the intent of all considerations of theory, especially as they relate to the teaching-learning process. There is only the level of actualization—of ideas, beliefs, values, and self—and its effect on youth and on the area of study involved.

The practice of a profession clearly involves commitment and dedication, depth of knowledge, and valid theoretical understanding. We are committed to the importance and significance of physical education because we *know* that it has rich and incomparable *meaning* in life and learning. Somehow this commitment must be expressed in our professional pride; with respect to that significance, none of us needs to feel the need to apologize for ourselves or our field, but we must examine and understand its importance so that it is more than just an emotionalized knowing. The development of physical education in any and every aspect depends on the expertise of its exponents in carrying out and in understanding the relationships of their activities. Again we must recognize and emphasize *significance* as an assumption of all our efforts. We must approach our task without defensiveness, secure in the knowledge that our role is a vital one, and aware that the theoretical understanding of it needs to be refined. There is no substitute for a deep and abiding belief in the vital value of physical education, which has characterized the field throughout its existence.

---

[2] Hilda Clute Kozman, Rosalind Cassidy, and Chester O. Jackson. *Methods in Physical Education.* (3rd ed.) Philadelphia: Saunders, 1958, p. 525.

We must meet the current educational challenge to our intellection, not with reluctance but with an acceptance of the need for the task: to examine and define physical education rationally.

Our professional endeavor must reflect our unreserved acceptance of the continual need to examine knowledge and belief in constructive actualizations of frameworks of valid principles. Despite the degree of our commitment to an idea, we must constantly evaluate it and, if necessary, modify or change it. We do this as individuals, as professionals in school and community, and as members of a profession. We must know ourselves so well that we can differentiate between our intellection and emotionalization and overcome our reluctance to give up pet theories when we must. It is our responsibility to keep up with new knowledge and new ideas and to be as impersonal as possible in our attitude and loyalty to conventional wisdom. Those who disagree with us must not be disparaged, and the nature of the disagreement must be thoroughly examined. We must continually reaffirm our common goals and concerns. The worthy intent of all physical educators must be seen as a common effort to refine understanding in a realm of ideas in which personalities are not allowed to confuse the issue. All of us must assume responsibility for the process of applying critical insight, and no one should confuse the issue by telling others how to think or what to believe. If we accept the view that perceptual determinants are related to learning and behavior, we will realize that "telling" is a wasteful way of dealing with people.

Problem solving, or some similar method of applying intelligence, can be considered as a basic assumption of professional approaches to the consideration of alternatives and the formulation of plans and policies. Even if telling people what to do and how to do it was once an effective guide to the development of behavior, today we would be at a loss to determine just what to tell them to do. This is a world of change—of new knowledge and new meanings—in which physical education, with its emphasis on rationality, is struggling to identify and clarify its discipline of knowledge. Each professional person in it must be willing and able to approach problems and decisions rationally. He must be able to single out and identify the problem that is most crucial or most relevant; he must be able to examine his assumptions in relation to that problem, construct hypotheses, plan solutions, carry them out, and evaluate them. These may be problems of theoretical relationships or knowledge or they may be problems related to the effectiveness of the teaching-learning situation. Whatever they are, they must be solved in a manner that permits the widest understanding and application.

The physical educator must be able to understand and fulfill the various roles he has assumed as a professional. Each of us in teaching has responsibilities to the school and society, to our subject-matter field, and to youth. The principles developed here should serve as bases for understanding and fulfillment of those responsibilities. The teacher must find ways to fulfill these various responsibilities and to be effective in terms of them. School experiences and student-teacher relationships should reflect concern for the individual and for the subject field. The teacher, by virtue of his position, is a director of learning and a counselor and guidance worker, and he has responsibility in other roles within the context of the school, community, and profession. The demands of each role are difficult and can be time-consuming; the teacher's task is to find ways in which to make his efforts most fruitful. Comparative physical education and an understanding of the field on an international as well as national level offer further challenges to the profession and to the individual physical educator. There is little question that the current international activities of professional organizations in physical education will flourish in terms of the understanding and generalization of conceptual ideation.

The physical education teacher should be committed to his continual effective actualization as an outgrowth of self-understanding, to theoretical understanding, and to the application of evaluative procedures. Self-evaluation is a familiar process to all of us. Whenever we say, "I am the kind of person who . . ." or "I teach this way because . . . ," we are providing the means for evaluating our behavior or choices. This kind of evaluation can be unproductive in that it simply expresses a judgment, or it can result in an analysis of self or situation that would lead to constructive improvement. As long as it is exercised without any relation to an understood standard or goal, it will be largely wasteful. We must learn to understand and accept goals for personal growth and action and to develop means for evaluating our progress toward them. Developing principles as essential truths and purposes leads to the construction of guides to action within the perspective of our own philosophical framework and the projection of our finest ideals of hope for ourselves and our profession.

INDEX

Adelphi Academy, 105
Aiken, Wilford M., 89
Allen, Catherine L., 217
American Association for the Advancement of Physical Education, 81, 105–107, 114
American Association for Health, Physical Education, and Recreation, 95, 114, 124–125, 141
    Division for Girls and Women's Sports, 125–126
    Division of Men's Athletics, 125–126
American Education Fellowship, 91
American Federation of Labor, 92
American Federation of Teachers, 92
American Philosophical Society, 38
American Physical Education Association, 116–117, 119
American Physical Education Review, 114, 116
Amherst College, 105
Anderson, Archibald W., 46
Anderson, Lewis F., 80
Anderson, William G., 105–106
Andrews, Gladys, 171
Association for the Advancement of Progressive Education, 88
Association of American Colleges, 75
Austin, Glenn, 52

Bancroft, Jessie H., 81
Barham, Jerry, 176
Barnard, Henry, 40–41, 42
Barrett, Joe, 208
Barrows, Isabel C., 108, 110, 111
Beard, Charles A., 94

Beck, Charles, 74
Beecher, Catherine E., 42, 74
Behaviorist psychology, 83–84
Bell, Carolyn, 208
Benne, Kenneth D., 46, 157
Bissell, Mary Taylor, 106–107
Blackwell, Gordon W., 55–56
Blaikie, William, 105
Bode, Boyd H., 96
Bolton, Frederick Elmer, 80
Boultwood, M. A., 119
    on Dewey, 58–59
Brameld, Theodore, 57, 98
Breed, Frederick S., 97–98
Brown, Camille, 170, 176, 211
Brubacher, John S., 60
Bruner, Jerome S., 147, 175
Bukh, 140
Burdick, William, 119
Butts, R. Freeman, 35, 38, 41, 49, 61, 119

Calkins, N. A., 71
Cardinal Principles of Secondary Education, 121
Carnegie Foundation, 91
Carter, James G., 40
Cassidy, Rosalind Frances, 123, 124, 170, 176, 211, 224
Caswell, Hollis L., 56
Chamberlain, Dean, 91
Chamberlain, Enid Straw, 91
Chase, Edward T., 153
Child, I. L., 197
Child and the Curriculum, The (Dewey), 89

228   Index

Children and Fitness, 125
Childs, John L., 59
Claxton, P. P., 118
Cleveland, Sidney E., 199
Clifton, Marguerite A., 199
Cohen, L. D., 198
Colonial era, 34–39
Columbia University, 88
Colvin, Stephen Sheldon, 84
Combs, Arthur W., 193
Commager, Henry Steele, 153
Commission of Life Adjustment, 98
Commission on the Relation of School and College, 89–91
Commission on the Reorganization of Secondary Education, 121–122
Committee on College Entrance Requirements, 78
Committee for Promoting Physical Education in Public Schools of the United States, 117–118
Conant, James B., 146
Conceptual understanding, 5–6
Conference on Fitness of American Youth, 124, 125
Conference in the Interest of Physical Training, 105, 108
Conference of the Mid-West Association of Physical Education for College Women, 168
Conference on Physical Fitness of Youth, 125
Conference on Values in Sports, 125
Connotations of Movement in Sport and Dance (Metheny), 170
Contemporary perspectives, 131–181
  premise of purposes, 146–165
    curricular, 158–160
    guidelines for learning experiences, 164–165
    human, 154–158
    social, 149–154
  problem of purposes, 133–145
    current, 136–138
    guidelines for learning experiences, 145
  promise of purposes, 166–181
    challenge of the discipline, 168–172

Contemporary perspectives, promise of purposes, guidelines for learning experiences, 180–181
    nature of the discipline, 173–177
    principles, 177–180
Council on Youth Physical Fitness, 125
Country Life Commission, 76
Counts, George S., 59, 91
Cozens, Frederick N., 124
Cratty, Bryant J., 171
Cremin, Lawrence A., 35, 38, 41, 42–43, 49, 70, 72, 83, 96, 122
  on Dewey, 88–89
Crooks, Janis, 219
Cubberley, Ellwood P., 42, 55, 75–76
Cuber, John F., 51–52
Culture-epochs theory, 80–83
Curricular premise, the, 158–160
Curti, Merle, 37, 41, 60, 71
Curtis, Henry S., 82
Curtis, S. J., 119
  on Dewey, 58–59

Dare the School Build a New Social Order? (Counts), 91
Declaration of Independence, 36
DeGarmo, Charles, 78
Delsarte culture, 113
Democracy and Education (Dewey), 58, 88, 119
Developing Democratic Human Relations through Health Education, Physical Education and Recreation, 125
Dewey, John, 44–45, 87–89
  on human intelligence, 58–59
  on play, 119
Disciplinary theory, 70–78
Drought, Neal E., 91
Dunton, Larkin, 112

Education for All American Children, 95
Education for All American Youth, 95, 96
Education of American Teachers, The (Conant), 146
Education Through Physical Education (Wayman), 123

Educational Policies Commission, 47, 50, 53, 152
  on ideals, 54
  theory for education, 94–96
Educational Services for Young Children, 95
Edwards, A. S., 84
Edwards, Newton, 54–55
Ehler, George W., 116
Eight-Year Study, 89–91
Eliot, Charles W., 77
Ellfeldt, Lois, 142, 170
Emerson, C. W., 113
Enesbuske, Claes J., 110
English physical exercise, 113
Experience and Education (Dewey), 89
Experience and Nature (Dewey), 89

Federal aid, 93–97, 101
Felshin, Jan, 208, 212, 219
Ferdun, Edrie M., 168, 208, 219
Fisher, Seymour, 199
Follen, Charles, 74
Foundations of Method (Kilpatrick), 88
Franklin, Benjamin, 37
Freud, Sigmund, 86
Froebel, Friedrich, 45

Galbraith, John Kenneth, 151
Garber, John P., 120
General Education Board, 91
German gymnastics, 109, 113, 124
German immigration, 74–75
German *Turnverein*, 75
Gestaltism, 86, 88
Gross, Ronald, 176
Guaranteed income, 153
Guitar, Mary Anne, 156
Gulick, Luther Halsey, 81, 82, 111, 113

Hall, G. Stanley, 80–81
Harper, Robert A., 51–52
Harris, William Torrey, 72–73, 76, 77, 108
Hartman, Betty G., 123
Hartwell, Dr. Edward Mussey, 78, 111, 112, 114
Harvard University, 75, 77, 110
Havinghurst, Robert J., 49, 54, 56, 60
Hemenway, Mary, 108–109, 111, 112
Hemenway Gymnasium, 105
Henry, Franklin M., 169, 172
Herbart, Johann Friedrich, 45, 78–79
Herod, Joyzelle, 199
Hetherington, Clark W., 114–115, 119–120
  on objectives of physical education, 121–122
Historical perspectives, 31–127
  physical education, 104–127
  school and society, 33–67
Historical perspectives, the colonial era, 36–39
  the common schools, 39–42
  foundations, 33–35, 67
  guidelines for learning experiences, 67
  new forces, 42–45
  principles, 62–67
  role of philosophical belief, 57–62
  the school explosion, 45–48
  the school as social institution, 48–56
  teaching and learning, 68–103
  basic assumptions, 91–93
  disciplinary theory, 70–78
  education and psychology, 80–87
  foundations, 69–73, 102
  guidelines for learning experiences, 102–103
  Herbartian contribution, 78–79
  national standards, 93–97
  new criticisms, 97–98
  new theories, 79–86
  nineteenth century contributions, 74–75
  principles, 98–103
  progressive movement, 87–91
Hitchcock, Edward, Jr., 75, 105, 110
Homans, Amy Morris, 108, 109, 111
Horne, Herman H., 97
How We Think (Dewey), 88
Human Nature and Conduct (Dewey), 89
Hutchins, Robert Maynard, 59–60, 98

Intercollegiate Association, 75

Jackson, Chester O., 224
Jahn, Friedrich Ludwig, 74

Index

James, William, 83–84, 87–88
Jefferson, Thomas, 37–38
Johnson, Lyndon B., 141
JOHPER, 114, 170
Journal of the American Association for Health, Physical Education and Recreation, 124

Kandel, I. L., 61
Kennedy, John F., 125
Kerber, August, 61–62
Kilpatrick, W. H., 88
"Kinecept," 142
"Kinestruct," 142
Kozman, Hilda Clute, 124, 224

Laboratory School, 87–89
Lawson, Reed, 84–85
Leonard, Fred E., 109, 111, 112
Lewin, Kurt, 86
Lewis, Dio, 75
Lieber, Francis, 74
Ling, Pehr Hendrick, 75, 109, 140
Locke, John, 78
Locke, Lawrence F., 170
Lynn, Minnie L., 115–116
Lyon, Mary, 42

McCord, Clinton P., 117–118
McKenzie, G. Tait, 82
MacLaren, Archibald, 107
Maguire, Joan, 208
Mann, Horace, 40, 42, 47, 70
Maritain, Jacques, 62
Martire, John G., 198
Massachusetts Law of 1642, 64
Mead, Margaret, 10, 48, 51, 54
Medical Gymnastics, 110
Mercer, Charles Fenton, 40
Metheny, Eleanor, 142, 170
Metzner, H., 109
Miel, Alice, 190
Moehlman, Arthur Henry, 36
Monroe, Paul, 35
Morgan, H. H., 44
Movement Behavior and Motor Learning (Cratty), 171
Movement Fundamentals—Figure, Form, Fun (Wessel), 171

"Movement Movement, The" (Locke), 170
Mowrer, Iona, 219
Murphy, Gardner, 86, 150
Mursell, James A., 39
Musial, Stan, 125, 141

Nash, Jay B., 124
National Academy of Sciences, 147
National Association for Physical Education of College Women, 170
National Association of Secondary School Principals, 95
National College Physical Education Asssociation for Men, 170
National Committee on Physical Education, 118
National Conference on Thrift Education, 63
National Council of Education, 63
National Defense Education Act (1958), 93
National Education Association, 45, 77, 100, 114
  membership growth, 92
  theory for education, 94–96
NEA: The First Hundred Years, 63
National Herbart Society, 78
National Kinesiology Council, 141, 170
National Leadership Conference, 125
National Physical Education Service, 118
National Society for the Promotion of Industrial Education, The, 45, 76
National Society for the Study of Education, 115
Neugarten, Bernice L., 54, 56
Newlon, Jesse H., 47–48
Nimkoff, Meyer F., 34, 46
Nixon, Eugene W., 124
Normal Institute for Physical Education, 75
North American Gymnastic Union, 113
Northend, Charles, 71

Oberteuffer, Delbert, 124, 179–180
Ogburn, William F., 34, 46
Ogden, John, 71
Ohio State University, 168

Index

Page, James A., 111–112
Parker, Francis W., 87
Perspectives
  guidelines for, 11–12
  principles of, 6–8, 13–27
    essential truths, 16
    guidelines for action, 16–17
    guidelines for learning experiences, 26
    process of, 13–27
      basic assumptions, 21
      evaluation, 26
      guidelines for learning experiences, 27
      hypothesis, 21
      identification, 20
      plan, 21–25
      problem statement, 20
  of students, 9–11
  of teachers, 8–9
  See also Contemporary perspectives; Historical perspectives; Projected perspectives
Pestalozzi, Johann Heinrich, 45, 70
Phenix, Philip, 191
Philosophical belief, 57–62
Physical education
  achieves foothold as a school subject, 73
  defensive aspect of, 134–135
  nineteenth century contributions, 74–75
Physical education, premises, 160–163
  threats to, 5
Physical Education Law of California (1917), 118–119
Physical Education for Today's Boys and Girls (Andrews, Saurborn, and Schneider), 171
Physical Educator, The, 124, 170
Playground Association, 120
Playground and Recreation Association, 118
Policies for Education in American Democracy, 95
Posse, Nils, 109–110
Profession, practice of, 217–226
  actualization guidelines, 224–226
  competence and excellence guidelines, 218–219
Profession, discipline of physical education, 220–222
  perception and person guidelines, 222–224
  role of physical education, 219–220
Progressive Education, 89, 91
Progressive Education Association (PEA), 88, 89, 91
Progressive Education at the Crossroads (Bode), 96
Progressive movement, 87–91
Progressive Physical Educator, The, 124
Projected perspectives, 185–226
  practice of profession, 217–226
    actualization guidelines, 224–226
    competence and excellence guidelines, 218–219
    discipline of physical education, 220–222
    perception and person guidelines, 222–224
    role of physical education, 219–220
Projected perspectives, practice of theory, 187–216
  basic assumptions, 209–210
  conceptual guidelines, 210–212
  contextual point of view, 208–209
  guidelines for learning experiences, 216
  objectives, 210
  process guidelines, 188–192
  program guidelines, 205–208
  teaching and learning guidelines, 192–205
Public and Its Problems, The (Dewey), 89
Purposes, premise of, 146–165
  curricular, 158–160
  guidelines for learning experiences, 164–165
  human, 154–158
  social, 149–154
  problem of, 133–145
    current, 136–138
    guidelines for learning experiences, 145
  promise of, 166–181

Purposes, promise of, challenge of the discipline, 168–172
   guidelines for learning experiences, 180–181
   nature of the discipline, 173–177
   principles, 177–180
Pusey, Nathan M., 51

Quest, 141
Quillen, James, 34, 49

Rafferty, Max, 135
Ralfe, C. H., 107
Raup, R. Bruce, 34
Ready, Marie M., 118
Reagan, Michael D., 153
Redfield, Robert, 45–46
Reed, Dudley B., 119
Reisner, Edward H., 43, 62
Report of the Committee of Ten on Secondary School Studies, 77–78
Research Quarterly, 170
Richey, Herman G., 54–55
Rotter, J. G., 197–198
Rousseau, Jean Jacques, 70
Rugg, Harold O., 43, 44, 88
Rupp, Wendy, 208
Russell, Ruth, 219

Sanborn, Marion Alice, 123
Sargent, Dr. Dudley A., 105, 110–111, 113, 117
Saurborn, Jeannette, 171
Schilder, Paul, 199
Schneider, Elsa, 171
School and society, 33–67, 149–154
   the colonial era, 36–39
   the common schools, 39–42
   foundations, 33–35, 67
   guidelines for learning experiences, 67
   new forces, 42–45
   principles, 62–67
   role of philosophical belief, 57–62
   the school explosion, 45–48
   the school as social institution, 48–56
School and Society (Dewey), 44–45
Schrader, Carl L., 120
Scott, William E., 91
Seaver, Edwin P., 112

Shapiro, Harry L., 46
Smith, B. Orthanel, 46
Smith, Cornie N., 198–199
Smith, Hope M., 199
Smith, Wilfred R., 61–62
Smith-Hughes Act (1917), 76, 92
Smith-Lever Act (1914), 76
Social Changes and Sports for Girls and Women, 125
Social Darwinism, 80–82
Social Studies in Secondary Education, 91
"Soft American, The" (Kennedy), 125
Spencer, Herbert, 79–80
Sports Illustrated, 125
Stanley, William O., 46
Stowe, Calvin, 40
Suffrage, 38
Swedish Educational Gymnastics, 109–110
Swedish gymnastics, 109–110, 112–113, 124
Swedish Movement Cure, 110
Swett, John, 40, 70, 73

Teaching and learning, 68–103
   basic assumptions, 91–93
   disciplinary theory, 70–78
   education and psychology, 80–87
   foundations, 69–73, 102
   guidelines for, 192–205
   guidelines for learning experiences, 102–103
   Herbartian contribution, 78–79
   national standards, 93–97
   new criticisms, 97–98
   new theories, 79–86
   nineteenth century contributions, 74–75
   principles, 98–103
   progressive movement, 87–91
Theory, practice of, 187–216
   basic assumptions, 209–210
   conceptual guidelines, 210–212
   contextual point of view, 208–209
   guidelines for learning experiences, 216
   objectives, 210
   process guidelines, 188–193

Theory, program guidelines, 205–208
    teaching and learning guidelines, 192–205
Thorndike, Ashley Horace, 83–84, 85, 87
Tocqueville, Alexis de, 36

United States Bureau of Education, 118
United States Office of Education, 92, 98, 100
University of California, 120
University of California at Los Angeles, 170
University of Nevada, 208, 212, 219
University of the State of New York, 117
University of Wisconsin, 120

Washburne, Carleton, 88
Wayman, Agnes R., 123
Wesley, Edgar B., 91, 92
Wessel, Janet A., 171
White, John S., 107

White House Conference on Children and Youth (1960), 45
White House Conference on Education (1956), 48–50
Whiting, J. W. M., 197
Wiley, Calvin, 40
Wilkinson, Charles B. ("Bud"), 125, 141
Willard, Emma, 42
Williams, Jesse Feiring, 123, 124
Wilson, Woodrow, 63, 117
Winship, George Barker, 75
Wirt, William, 87
Withers, William, 44
Wood, Thomas D., 81, 114–115, 119–120, 123
Woody, Thomas, 47
Wriston, Henry M., 155

Yale University, 75
Young Men's Christian Association, 111, 113
Youth and Fitness, 125
Youth Fitness Test Manual, 124